Sensibility and Singularity

SUNY series in
Contemporary Continental Philosophy

Dennis J. Schmidt, editor

Sensibility and Singularity

The Problem of Phenomenology in Levinas

John E. Drabinski

STATE UNIVERSITY OF NEW YORK PRESS

Published by
State University of New York Press, Albany

© 2001 State University of New York

Printed in the United States of America

For information, address the State University of New York Press,
90 State Street, Suite 700, Albany, NY 12207

Production by Judith Block
Marketing by Patrick Durocher

Library of Congress Cataloging-in-Publication Data

Drabinski, John E., 1968–
    Sensibility and singularity : the problem of phenomenology in Levinas
/ John E. Drabinski.
        p.   cm. — (SUNY series in contemporary continental philosophy)
    Includes bibliographical references and index.
    ISBN 0-7914-4897-5 (alk. paper) — ISBN 0-7914-4898-3 (pbk. : alk. paper)
    1. Levinas, Emmanuel.   2. Husserl, Edmund, 1859–1938—Influence.
    I. Title.   II. Series.

B2430.L484 D73 2001
194—dc21   00-032227
                                                             CIP

10   9   8   7   6   5   4   3   2   1

In memory of
Bill Hargrove and Stephanie Walsh

And for
Maria Cimitile

Contents

Acknowledgments

Parts of chapter 2 appeared in *International Studies in Philosophy* XXX, 4 (1998): 23–38. I would like to thank the editor, Professor Leon Goldstein of Binghamton University, for allowing me to reprint those materials.

I offer this work in memory of Bill Hargrove and Stephanie Walsh, without whom this world is all the more difficult. From my first memories, they were instructors in the art of writing and in the work of generosity, both of which were lived by authentic spirits. Whatever the passage of time, whatever the fading of memories, their instruction will always be the beginning of my intellectual and moral life.

The following project had its beginnings in my dissertation written at the University of Memphis under the direction of Robert Bernasconi. But the trail of teachers begins, of course, before the Memphis faculty. At Seattle University, Robert Cousineau met my first essay in continental philosophy with the question "Please! Do you believe this nonsense?" Haunted by its bluntness, but moved by its imperative, it is a question I still ask myself after every paragraph I write. Jim Risser and Ken Stikkers continue to be important teachers and friends. Burt Hopkins and Marylou Sena taught me how to see phenomenologically and stirred in me an independence of thinking, a gift for which I will always be indebted.

I consider myself privileged to have worked with the faculty at the University of Memphis. Tina Chanter and Len Lawlor were responsible for much of my training in contemporary French philosophy, pushing and pulling my thinking back and forth across the border between phenomenology and postphenomenology. Their scholarship remains for me a model. Tom Nenon was a loyal teacher and friend whose advice and guidance went (and still goes) beyond written pages and structures of argument. I thank him for his philosophical and human contributions to my time in Memphis. John Llewelyn's seminars were decisive for my understanding of Levinas, Derrida, and the complexity of our moral life. Perhaps more importantly, though, I thank him for his dedication to the Memphis students, his careful readings of our work, and the time he always reserved for conversation and instruction.

I reserve a special expression of gratitude for Robert Bernasconi. It was good to have a fellow lover of Southern soul music during my years in Memphis, someone who already knew names like Ann Peebles, James Carr, Syl Johnson, and others. His philosophical work, both written and in his seminars, altered my philosophical orientation from my first semester forward. The combination of philosophical rigor and sensitivity to questions of justice in his work is a model against which I suspect I will always measure my own. His support, from my first fumblings toward a dissertation project to my years as a job candidate, was quiet and unwavering. There were countless moments in my graduate and postgraduate life where this support was the difference between being merely discouraged and giving up.

The present project was conceived and completed while living the absurd life of a philosopher on the academic job market. I have continued to write in part because of my love for ideas. But that love of ideas is not enough to sustain a spirit living the cruel life of the job search. Friendship has often been enough (and at times the only) reason to go on writing and reading. So, a word of thanks to dear friends. Amit Sen, Jim Hanas, Amy Morgenstern, Kevin Thompson, and Max Maloney have all been voices cynical, encouraging, sarcastic, and always refreshing. Amit and Max have been especially important in my development as a thinker, always asking too many questions, and always too suspicious. It is no understatement that I would be much less a philosopher and human being were it not for their presence in my graduate school life.

This work is dedicated to Maria Cimitile. I have anguished more about how to say thank you to her than I have about any philosophical or moral enigma. But words for this thanks break off. So let me fail with affection and with familiar words. Thank you, Maria, for always asking more of me than I could ever ask of myself.

Abbreviations

All references to the writings of Emmanuel Levinas and Edmund Husserl are included in the text according to the following table of abbreviations. All citations in the text abbreviate the title of the original language edition. Following the abbreviation of the original language edition is, first, the pagination of the original language edition and, second, the pagination of the English translation (where available). Translations have frequently been modified and are not noted in the text.

Works by Emmanuel Levinas

Books by Levinas Cited in This Study

AE	*Autrement qu'être, ou au-delà essence.* The Hague: Martinus Nijhoff, 1974; *Otherwise than being, or Beyond Essence*, trans. Alphonso Lingis. The Hague: Martinus Nijhoff, 1980.
DEE	*De l'existence à l'existant.* Paris: Vrin, 1992; *Existence and Existents*, trans. Alphonso Lingis. The Hague: Martinus Nijhoff, 1974.
DL	*Difficile liberté.* Paris: Éditions Albin Michel, 1976; *Difficult Freedom*, trans. Seán Hand. Baltimore: Johns Hopkins University Press, 1990.

DMT   *Dieu, la mort et le temps*. Paris: Éditions Grasset & Fasquelle, 1993.

DQVI   *De Dieu qui vient à l'idée*. Paris: Vrin, 1982.

EeI   *Éthique et infini*. Montpellier: Fata Morgana, 1980; *Ethics and Infinity*, trans. Richard Cohen. Pittsburgh: Duquesne University Press, 1988.

HS   *Hors sujet*. Montpellier: Fata Morgana, 1987; *Outside the Subject*, trans. Michael Smith. Stanford: Stanford University Press, 1994.

NP   *Noms propre*. Montpellier: Fata Morgana, 1975.

TA   *Le temps et l'autre*. Paris: Presses Universitaires de France, 1992; *Time and the Other*, trans. Richard Cohen. Pittsburgh: Duquesne University Press, 1987.

TeI   *Totalité et infini*. The Hague: Martinus Nijhoff, 1961; *Totality and Infinity*, trans. Alphonso Lingis. Dordrecht: Kluwer Academic Press, 1995.

TIPH   *Théorie de intuition dans la phénoménologie de Husserl*. Paris: Vrin, 1963; *Theory of Intuition in Husserl's Phenomenology*, trans. Adrian Orianne. Evanston: Northwestern University Press, 1970.

Articles by Levinas Cited in This Study

BI   "Beyond Intentionality." In *Philosophy in France Today*, ed. Alan Montefiore. Cambridge: Cambridge University Press, 1983, 100–115.

CNI   "La conscience non-intentionelle." In *Entre nous: Essais sur le penser-à-l'autre*. Paris: Éditions Grasset & Fasquelle, 1991, 132–142. Translations mine.

DCV   "De la conscience à la vielle." In *De Dieu qui vient à l'idée*. Paris: Vrin, 1982, 34–61. Translations mine.

DP   "Dieu et la philosophie." In *De Dieu qui vient à l'idée*. Paris: Vrin, 1982, 93–127; "God and Philosophy," trans. Richard Cohen and Alphonso Lingis. In *The Levinas*

Reader, ed. and trans. Sean Hand. Oxford: Basil Blackwell, 1989, 167–189.

EFP	"Ethics as First Philosophy." In *The Levinas Reader*, ed. and trans. Sean Hand. Oxford: Basil Blackwell, 1989, 75–87.
EP	"Enigme et phénomène." In *En découvrant l'existence avec Husserl et Heidegger*. Paris: Vrin, 1975, 203–217; "Phenomenon and Enigma," trans. Alphonso Lingis. In *Collected Philosophical Papers*, ed. and trans. Alphonso Lingis. The Hague: Martinus Nijhoff, 1987, 61–74.
FHP	"Fribourg, Husserl et la phénoménologie." In *Les imprévus de l'histoire*. Montpellier: Fata Morgana, 1994, 94–106. Translations mine.
IM	"Intentionalité et métaphysique." In *En découvrant l'existence avec Husserl et Heidegger*. Paris: Vrin, 1975, 137–144. Translations mine.
IS	"Intentionalité et sensation." In *En découvrant l'existence avec Husserl et Heidegger*. Paris: Vrin, 1975, 145–162. Translations mine.
LB	"Lévy-Bruhl et la philosophie contemporaine." In *Entre nous: Essais sur le penser-à-l'autre*. Paris: Éditions Grasset & Fasquelle, 1991, 53–68. Translations mine.
LC	"Liberté et commandement." In *Liberté et commandement*. Montpellier: Fata Morgana, 1994, 27–48; "Freedom and Command," trans. Alphonso Lingis. In *Collected Philosophical Papers*, ed. and trans. Alphonso Lingis. The Hague: Martinus Nijhoff, 1987, 15–24.
LeP	"Langage et proximité." In *En découvrant l'existence avec Husserl et Heidegger*. Paris: Vrin, 1975, 218–236; "Language and Proximity," trans. Alphonso Lingis. In *Collected Philosophical Papers*, ed. and trans. Alphonso Lingis. The Hague: Martinus Nijhoff, 1987, 109–126.
MT	"Le Moi et la totalité." In *Entre nous: Essais sur le penser-à-l'autre*. Paris: Éditions Grasset & Fasquelle, 1991, 23–48; "Ego and the Totality," trans. Alphonso

Lingis. In *Collected Philosophical Papers,* ed. and trans. Alphonso Lingis. The Hague: Martinus Nijhoff, 1987, 25–46.

ŒH   "L'œuvre d'Edmond Husserl." In *En découvrant l'existence avec Husserl et Heidegger.* Paris: Vrin, 1975, 7–52.

NS   "Notes sur le sens." In *De Dieu qui vient à l'idée.* Paris: Vrin, 1982, 231–257. Translations mine.

PE   "La Philosophie et l'éveil." In *Entre nous: Essais sur le penser-à-l'autre.* Paris: Éditions Grasset & Fasquelle, 1991, 86–99; "Philosophy and Awakening." In *Who Comes after the Subject?,* eds. Eduardo Cadava, Peter Connor, and Jean-Luc Nancy. New York: Routledge, 1991, 206–217.

PEA   *"Totalité et infini:* Préface à l'édition allemande." In *Entre nous: Essais sur le penser-à-l'autre.* Paris: Éditions Grasset & Fasquelle, 1991, 231–234. Translations mine.

PEQA   "La pensée de l'être et la question de l'autre." In *De Dieu qui vient à l'idée.* Paris: Vrin, 1982, 173–188. Translations mine.

RR   "La ruine de la représentation." In *En découvrant l'existence avec Husserl et Heidegger.* Paris: Vrin, 1975, 125–136. Translations mine.

RTP   "Réflexions sur la 'technique' phénoménologique." In *En découvrant l'existence avec Husserl et Heidegger.* Paris: Vrin, 1975, 111–124. Translations mine.

SLI   "Sur les *Ideen* de M. E. Husserl." In *Les imprévus de l'histoire.* Montpellier: Fata Morgana, 1994, 45–93.

SS   "Signification et sens." In *Humanisme de l'autre homme.* Montpellier: Fata Morgana, 1972, 15–70; "Meaning and Sense," trans. Alphonso Lingis. In *Collected Philosophical Papers,* ed. and trans. Alphonso Lingis. The Hague: Martinus Nijhoff, 1987, 75–108.

TeH   "Transcendence et hauteur." In *Liberté et commandement.* Montpellier: Fata Morgana, 1994, 49–99; "Transcendence and Height," trans. Tina Chanter, Nick Walker, and Simon Critchley. In *Levinas: Basic Writings*, eds. Adriaan Peperzak, Simon Critchley, and Robert Bernasconi. Bloomington: Indiana University Press, 1996.

TrA   "Trace de l'autre." In *En découvrant l'existence avec Husserl et Heidegger*. Paris: Vrin, 1975, 187–202; "Trace of the Other," trans. Alphonso Lingis. In *Deconstruction in Context*, ed. Mark Taylor. Albany: State University of New York Press, 1988.

VDVT   "Vérité du dévoilement et vérité du témoignage." In *La témoignage*, ed. E. Castelli. Paris: Aubier-Montaigne, 1972, 47–59; "Truth of Disclosure and Truth of Testimony," trans. I. MacDonald and S. Critchley. In *Levinas: Basic Writings*, eds. Adriaan Reperzak, Simon Critchley, and Robert Bernasconi. Bloomington: Indiana University Press, 1996, 98–107.

Works by Edmund Husserl Cited in This Study

EU   *Erfahrung und Urteil,* hrsg. Ludwig Landgrebe. Hamburg: Meiner Verlag, 1985; *Experience and Judgment*, ed. Ludwig Landgrebe and trans. James Churchill and Karl Ameriks. Evanston: Northwestern University Press, 1976.

Hua I   *Cartesianische Meditationen und Pariser Vorträge,* hrsg. Stephan Strasser. *Husserliana: Band I*. The Hague: Martinus Nijhoff, 1950; *Cartesian Meditations*, trans. Dorion Cairns. The Hague: Martinus Nijhoff, 1970.

Hua III   *Ideen zu einer reinen Phänomenologie und phänomenologischen Philosophie: Erster Teil*, hrsg. Karl Schuhmann. *Husserliana: Band III*. The Hague: Martinus Nijhoff, 1950; rev. 1976; *Ideas Pertaining to a Pure Phenomenology and a Phenomenological Philosophy: Book One*, trans. Fred Kersten. The Hague: Martinus Nijhoff, 1983.

Hua IV   *Ideen zu einer reinen Phänomenologie und*
            phänomenologischen Philosophie: Zweite Teil, hrsg. Marly
            Biemel. *Husserliana: Band IV.* The Hague: Martinus
            Nijhoff, 1952; *Ideas Pertaining to a Pure Phenomenology*
            and a Phenomenological Philosophy: Book Two, trans.
            Andre Schuwer and Richard Rojecwicz. The Hague:
            Martinus Nijhoff, 1988.

Hua V   *Ideen zu einer reinen Phänomenologie und*
            phänomenologischen Philosophie: Drittes Teil, hrsg. Marly
            Biemel. *Husserliana: Band V.* The Hague: Martinus
            Nijhoff, 1971; *Ideas Pertaining to a Pure Phenomenology*
            and a Phenomenological Philosophy: Book Three, trans. Ted
            Klein and William Pohl. The Hague: Martinus Nijhoff,
            1982.

Hua IX   *Phänomenologische Psychologie,* hrsg. Walter Biemel.
            Husserliana: Band IX. The Hague: Martinus Nijhoff,
            1962; *Phenomenological Psychology: Summer Semester*
            1925, trans. John Scanlon. The Hague: Martinus
            Nijhoff, 1989

Hua X   *Zur Phänomenologie des innern Zeitbewußtseins,* hrsg.
            Rudolf Boehm. *Husserliana: Band X.* The Hague:
            Martinus Nijhoff, 1966; *On the Phenomenology of the*
            Consciousness of Internal Time: Lectures 1893–1918, trans.
            John Brough. The Hague: Martinus Nijhoff, 1991.

Hua XI   *Analysen zur passiven Synthesis,* hrsg. Margot Fleischer.
            Husserliana: Band XI. The Hague: Martinus Nijhoff,
            1966.

Hua XV   *Zur Phänomenologie der Intersubjektivität: Drittes Teil,*
            hrsg. Iso Kern. *Husserliana: Band XV.* The Hague:
            Martinus Nijhoff, 1973.

Hua XVII   *Formale und transzendentale Logik,* hrsg. Paul Janssen.
            Husserliana: Band XVII. The Hague: Martinus Nijhoff,
            1974; *Formal and Transcendental Logic,* trans. Dorion
            Cairns. The Hague: Martinus Nijhoff, 1974.

Hua XVIII   *Logische Untersuchungen,* hrsg. Elmar Holenstein.
            Husserliana: Band XVIII. The Hague: Martinus Nijhoff,

1975; *Logical Investigations,* trans. J. N. Findlay. New Jersey: Humanities Press, 1970.

Hua XIX/1   *Logische Untersuchungen,* hrsg. Elmar Holenstein. *Husserliana: Band XIX/1.* The Hague: Martinus Nijhoff, 1984; *Logical Investigations,* trans. J. N. Findlay. New Jersey: Humanities Press, 1970.

Hua XIX/2   *Logische Untersuchungen,* hrsg. Elmar Holenstein. *Husserliana: Band XIX/2.* The Hague: Martinus Nijhoff, 1984; *Logical Investigations,* trans. J. N. Findlay. New Jersey: Humanities Press, 1970.

Introduction

The work of Emmanuel Levinas has begun to make a significant impact on contemporary thought. Despite the fact that he has been writing in a thoroughly contemporary vein since the 1940s, his writing has only recently come to impress itself upon philosophy, theology, literary theory, Judaic studies, and related fields. The locus of his impact lies in the varied languages of otherness that his thought makes possible. The centrality of otherness—this is the ultimate meaning of Levinas's work. And this alterity has proved a productive thought. Its fecundity derives in large part from the difficulty of thinking after the death of metaphysics, of accounting after the faltering of epistemology, and ultimately of questioning our moral life in the ashes of morality. If the history of Being, critical theory, and the catastrophes of the twentieth century have put in question the powers of subjectivity, then the task of philosophy (and theory in general) is to think about how to think in the wake of so many deaths. Levinas has been engaged in precisely this sort of task since the 1940s. It should be no surprise then that his thought is beginning to cast a shadow. What is surprising, however, is that it has taken so long for this shadow to be cast.

But the reception of his thought, especially in the English-speaking world, has been slow to appreciate—if not wholly remiss in recognizing the impact of Levinas's work on the classical phenomenological tradition. This peculiar gap has been made only more pronounced by the lack of a single book-length study of Levinas and classical phenomenology.[1] A simple glance at his work and philosophical itinerary seems to point to a constant problem: Husserl's phenomenology. Levinas, on the advice of his mentor-teacher Jean Hering, left Strasbourg for Freiburg to study phenomenology with Husserl, beginning with Husserl's 1928 lectures on phenomenological psychology. In addition to his translation of Husserl's *Cartesianische Meditationen*, Levinas also contributed some of the first and finest of the studies of Husserl's phenomenology to the French philosophical scene. In both his major works, *Totality and Infinity* and *Otherwise than being*, Levinas will situate his descriptions squarely within the horizon of Husserl's thought. As late as 1984, in the essay "Ethics as First Philosophy," Levinas will ask us to, along with him, begin again with Husserl. This is not to say that Levinas has an unwavering regard for Husserl. It is, rather, to say that Husserl's phenomenology is the one constant *problem* in Levinas's philosophical work. Husserl's phenomenology is *problematic* for Levinas. But it is perhaps also *the problematic* of Levinas's enigmatic philosophical method. What sense are we to make of this relation? Who is Husserl to Levinas?

A few perspectives on this issue have become all but standard Levinas-interpretation. There is the considered view that the early Levinas falls under the spell of Heidegger's critique of phenomenology and only later turns to Husserl to "leave the climate" of Heideggerian philosophy. Thus the early work from *Theory of Intuition* up through *Totality and Infinity* bears the mark of Heidegger's revolution in thought. Levinas's obvious discontent with the "intellectualism" of Husserl's phenomenology, so the story goes, stems from his encounter with the Heidegger of *Being and Time*. Indeed, Husserl will employ the most un-Levinasian terms in describing the aim of phenomenology: *philosophia prote, rizomata panton*, or, simply, *prima philosophia*. Husserl always anchors these visions of philosophy in transcendental subjectivity. Heidegger complicates matters. The in-the-world-being of Dasein introduces a decisive and fundamental ambiguity into philosophical reflection. To be in the world is to always already be ahead of one's self. So presence to self—which, after *La voix et le phénomène*, seems the very foundation of Husserl's thought—is never completely transparent. And, this nontransparency of one's presence to self is doubtless the horizon in which Levinas works.

This story has very significant gaps. It cannot be disputed that Heidegger alters Levinas's understanding of phenomenology. In the 1930s and 1940s, Levinas will talk of Heidegger's work as "revolutionary." But this does not mean that Heidegger's work determines much of Levinas's itinerary. Quite to the contrary, I would argue that Levinas's concern with Heidegger is, in fact, not very Heideggerian. There is little or no positive talk of Being or historicity, of facticity or resoluteness. What Levinas calls "being" in, for example, *De l'existence à l'existant* bears little or no resemblance to the meaning of Being in general. Rather, it looks a lot more like sensibility. Historicity plays little role in Levinas, except in the sense of the nonnarrative history of the I, which places the oneself in the immemorial. This history does not place us back in the world. This history does not return us to our thrown situatedness. Levinas's is not Heidegger's history. Facticity is asymmetrical sociality for Levinas, not a clue to the care structure of subjectivity. Death is not an event of freedom. It is subjectivity dedicated to the death of the Other. And even with those themes from Heidegger's work that Levinas takes up explicitly—e.g., ecstatic time—it is altogether unclear if they are different from Husserl's reflections on the same.

This should not surprise us if we actually listen to how Levinas first expresses the influence of Heidegger: "But such a powerful and original philosophy as Heidegger's . . . is to some extent only the continuation of Husserlian phenomenology" (TIPH, 15/xxxiv). This assessment, formed in part on the basis of participation in Heidegger's Winter 1928–1929 seminar, would no doubt trouble Heidegger scholars today. What is important, however, is not what it says about Heidegger, but what it says about Levinas's understanding of Heidegger and hence Heidegger's influence on Levinas. What is revolutionary about Heidegger's work, for Levinas, is Heidegger's *husserlianism*.[2] The transcendence of the subject in *Theory of Intuition*, which aims above all to free Levinas from Husserl's intellectualism, is described in terms of the practical intentionality of affective life. This aim sets Levinas on a path from which he will not, in any significant manner, diverge. Though Levinas's work will shift in terminology and even in the implications of his findings, affectivity—whether sensibility, proximity, materiality— remains the point of departure. Although this turn to affectivity certainly bears marks of Heidegger's understanding of *Befindlichkeit* in *Being and Time*, the language of Levinas's analysis is distinctly Husserlian. Levinas's talk is of nonrepresentational modes of intentionality (cf., TIPH, 75/44f), not of attunement and facticity. Affective, practical intentionality, for Levinas, seems less a commentary on ¶29 of *Being and Time* than a discussion of nonpositional modes of awareness.

So who is Husserl to Levinas? If we assume that Husserl, not Heidegger, is the one who most decisively directs Levinas's philosophical itinerary, then who is Husserl and what is phenomenology? to Levinas? Levinas-interpretation has produced two basic alternatives to this Heidegger narrative. The first argues for something like a "supplemental" influence. This story contends that there is a fundamental lack at the heart of Husserl's work and that another thinker fills this shortcoming for Levinas. Ethics is first philosophy for Levinas, "grounded," as it were, in the asymmetrical relation without relation. The science of *rizomata panton* is grounded in a nonworldly ego for Husserl. Levinas must therefore seek an external source to arrive at and put the Other first. Levinas needs a supplement to Husserl. The primary figure of this supplement is, justifiably, Franz Rosenzweig. I say "justifiably" because Levinas himself remarks quite famously in *Totality and Infinity* that Rosenzweig's *Stern der Erlosung* is "a work too often present in this book to be cited" (TeI, xvi/28). Richard Cohen's work has been exemplary of this line of thought.[3] Cohen writes that Levinas's "acknowledgement" of Rosenzweig's work "*interrupts* one extended discussion of phenomenology"[4] with the weight of morality. Further Cohen writes that

> the mercy and justice which Rosenzweig's *Star* sets up . . . also inspire Levinas in his opposition to the noetic-noematic totality of phenomenology. . . . The inspiration of the concluding words of the *Star* is intended not merely as another philosophical discourse, nor merely as another philosophical intuition, but rather as a *call to and from above.*[5]

To a certain extent, this is a story beyond dispute. It would be naive to excise Rosenzweig from Levinas's constellation of influences. (Even without reverence for the *Star* in *Totality and Infinity*, one could exchange the Judaic tradition for the name Rosenzweig.) But, it is in dispute whether this encounter with Rosenzweig, as Cohen puts it, "*frees* Levinas from phenomenology by deepening his appreciation for ethics and justice."[6] One can surely admit that Rosenzweig awakens Levinas to a certain sensitivity to ethics and justice, but it is another matter altogether to claim that this "frees" Levinas from phenomenology. And this latter claim is surely complicated by Levinas's remarks at both the opening of *Totality and Infinity* and the close of *Otherwise than Being* that his work "owes everything to the phenomenological method" (TeI, xvi/28) and is "faithful to intentional analysis" (AE, 230/ 183). Is it necessary to free Levinas from phenomenology? What would that mean in light of these remarks from his two landmark works?

It is not necessary to throw another thinker into the mix in order to place Levinas outside phenomenology, as the "supplement" story seeks to. Perhaps, as some have argued, the matter of morality itself pushes Levinas to, in Jan de Greef's words, "abandon light in order to continue description in ethical terms, that is, in non-phenomenological terms."[7] Ethics itself, one might say, prompts Levinas to leave the climate of Husserl's thought. The ruptures and interruptions of moral consciousness are too much for phenomenology to contend with. Phenomenology, as this story tells it, brings us to the precipice of ethical life, but only to the precipice. To fully engage the ethical relation, one has to leave phenomenology for an ethical (metaphysical?) language. Again, de Greef's work is representative of this reading of Levinas:

> Levinas will describe alterity [in terms of] the *idea* of a "rupture" or an "absence" of horizon. It is in this way that phenomenology itself . . . makes possible thinking the beyond of its limits and beyond the conditions of visibility as rupture and the absence of horizon, and, above all, thinking this rupture of horizon as the proper determination of alterity.[8]

Stephan Strasser echoes this sentiment when he writes that "Levinas has changed the phenomenological perspective by adding to it a dimension of depth."[9] This change alters the content of what is described such that the language of phenomenology can no longer be said to contain it. Perhaps, then, as Jacques Colette has put it, Levinas's thought retains only the "phrasings" of phenomenological research while at the same time breaking with its most fundamental propositions.[10] If Husserl's work is condemned to idealism, then it would seem that the very idea of exceeding conditions of visibility requires dispensing with phenomenology. Depth, departure from light, and the rupture of horizon—it is also futile to dispute this aspect of Levinas's thought. He is surely concerned with the limits of Husserl's descriptions, specifically how they limit our ability to account for the intrigue of the interhuman. This justifies, at least in part, positing a break with the fundamental propositions of Husserl's philosophy. The ethical relation is not a theme. There is no Eidos between the oneself and the Other. The transcendental subject does not constitute the interruption it undergoes. So, one might be led to conclude that phenomenology must be exceeded by an antiphenomenology, a thinking beyond. Perhaps something postphenomenological is necessary. But, as we asked of Cohen's comments, how does this story square with Levinas's rather decisive expressions of sympathy with Husserl? Is Husserl not something more than the ladder subsequently discarded?

There is, then, a question shared by both the "supplement to phenomenology" and the "beyond phenomenology" stories of the Husserl-Levinas relation: Is Husserl's phenomenology something to be discarded? The central thesis of the present work is that such discarding is both unwarranted and philosophically naive. What is most troubling on both accounts is the problematic construal of phenomenology as a doctrine. Phenomenology has never been a system. It has always been a method, and one subjected to constant reassessment. Husserl's project of *philosophia prote* aimed, not at firm foundations, but at the infinite task of purging descriptions of their metaphysical presuppositions. Phenomenology is, in some sense, never fixed. Self-critique is coextensive with practice of the method. The method entails descriptive intentional analysis, which accounts for the complexities, in their fullness, of our presence to the world.

We should not be surprised that this becomes Levinas's method. Intentional analysis is a method of description, and the concrete, deformalized investigations provide the site for purging metaphysical presuppositions. Intentionality is important for Levinas simply because it puts us in sensual contact with the matters described. There is no distance in intentionality; intentionality is already proximity, the irreducibility of relation. Intentional analysis, as he says in *Totality and Infinity*, is the search for the concrete. This contact, this irreducibility of relation, discloses the (unsuspected) horizons within which Levinas's work works. It is important as well that, at their outset, these horizons do not invoke prior juridical constraints. As unsuspected, the horizons that animate Levinas's work are susceptible to surprise. The phenomenological method, in Levinas's hands, is transformed into a way of accounting that encounters, with all due weight and height, the *sense* of disruption, surprise, and interruption. Levinas says:

> The phenomenological method enables us to discover sense (*sens*) within our lived experience; it reveals consciousness to be an in-

tentionality always in contact with objects outside of itself, other than itself . . . The phenomenological method permits conscious-ness to understand its own preoccupations, to reflect upon itself and thus discover all the hidden or neglected horizons of its intentionality . . . One might say that phenomenology is a way of becoming aware of where we are in the world, a *sich besinnen* which consists of a recovery of the origin of sense *(sens)* in our lifeworld or Lebenswelt.[11]

As the method of intentional analysis, phenomenology does not place us once removed from the concreteness of life. Phenomenology is intentionality—which is to say, phenomenology is those myriad hori-zons, suspected and unsuspected, of contact. Contact returns us, we might say, to the things themselves.[12]

Still, in this description of phenomenology, Levinas invokes *sich besinnen* as coextensive with contact. Does this not complicate matters? Does not Levinas seek, if nothing else, to break us out of those self-enclosed notions of presence lying at the foundations of the history of subjectivity? Does it really make sense to situate Levinas's thought within a method of self-reflection? This brings us to another important misunderstanding of the Husserl-Levinas relationship. The fact that the other human is the centerpiece of Levinas's work tempts us to see his break with Husserl in terms of a confrontation with the account of intersubjectivity in the *V. Cartesian Meditation*. We might be further tempted in this regard by the fact that Levinas's first contribution to Husserl studies was his *Méditations Cartésiennes* translation, coupled with the fact that Levinas attended Husserl's lectures on intersubjecti-vity during Winter Semester 1928-1929. But Levinas's work in truth does not rewrite the problem of intersubjectivity.[13] Rather, Levinas's work is, as he says in *Totality and Infinity*, a defense of *subjectivity*. It is neither a phenomenology of the Other nor a phenomenology of how intersubjectivity works. His defense turns phenomenology back, with Husserl, to the subject. To be sure, Levinas will rethink what it means to be a subject in the ethical relation, but, and this is crucial, this re-lation is always understood by him on the basis of the subject accused. "There is an intrigue of the other in the same which," Levinas writes, "does not amount to an openness of the other to the same . . . Subjecti-vity is structured as the other in the same, but in a way different from that of consciousness" (AE, 31–32/25). The descriptive demand is to

attend to a *sich besinnen* of the other in the same. To describe otherwise—
that is, to describe the Other itself—would risk usurpation of the place
of the Other. To account for the Other in terms of its unsettling of my
life is to account for a subjectivity in question, my moral consciousness,
ethical subjectivity itself. This is the locus of Levinas's concerns.

Hence, in Levinas's hands, phenomenology will forgo the violence
of describing the Other as such in the name of describing the subject
subjected to the interruption of the Other. Levinas will say in this vein
that he does not want to write an ethics, but wants only to account for
the *sens* of ethics. We shall have more to say about Levinas's notion of
sens below in chapter 1, but here we might consider a revealing remark
on the matter. Levinas asks: "Can the alterity of the other not bestow
sense otherwise (*prendre sens autrement*), in the positive modality of the
unique and the incomparable?"[14]

The *sens* bestowed from the unique and the incomparable is ethical sense: my sense of myself as a moral consciousness, the sense of
ethical subjectivity. Levinas's conception of a bestowal of sense from
the alterity of the Other both alters and preserves something fundamental about phenomenology: a *sich besinnen* which, in this case, uncovers
the origin of ethical sense in the accusing face. Levinas preserves
Husserl's claim that subjectivity is the space in which phenomenological understanding occurs. Levinas, like Husserl, describes subjectivity,
not the Other itself and not this "third thing" called *inter*subjectivity.
Levinas's alteration of phenomenology lies in the peculiar mode of
understanding that such ethical *sich besinnen* entails. I do not thematize
the Other, nor do I thematize myself immanently. Rather, in moral consciousness, I come to myself as already called by the other, already
interrupted, already, as Levinas will say in *Otherwise than Being,* trau-
matized and obsessed. The recurrence of the oneself is the experience,
with all due qualifications on the term, to which Levinas gives testimonial description.[15] My traumatic awakening initiates an account of
what comes to be called ethical subjectivity. The Other, we might say,
traumatically provokes the *intersubjective reduction*. This reduction
begins the phenomenological accounting for how one awakens to one's
self, in moral consciousness, already possessed and obsessed by the
Other. What is the sense and origin of this traumatic awakening? This
is Levinas's most originary phenomenological question.

In asking this question, Levinas situates his work within the issue of the status and origin of sense. We cannot understand this prob-

lematic in Levinas with any thinker other than Husserl. It is Husserl alone who has turned philosophy toward the original institution(s) of sense, toward the problem of, in a term he and Levinas will share, *Sinngebung*. Levinas's understanding of *Sinngebung* comes directly from Husserl, and it is always, phenomenologically, a problem of subjectivity. Intersubjectivity concerns the constitution of objectivities. If Levinas confronts Husserl's *V. Cartesian Meditation* at all, and he mentions that text only a couple of times by name, it is only in those places where Husserl discusses analogizing apperception and pairing. It is important to realize that at that point in the analysis, Husserl is firstly occupied with the question of the origin of the subject's awareness of self.[16] The problem of objectivity (of intersubjectivity) only enters as an unwitting prejudice, one that compromises what a phenomenology of the encounter with the Other discovers. This is what Levinas exposes when he opposes his asymmetry to Husserl's symmetry.

The problem of sense, a Husserlian problem through and through, changes the terms of the Levinas-Husserl relation. This problem around which this relation clusters is that of intentionality and genesis. To state it precisely: How does sense emerge from our sensible contact with the world? Now it should be said that Levinas will put forth an account enormously different than any we might find in Husserl's works. Husserl's phenomenology is *the* problem of Levinas's philosophical work. It is a problem both in terms of something to be surmounted and something to be extended. Levinas's original descriptions are both parasitic on and independent of Husserl, drawing vitality from his findings while at the same time standing in a wholly other horizon. Phenomenology is a problem for Levinas. But to claim, on this basis, that Levinas points us *beyond* phenomenology is to miss the heart of the matter: the method of intentional analysis. Intentional analysis may at first appear to be a formal method, but the sense of the method lies in its deformalization, the *mise en scène* of contact and sensibility. To rethink what that method discovers when purged of certain prejudicial, operative concepts is not postphenomenological. Rather, and quite to the contrary, it is wholly and eminently Husserlian in its spirit and approach. And, if this contact itself signals the ethical within experience, we need not seek out supplements to phenomenology. The living-presence of the Other—and whatever its approach does to experience—institutes a relation, and consequent sense, that

Levinas calls ethical. Phenomenology, put in contact with the sensibility of the face, is sufficiently sensitive to the ethical intrigue of the interhuman.

This problem of relation and sense must be taken up systematically. To this end, we will have to remain sensitive to how Levinas constantly begins again with Husserl. If Husserl proclaimed himself the perpetual beginner in philosophy, we might be well justified in calling Levinas a perpetual beginner with Husserl. Thus, in the following chapters we will have to continually restage Levinas's encounter with Husserl. Restaging is necessary for the simple reason that Levinas will *reread* Husserl and the Husserlian method of intentional analysis in each phase of the evolution of his thought. Levinas calls this, to borrow a phrase from "La ruine de la représentation" his "long frequenting of Husserlian labors" (RR, 128). Though this rereading of Husserl will reflect changes in Levinas's thought, there is a constant to these frequentings: the problematic of thinking the genesis of sense otherwise. This problematic sits squarely within the question of sensibility, and, ultimately, Levinas will transform this sensual presence to world into a legitimate sense of singularity. The singularity of both the Other and of the I—this is the *sens* of the ethical.

The opening chapter of the present study will serve a dual function: firstly, to introduce the basics of the phenomenological disposition Levinas takes up, and, secondly, to remark on the methodological backdrop of Levinas's confrontation with Husserl. It will be important there to distinguish between Husserl the programmatic thinker and Husserl the phenomenological philosopher. We must be sensitive to the difference between phenomenology as a possibility and phenomenology as interpreted, by Husserl, as transcendental subjectivity. The problem of the reduction, as treated in *Theory of Intuition*, will be our methodological focus. The second chapter will offer a close reading of the Husserlian problematic at work in Levinas's writings from the 1940s and 1950s. The aim of this reading is to appreciate Levinas's engagement with Husserl, as well as to see how this work prepares the phenomenological ground exploited in *Totality and Infinity*. Chapter 3 deploys that preparatory work through a treatment of the interwoven problems of signification, relationality, and sense in *Totality and Infinity*. What emerges from *Totality and Infinity* is subjectivity in question, a subject separated from its origin, and so a subject structured through the relation of passivity.

But passivity is not fully explicated in *Totality and Infinity*. Though it lies at the very basis of what is said in that text, the problem of the temporal dimension of the passive relation remains wholly unexamined. This task is taken up by Levinas in his essays on Husserl and the Husserlian problematic of time in the 1960s. These essays comprise the subject matter of our fourth chapter. These essays, clustered between *Totality and Infinity* and *Otherwise than Being,* open up the question of relation by asking the question of the temporal structure of the interval. The result is diachronic time. Our final chapter reads *Otherwise than Being* under the guidance of these interim essays and their phenomenological discoveries. The result is an account of a phenomenologically justified language of alterity in *Otherwise than Being* that, far from distancing Levinas from Husserl, brings them into an important proximity. Further, this account of how the language of alterity is justified by Levinas will show us both how and why Levinas so dramatically alters his ethical language from *Totality and Infinity* in *Otherwise than Being.*

This alteration is not done by fiat. It is an alteration undertaken (and undergone) out of a phenomenological necessity first disclosed in *Totality and Infinity.* Both texts concern the passivity of the subject in sensibility. In *Totality and Infinity,* that passivity places the subject in a plenitude of sense that overflows any grasping, aiming, wanting. The passivity of *Otherwise than Being,* however, does not discover such abundance. The passivity structured by the trace, a crucial structural item missing in *Totality and Infinity,* places the subject late to itself and its obligations. The sense of ethics has been altered significantly. I am no longer simply insufficient in powers standing before the other. According to *Otherwise than Being,* I have already failed, even prior to the encounter.

A final remark on the nature of this project. The primary task I hope to accomplish is really quite modest: to make Levinas's relation to Husserl explicit. Why pay such sustained attention to this relation? First, Levinas is, historically, an important commentator on Husserlian phenomenology and his criticisms and extensions of it have yet to be taken seriously in the English-speaking philosophical world. The historical and philosophical importance of his Husserl-interpretation warrants our attention. Second, Levinas's work is a critical extension of Husserlian phenomenology. He does not simply critique certain oversights in Husserl's work, but, more importantly, he develops marginal strands of that work in unique and important ways. In this development, Levinas exposes our moral life with a depth and complexity that, to my mind, is unprecedented in the phenomenological tradition. Levinas's place in the phenomenological movement (in this two-fold sense) cannot be understood until we understand the precise terms of the relation his work holds to Husserl's phenomenology.

Further, there is the question of the status of Levinas's own philosophical claims. How can he justify the claim that "the Other comes to teach me," that the Other is singular and unique, that ethics is first philosophy? These claims are of such enormous importance that to leave them without concrete legitimation is to both pass over an indispensable part of Levinas's work *and* open his thought to unwarranted dismissals. Phenomenology, in my view, offers the most significant, concrete mode of legitimation for these questions. It is not enough to be moved by Levinas's evocations. There must be philosophical legitimacy to what is evoked, and I think phenomenology has a powerful claim on that legitimacy in Levinas's work. Phenomenology is the point of access and the term of justification for Levinas's first philosophy, ethics. To document Levinas's relation to Husserl, then, is not simply to document an historical relationship. It is also to draw out something about the matter of moral life itself through phenomenological reflection and to demonstrate, concretely, the claim that that life has on the subject.

And this is not simply a question of the development and justification of Levinas's thought. This is neither merely a question of who Levinas is to Levinas nor merely a question of who Husserl is to Levinas. The matter at issue is subjectivity—its sense and its origin. Levinas's work begins here with the most intimate and disturbing question philosophy can ask: Who am I before the Other? What is my place in the world?

One

Unsuspected Horizons

On the Husserl Question

Phenomenology inaugurates a new style of philosophy.

—Levinas

The relationship between phenomenology and empiricism is complicated. While on the one hand Husserl's reflections show a pervasive preference for the Cartesian path into phenomenology, it is also true that empiricism bears a most striking resemblance to phenomenological research. There is a danger to empiricism, however, that qualifies any resemblance. Empiricism conflates impression or sensation with appearance, and this conflation conceals what, strictly speaking, appears within the properly phenomenological attitude. Phenomenology is an empiricism in the sense that it returns philosophy to experience. But it is not just any experience to which we are returned. Phenomenology returns us to experience as it is *lived*. Empiricism puts fragments and particulars at the basis of experience reflected upon, whereas phenomenology puts the interwoven *morphe* and *hyle* at the basis of experience as lived. This leads Husserl in §6 of the "Epilogue" to *Ideas II* to write that, although Hume's work is quite close to the phenomenological disposition, it is in the end a "sensualistically perverted" transcendental phenomenology (Hua IV, 156/423).

Though he is certainly not a Humean, we might well say the same of the philosophical work of Levinas. Particularity and singularity lie at the basis of the experience *his* work evokes. From the outset of his philosophical itinerary, Levinas has insisted on the phenomenological character of his work, even in its most pronounced departure from Husserlian descriptions. He has demanded that his philosophical work be seen as phenomenological despite the fact that, by his own admission, it does not always follow the rules laid down by Husserl and does

13

not share Husserl's "obsession" with representation and theory. The fact that Levinas will come to characterize his own position as a phenomenology of the noumenal (cf., LC, 43/21) clearly distinguishes the aim of his work from that of Husserl, who sought the *logos* of the phenomenal. Levinas will always emphasize his distance from the Husserlian program, but will exceed it only by way of the horizons Husserl's labors open up. This exceeding is phenomenology itself. This exceeding takes its point of departure within the myriad horizons of a phenomenological empiricism. Much of the task of the present work is to document the meaning of this departure and how it is rooted squarely within a set of distinctly Husserlian problematics.

In what sense can Levinas's work be called phenomenological? And, indeed, how can a work that is so critical of the primacy of identity and theory be aligned with Husserl, whose work is nothing if not the rigorous pursuit of the Eidos? If Levinas's work is a sensualistic perversion of the transcendental, then in what sense can it still be a phenomenology? If phenomenology inaugurates a new style of philosophy, as Levinas will say in 1959, then it must also be said that Levinas inaugurates a new style of phenomenology. This new style is not brought about through the wedding of the transcendental with another set of privileges, the arguments of numerous commentators notwithstanding, but rather only through the explosion of the horizons of phenomenology from within phenomenology itself. Levinas puts phenomenology in tension with itself and develops his own position out of this tension. So the centrality of phenomenology for Levinas's work must be emphasized. This emphasis has its locus in Levinas's reworking of Husserlian horizons, which the present work documents. The enigma of sensibility produces what may be called a sensualistically perverted transcendental phenomenology. The decisive nuance here is that this perversion is authorized by the very phenomenology it perverts. This authorization has manifold features, all of which will come to mark the phases of Levinas's constantly renewed debate with Husserl.

To establish the basic parameters of this new style of phenomenology, we first need to ask what general thematic concerns unite Levinas with Husserl. We must ask what makes Levinas's work eminently phenomenological. To begin with, it is noteworthy that both thinkers demand the intertwining of the question of sense with relationality or intentionality and subjectivity. As early as his "Sur les *Ideen* de E. Husserl," Levinas will underscore the basic feature of intentionality: Concretely, the question of intentionality insists on the primacy of relation, where we understand this relationality to be *constitutive of the very meaning of subjectivity* (SLI, 62). Further, to ask what it means to be a subject is already to implicate the problem of sense with intentionality. Intentionality, the relationality constitutive of subjectivity, is "secured" or "grounded," in the end, in the logic of sense-bestowal. Thus, the problem of the directional flow of sense, where it comes from and how it is generated (which answers the question of the relational structure of primordial subjectivity), will be what occupies much of our attention in the following study. The problem of sense-bestowal emerges from the concretion of phenomenology's transcendental project. In this regard, Levinas and Husserl are bound to the phenomenological demand to return to the concrete, as well as the necessity of establishing the transcendental character of what is rendered as concrete in explicating the structure of lived-experience. In spite of the fact that Levinas's language of alterity will contest the letter of Husserl's work at virtually every moment, the two share a common logic and spirit: the return to sense-bestowal and the primacy of relation. This is the logic that constitutes any genuinely radical philosophy. As we shall see, Levinas's work enacts a reversal of the Husserlian position, but (perhaps paradoxically) this does not amount to a repudiation of the strategies of phenomenology. To the contrary, Levinas will show us both how this reversal is necessitated by the methods and matters of phenomenology itself and how only the structures of sense-bestowal can render the reversal adequately. Thus, we will have to show exactly how this reversal is demanded and how Levinas's inverting of the Husserlian world is only accomplished from within the horizons of phenomenology as a radical philosophy.

Levinas's work is for the most part critical of Husserl's phenomenology. This fact is evident upon even the most cursory glance at Levinas's writings. But the fact that his critique of Husserlian phenomenology is still necessarily phenomenological opens the general question of the function of critique. To put it simply, given the pursuit of the enigmatic that characterizes Levinas's lifelong work, there are legitimate rhetorical reasons for considering Levinas's relation to phenomenology as primarily, and for the most part, critical. Indeed, Levinas will often portray Husserl's phenomenology as a foil to his own researches. What in Husserl's thought is a dominating preoccupation with the formalistic question of method seems, at best, only marginally present in Levinas's original work. However, to construe this relation as one of opposition is to fundamentally misunderstand the status of phenomenology in Levinas's work. It is to fail to appreciate what is radical about phenomenological philosophy. In pursuing what is radical in phenomenology, Levinas's explosion of phenomenological matters and methods is written into the very demand that phenomenology seek what is without presupposition and purge its descriptions of metaphysical structures. Relentless self-critique, self-overcoming, and self-transformation are demanded by the very idea of a rigorous science. Now, it is quite clear that the rhetoric of rigor and science will fall by the wayside in Levinas's work. He no doubt spends his philosophical career problematizing the legitimacy of the first position of identity, but the method and matter of Husserl's phenomenology will be both the matter of his point of departure and the method of his contestation of the primacy of identity.[1] Because phenomenology is defined by self-critique and self-overcoming, the present study may legitimately contend that the strict opposition of Levinas to Husserl misconceives both the methodological status of Levinas's work and the possibilities of phenomenological "reflection."[2] In those moments where he is most critical of Husserl, Levinas, paradoxically, is perhaps the most phenomenological.

With this much said, the following question still stands: What is the meaning of "phenomenology" in the context of Levinas's work? To answer this question it is imperative that we gain clarity regarding the essence of phenomenological inspiration, as well as what is shown in the concrete experience of phenomenology. The irreducible items of this experience and inspiration are captured in the intertwined function of intentionality and sense. Presently, our first concern will be with the general structure of this problem. Throughout Levinas's reading of Husserl's phenomenology, the structural relation between intentionality and sense is essential. It establishes the very logic at work both in the transcendental/formal and concrete/sensual moments of phenomenological researches. We will follow this problematic with consideration of the thematic orientation prevailing in Husserl's treatment of the question of intentionality and sense. This consideration will highlight the method of reflection against which Levinas's work will labor. A glance at the brief critical concerns regarding Husserl's treatment of intentionality and sense in Levinas's *Theory of Intuition* will conclude our first foray into Levinas's phenomenology. Reading Levinas's early critical concerns set the stage for more fully developed problems of transcendence and sensibility from the 1940s and 1950s. The present chapter aims at the formal task of setting out the (exploded) boundaries of the phenomenology within which Levinas first encounters and subsequently rewrites the Husserlian prerogative. First, then, let us gain some clarity regarding the scope of phenomenology and the point of departure for its general project.

Intentionality and Sense

For Husserl, the problem of intentionality is both the matter (Hua III, 167ff/199ff) and the method (Hua IX, 270) of phenomenology. Intentionality defines the "nature" of consciousness or subjectivity. Intentionality is not a property of consciousness, but wholly and simply consciousness itself. Though the Husserlian conception of intentionality is dominated by the thematic structure of consciousness of a proposed something, and thereby ultimately refers back to a spontaneous ego, the problem of intentionality as such is the problem of relation. That which is given in experience is constituted by a set of relations. The relations themselves constitute the form and content of subjectivity or consciousness. Subjectivity is this relation. The subject does not adopt an intention, but rather is the relation itself. The matter of phenomenology, its thematic orientation, and its method are guided by this irreducible relationality.

The relationality named by the general problem of intentionality brings us to the primordial construal of the phenomenological field. As Levinas will argue in the third chapter of *Theory of Intuition*, intentionality and the primordial phenomenological field are inseparable (TIPH, 65–85/37–51). The first book of the *Ideas* names this field the stream of lived-experience (*Erlebnis*). Husserl writes that

> [b]y lived-experience in the broadest sense we understand everything and anything to be found in the stream of lived-experience; accordingly not only the intentive lived-experiences, the actional and potential *cogitationes* taken in their full concreteness, but also whatever is to be found in the way of really inherent moments in this stream and its concrete parts. (Hua III, 65/75)

This "but also" qualification introduces an important set of concerns for Levinas. Such a qualification will allow Levinas to retain, despite his sustained critique of the traditional concept, a sense of the term experience. The broadest sense of *Erlebnis* is not delimited by the positional and actional conceptions of the ego. That is, *Erlebnis* does not designate only what the ego actively seeks and produces. *Erlebnis* has also its dimensions of passivity. All modalities of relation—active and passive—are set in this original field of phenomenology. The concrete parts and inherent moments constitutive of the meaningfulness of lived-experience are already operative in the stream of experience. In the *Cartesian Meditations*, Husserl calls this field, in its full concretion, the "monad." Though the term "monad" is rather awkward and misleading, Husserl is simply designating as monadic the whole of concrete life and its constitutive parts. The monad, or subjectivity in the comprehensive sense of the matrix of intentionalities,

> includes the whole of actual and potential conscious life, [and] it is clear that the problem of explicating this monadic ego phenomenologically (the problem of his constitution for himself) must include all constitutional problems without exception. (Hua I, 102–103/68)

All constitutional problems lie within the scope of phenomenological research. What this means is that the field within which phenomenology works is unconstrained in theme. The primordial field is thus composed of a multiplicity of horizons. The horizons are intentionally constituted—relationally structured. All horizons demand an explication concrete and free of naive metaphysical adventure (Hua I, 166/139). Out of this concretion emerge both passive and active modalities of relation, which is to say, passively bestowed and actively instituted intentions.

The principle of concretion is a principle that Levinas will adopt as the centerpiece of his phenomenology. And this concretion will transform Husserl's construal of the things themselves. Levinas's return to the concrete things themselves will have dramatic consequences for the idealistic construction of intentionality. We shall have more to say about this concretion later, but for now we note the immediacy and unconstrained character of the original phenomenological field. At its outset, the field of phenomenology is not constrained by a particular prerogative. Indeed, the field is unconstrained precisely because of a lack of preconceived construals of its structure(s). Lived-experience is in its original manifestation open and pregnant. The project of a phenomenological idealism, as Levinas understands it, closes the horizons of this openness, thereby constraining what appears to the idealist according to the work of the transcendental ego.

This closing and its subsequent compromises quite clearly trouble Levinas. For Levinas, the idealism that inheres in Husserl's work will always compromise the scope of his descriptions—the programatic claims made regarding the possibilities of this original phenomenological field notwithstanding. However, this compromise is *not* wholly negative. Rather, it opens upon another positivity. There remain open horizons forgotten and betrayed in the privilege of the idealist's mode(s) of relationality. The task of a radical phenomenology, one that displaces and replaces the transcendental, is to recall with all due constitutive force what is both forgotten and indispensable. Levinas writes:

> Phenomenology is the recall of these forgotten thoughts, of these intentions; full consciousness, return to the misunderstood implied intentions of thought in the world . . . It is the presence of the philosopher near to things . . . Recalling the obscured intentions of thought, the methodology of phenomenological work is also at the origin of some ideas (*idées*) which seem to me indispensable to all philosophical analysis. (EeI, 20–21/30–31)

The "ideas" Levinas has in mind originate in a consideration of intentionality. To be more precise, these indispensable and forgotten ideas emerge from a consideration of the relationality constitutive of affective life—our affective presence to the world. This affective presence turns us to a concrete consideration of what animates consciousness (what Levinas will later call *psychism*),[3] both in and outside of accomplished egoic life. Levinas writes:

> [Phenomenology] consists in respecting the intentions which animate the psychic and the modalities of appearing which conform to these intentions, modalities which characterize the diverse beings apprehended by experience. It consists in discovering the unsuspected horizons within which the real is apprehended by

representative thought, but also apprehended by concrete, pre-predicative life. (DL, 406/292)

The horizons of phenomenology do not solely include those apprehended in acts of active synthesis. Rather, the unsuspected horizons within which thought is caught include the concrete pre-predicative life of the ego. Intentional analysis will also always be directed toward the relations constitutive of that life. Intentional analysis must exceed the constraints of egology, and this exceeding is demanded by the situation in which phenomenology already finds itself. Levinas's critique of Husserl, which comes from within this explication of pre-predicative life, is immanent to phenomenology. Husserl generates the very critical tools that Levinas puts into action.

A phenomenology aimed at describing this pre-predicative life (with all qualifications due regarding the term "description") opens up the possibility of another *practice* of phenomenology. That is, the exploration of the relational structures of pre-predicative life explodes the limitations imposed by the idealist's closed system of predelineated horizons. To do phenomenology, then, is not necessarily to find oneself constrained by a closed system of horizons. Phenomenology may also be a description of how the noumenal lends itself to appearance and the perhaps absurd logic of that lending. This is precisely what Levinas means by his call to a phenomenology of the noumenal. *This* extension of the practice of phenomenology is not bound by the abstract notion of signification on which any idealism turns. Doing phenomenology in this Levinasian sense

is not only . . . to guarantee the signifyingness of a language threatened in its abstraction or in its isolation. It is not only to control language by interrogating the thoughts which offend it and make it forget. It is above all to search for and recall, in the horizons which open around the first "intentions" of the abstractly given, the human or interhuman intrigue which is the concreteness of its unthought (it is not purely negative!), which is the necessary *mise en scène* from which abstractions are detatched in the said of words and propositions. It is to search for the human or interhuman intrigue as the fabric of ultimate intelligibility. And perhaps it is also the way for the wisdom of heaven to return to earth. (TeI, 28/158)

This passage is remarkable for the very reason that in it Levinas tells us how the abstracts concerns of idealism are so radically transformed by their own forgotten horizons that they *already* point the way to "the return of the wisdom of heaven to earth." In this remark, Levinas employs the figure of heaven in order to evoke the transcendence of the face of the Other and the language of earth in terms of the sensible relation. It is phenomenology that leads us to this transcendence. Phenomenology describes the peculiar relationality such transcendence manifests. Phenomenology remains a pregnant possibility because it always demands a return to the originary stagings that precede what is abstractly given as representation. This is a significant series of remarks. They qualify Levinas's often quick identification of phenomenology with representation. In particular, what we learn from this passage is that the phenomenology set out as an explication of representation is always already exceeded and superseded by the call to the original *mise en scène* from which representation first arises. The complexities of this original, pre-reflective, and concrete *mise en scène* form the horizons forgotten by idealism. But, and this is the decisive twist, those unsuspected horizons remain irreducible relations constitutive of sense.

It is important to here hesitate and consider the meaning and significance of Levinas's evocation of the "horizons" of phenomenology. If we are conceiving Levinas's work as a certain kind of phenomenology, then the problem of horizon calls for careful definition. First, the significance of the notion of a *forgotten* horizon is that it allows Levinas to claim that his concerns have a certain and decisive immediacy for the phenomenological project. That is to say, if the horizons that occupy Levinas's work with and against idealism are already implicated in the original field within which idealism is motivated, then the critique and surmounting of the terms of idealism are immanent to Husserlian phenomenology. The critique and surmounting are genuinely built into the idealist project of phenomenology. The unsuspected horizons surround and often offend its researches. The horizons are unsuspected precisely because, like anything unsuspected, they are not *fore*seen. Husserl does not *fore*see these horizons because his prerogative puts another kind of foreseeing first. But what is unforeseen, in this case, retains a secret constitutive force. The Levinasian prerogative will see—albeit in a very peculiar manner—what Husserl forgets.

But Levinas's employment of the notion of horizon is neither unproblematic nor without qualification. The meaning of this Levinasian horizon is far from clear. Indeed, in *Totality and Infinity* for example, Levinas will outright reject the positivity of the phenomenological notion of horizon for his own work. In this vein, he will write that

> [a]n existent is comprehended in the measure that thought transcends it, measuring it against the horizon whereupon it is profiled. The whole of phenomenology, since Husserl, is the promotion of the idea of *horizon*, which for it plays a role equivalent to that of the *concept* in classical idealism . . . The existing of an existent is converted into intelligibility, its independence is a surrender in radiation. (TeI, 15/44–45)

In this account, Levinas sees the problem of horizon as inseparable from the problem of mediation and the medium of truth. The notion of horizon that is coextensive with mediation and truth is one determined by the activity of projection—whether that be the projection of the constituting ego, the practical interests of Dasein, or the openness of Being. This projection plays a conditioning role wherein what appears (the existent) is always already determined in and through projection.

The Levinasian notion of horizon seeks a phenomenological account capable of returning the "wisdom of the heavens to earth." So it cannot be determined by a projection set out from the subject. The concrete relation Levinas describes is marked by its lack of mediation, its singularity, and its immediacy. To this end, the problem of signification is our first clue to a positive notion of horizon. The concrete relation is first indicated by a signification, a signification out of which a notion of sense is generated as *not* construed by the active projections of the ego. Concrete signification points to another horizon that surrounds, but is not reducible to, the horizons of transcendental subjectivity. Forgotten by idealism, this horizon is understood by Levinas in terms of a horizon of sense. Thus, this horizon bears within it the problem of constitution. The problem of constitution is the problem of intentionality. Constitution asks about the problem of relations constitutive and generative of a particular sense. How the logic of this constitution and generation works is the task of the following chapters, but at this point it is important to pause and note that the horizons forgotten by idealism are horizons of relations that bestow sense. Indeed, as Levinas will claim in the "Preface" to *Totality and Infinity*, the unsuspected horizons in which idealism is planted and which surround its projections do in fact bestow sense (TeI, xvi/28). The horizons to which Levinas's work is dedicated are not horizons of meaning; they are horizons of sense.[4] We will carefully distinguish sense from meaning in Levinas's work below, but it is important to state here the claim that relations that concretely bestow sense are not determined by mediation and the medium of truth. In the positive sense that Levinas wants to give it, we can think of horizon as intentionally structured without necessarily conflating that relationality with the active and positional subject. Sense is bestowed otherwise than idealism through a horizon of relations first signified in the concrete.

Now, it should be said that Levinas's concern in his own work will always be with the problem of alterity and the necessity of articulating its *first* position. This brings us to the obvious question: Is intentionality genuinely adequate to the radical nonadequation of the thought of alterity? How can intentional analysis legitimately be ascribed to the language of alterity? This difficulty is due in part to Levinas's own self-understanding. In his rejection of the rules of Husserl's method and the parameters set by the Husserlian conception of the transcendental, Levinas will nevertheless retain the methodological work of intentional analysis as that which recovers the forgotten sense in phenomenology (cf., DQVI, 139–143). The reversal of intentionality, which ruptures the boundaries of the theoretical, is accomplished in the setting out of the intention from the Other. This is still a relation, still an intention, but it must be said otherwise (DQVI, 141). Intentional analysis must come to terms with the structure of the language of this saying. On this intentionality, Levinas notes in *Ethics and Infinity* that "[t]he relationship with the Other can be sought as an irreducible intentionality, even if one must end by seeing that it ruptures intentionality" (EeI, 23/32). Levinas puts two senses of intentionality to work in this remark. First, the irreducible intentionality. This intentionality manifests the general feature of intention—that of relationality. The relation to the Other is irreducible. This will be the site of the weight of concern alterity places on the Same, wherein I cannot evade the Other and cannot reduce or neutralize the relation. The intentionality interrupted and ruptured is the interpretation of relation in terms of positionality and the noesis-noema structure, both of which are interpreted by Levinas in terms of the economy of representation. The rupture is manifested in saying relation otherwise than the theoretical.

The saying of relation "otherwise" than the theoretical, as Levinas will put it, departs from the straightforward immediacy of the horizons of lived-experience. This general phenomenological point of departure, then, becomes the problem of how to make sense of the subject's presence to world—that is, where we understand "world" to be the "universal horizon of all experience," as Landgrebe has put it.[5] Phenomenology is concerned explicitly with the question of how we ought to construe the relationality constitutive of this presence to world. In Mohanty's phrase, phenomenology is the attempt to understand the "cunning of intentionality" that has secretly constituted the sense of the relation.[6] The Husserlian words for this presence to world are the thematizing modalities of relation: *Erlebnis*, absolute subjectivity, and pure consciousness. The Levinasian words for this presence will be the affective modalities of presence to world: transcendence, sensibility, and proximity. For both Levinas and Husserl, the presence of the subject to world is always exceeded by the intentional horizons implicated in the explicit collection of significations. What is signaled in lived-experience is the starting point of exposition for both thinkers. What is signaled in lived-experience—the things themselves—will be the locus of Levinas's debate with Husserl and thus the debate is immanently and eminently phenomenological. Further, though intentionality is constitutive of our presence to world, this intentionality or horizon of intentionalities cannot be conceived solely as a static structure. Rather, the matrix of relations constitutive of presence to world effects a production of sense. This production of sense points us beyond the horizon of intentions explicated in static analysis and toward the problem of sense-genesis. This brings us to yet another question: What, in general, is the status of "sense" as both a static and genetic item in the presence of the subject to world? How is it possible for Levinas to retain the phenomenological notion of "sense" in his own descriptions?

In describing his own project, Levinas will write that ". . . my task does not consist in constructing an ethics; I only seek its sense" (EeI, 85/90). What does it mean to seek the sense of ethics? Ethics is concretely produced in the presence of or proximity to the Other. How is it possible to assign the term "sense" to this proximity, in light of the fact that the term is so typically bound up with the thematic orientation of the noesis-noema correlation? Here we come up against a crucial set of distinctions in phenomenology between modalities of meaningfulness, all of which turn on how we understand the relation between the problem of the structure of constitution and the primordial relational problem of intentionality. It is crucial for our attempt to develop what might be a Levinasian phenomenology to distinguish these modalities of meaningfulness, as we hope to show that Levinas will not abandon the transcendental logic of constitution. He will of course abandon the dominant form of constitution that obtains in idealism—constitution as set out from the active transcendental ego—but the logic of constitution, under the rubric of the genetic and a reversed model of sense-bestowal, is maintained. As we have already indicated, Levinas will also not abandon the problem of intentionality as the problem of relation, although he will abandon the dominant form of intentionality in idealism: the intentionality set out from the ego. The relation of constitution generates a sense. For Levinas, ethics will always be a relation and a sense that is constituted otherwise than idealism. What sense, then, are we to make of the appeal to "sense"?

There are three basic modalities of phenomenological meaningfulness: *Sinn*, *Bedeutung*, and *Meinung*. Simply put, to seek the *Sinn* of the ethical is not the same as to seek a *Bedeutung* or a *Meinung* of the ethical. Levinas is quite careful in this regard. The choice of the phenomenological notion of sense as *Sinn* as the character of what is produced in the ethical relation—instead of and in direct opposition to *Bedeutung* and/or *Meinung*—is significant. From the outset, Levinas translates the German word *Sinn* as *sens* and it is only *sens* that will hold a primary positive phenomenological position. In his treatment of the problem of sense in *Theory of Intuition*, Levinas will translate the German *Sinn* into the French *sens* (TIPH, 90/56). This is consistent with his translation of the Fourth and Fifth of Husserl's *Cartesian Meditations*, where he all but exclusively renders *Sinn* as *sens*. In his remarks on *Sinn* from the *Theory of Intuition*, Levinas notes that the phenomenological notion of sense must be distinguished from the more restricted notion of sense as a noematic core and thus sense as a noetic correlate (TIPH, 90/56). This distinction is decisive. *Sinn* or *sens* is neither reducible to a correlate of one act (noesis) nor to one modality of constitution (noema). Sense will always require an adjectival and contextual qualification. This adjectival and contextual qualification attaches sense to its generative source thereby making sense a more pluralistic or fluid structural item than meaning. Sense can be attached to a multiplicity of sites of genesis. Thus, even when, in his translation of the *Cartesian Meditations*, Levinas on one occasion renders *Bedeutung* as *sens*,[7] the context of the translation keeps it in line with the philosophical point of our discussion. That passage pertains to the status of "meaningful" descriptions of empirical *Bedeutung*. Levinas translates *empirische Bedeutung* as *sens "empirique"* and thus the phenomenological status of what is at issue requires an adjectival and contextual qualification. The phenomenological position of sense is therefore held fast.

The other words that come to stand for "meaning" and with which "sense" could easily be confused are distinguished according to their structural status. Levinas's translations of *Sinn, Meinung,* and *Bedeutung,* along with his implicit quarrels with other translators, can tell us a lot about how he understands the problem of *Sinn* and its difference from the problem of *Meinung* and *Bedeutung.* The latter two ultimately either refer to the question of the propositional models of intentionality set out from the ego *(Meinung)* or to the economy of manifestation *(Bedeutung).* As early as his first essay on Husserl in 1929, "Sur les *Ideen* de M. E. Husserl," Levinas will translate the German term *meinen* with *penser* (SLI, 83) and Husserl's *bedeuten* and *Bedeutung* into the French *signifier* (SLI, 83) and *signification* (SLI, 53). In a footnote to *Otherwise than Being,* Levinas will translate the substantive form of *meinen* as *vouloir-dire,* which somewhat departs from his translation in 1929. The translation in *Otherwise than Being* aims at distinguishing the phenomenal status of *vouloir-dire* from *visée.* Levinas's target here is Paul Ricœur, who renders *Meinung* as *visée* in his translation of *Ideen I.* For Levinas, Ricœur's translation is too blatantly voluntaristic and thereby fails to be attentive to the neutralization of the will that phenomenology attempts to institute through the reduction. Suzanne Bachelard, for her part, renders *Meinung* as *intention* in the translation of *Formale und Transzendentale Logik,* which is close to the sense Levinas wants to capture in his 1929 translation. But, the French *intention* is still too broad. Not all intentions are inextricably bound to thought. *Meinung* as *intention* risks conflation of thought with intentionality, thereby forestructuring any phenomenological account of relation. Levinas's translation of *meinen* into *penser* locates the modality of meaningfulness appropriate to *Meinung* within thought. But *meinen* as *penser* does not, as does Bachelard's translation, reduce all intentions to the intellectual sphere. According to Husserl, sense is not reducible to an attitude or disposition of the positional ego (Hua III, 191/224); the same cannot be said of *Meinung.*[8] The essence of *Meinung* sought in Levinas's revised translation of it as *vouloir-dire* is of course captured in the *vouloir,* the wanting of the wanting-to-say. The will is secretly at work in the intention. The intending will and thought animate, however clandestinely, what has meaning. This translation of *Meinung* locates meaning as a correlate of an attitude or disposition. Meaning is distributed from a position of the ego. Levinas's translation of *Meinung* as *vouloir-dire* therefore neither reduces intentionality to the intellectual—it is not *intention*—nor does it ascribe a necessary voluntarism to all modalities of meaningfulness.

The translation of *Bedeutung* as *signification* is perhaps less complicated. The phenomenal and structural status of *signification* is one of dependency; signification is founded on a sense and points to sense in its signifying. The signifyingness of signification derives its sense from *Sinn* or *sens*. This much is evident from Husserl's work on *Bedeutung* in *Ideas I* and the First of the *Logical Investigations*, where *Bedeutung* is described in its expressive manifestation of *Sinn* (cf., Hua III, 257/295). What is to be gained from Husserl's analysis is that *Bedeutung*, by itself, is always reducible to the economy of manifestation. Manifestation is not freestanding. It points to a prior constitution. In Levinas's account, and here he is eminently phenomenological, it is not enough to end with the modality of signification. We need a further account of the sense signified in manifestation, even where manifestation is freed from the logic of thematization. Sense and signification are interwoven. "It is phenomenologically irreducible," Levinas declares, "sense signifies."[9] And so too the converse. Just as every sense signifies, every signification has a sense. To explicate signification is to explicate the sense, however it is constituted, of what signifies.

Now, this account of sense will be a site of contention between Husserl and Levinas. The former will, quite famously, seek the genesis of the sense that underpins signification in the ego. The latter seeks the genesis of sense in an origin prior to accomplished egoic life. And, this relation between *signification* and *sens* explains why the terms retain a positive position in Levinas's exposition of the intentionality proper to the ethical relation. To be sure, *signification* will be transformed, along with *sens*, in the course of the exposition of the ethical relation, but *visée/vouloir-dire/pensée*, as modalities of meaningfulness, will for Levinas always be aligned with idealism and the philosophy of the Same. These translations of *Meinung* do not take an adjectival form. "Aimed at," "wanting to say," and "thought" are wholly active and point to a constituting ego. *Signification* and *Bedeutung* are founded on *sens* and this *sens*, while it always takes us to the point of its genesis, does not always and of necessity point to the ego of the Same. All sense refers us to sense-bestowal, but all sense-bestowal does not refer us to the transcendental ego. Sense and signification may be produced out of the relation of passivity.

At this point it may be objected that *Meinung* is actually more productive, as one might say that the other who interrupts my life institutes a reversed relation of *Meinung*. And of course this relation would be anchored, not in the ego, but the Other. The distinction between analyses of intersubjectivity and subjectivity is decisive here. An analysis of intersubjectivity might proceed on the basis of the presentational clues in the Other's body, seeking, in various modes of empathy, the intentions of the Other. Perhaps through gestures, perhaps through dialogue, an analysis of intersubjectivity might try to how the Other *means* or *intends* a set of demands for me. But this is not Levinas's concern. Levinas is concerned first with the condition of the subject at the origin of responsibility. This is what it means to write an ethics of ethics, to seek the ethical, or, more astutely, to establish the *sens* of *l'éthique*. To ask what the Other intends me to give, what s/he asks as my response, is to write—if only for myself—an ethics. The sense of the ethical lies only within the boundaries of the oneself as accused. To ask outside this boundary is to put myself in the place of the Other. Such displacement is quite literally violence *par excellence*. But, to ask the sense of the ethical, and even to ask whence its bestowal, puts the Other at a distance—a separation—marked by respect. This relation only reintroduces the Other as the origin of *sens unique*. It is a relation, to be sure, but a relation in which my grasp is halted at the limit of myself as the subjected subject.

Intentionality and sense—as well as signification, as the expressive clue to investigation—are thus adequate to the demands of the ethical relation. But, as we have already noted, this sense and this relation must be understood or said otherwise than the constraints of Husserlian idealism. Sense and relation are transformed by Levinas, not through another thinker or a supplement to phenomenology, but in his very confrontation with Husserl. This is a confrontation over the *Sinn* of the things themselves. In order to set the context of this confrontation, let us turn to some of the general features of Husserl's constraining of intentionality and sense and hence his circumscription of our presence to the world.

The Limits of Idealism

How does Levinas understand Husserl's rendering of the relation between intentionality and sense? How does this rendering serve to delimit the scope of *Erlebnis*? In Levinas's work that is *critical* of Husserl, he is primarily concerned with the delimitation of lived-experience in the idealism of *Ideas I*. The structures of Husserl's idealism and the essential stages that lead to it must be outlined so that the context of Levinas's work may be appreciated.

As we noted at the outset, intentionality is the matter and method of phenomenology for Husserl. Husserl will also claim in the *Ideas I* that the phenomenological method operates exclusively in acts of reflection (Hua III, 144/174). What is discovered in acts of reflection is, to use Mohanty's phrase, the cunning of intentionality. In other words, the constitutive and synthetic work that labors in the implicit is made explicit in phenomenological reflection. Reflection in phenomenology is not an inner-perception that turns away from the world of lived-experience. Reflection is rather an attempt to render present to the ego's ray of regard the implicit relations of constitution borne by experience itself. This, for Husserl, is inherent in the kind of being properly ascribed to *Erlebnis*. He writes:

> The kind of being belonging to lived-experiences is such that a seeing regard of perception can be directed quite immediately to any actual lived-experience as an originary living present. This occurs in the form of *"reflection,"* which has the remarkable property that what is seized upon perceptually in reflection is characterized fundamentally not only as something which exists and endures while it is being regarded perceptually, but also as something that *already existed before* this regard was turned to it. (Hua III, 83/98)

This is the concrete sense of reflection. It is not a turn inward, but a thematization of what was already there in pre-reflective life. The "already" of this conception of reflection is decisive, as it guarantees the integrity of the coinciding of the reflected and the reflecting.

Phenomenological reflection is not limited to the thematizing the flow of experience. Reflection becomes philosophically significant when it seizes upon invariance. Reflection is guided by the search for the

Eidos. The methodological point of access to the reflective attitude is the phenomenological reduction and the *epoche*, both of which put out of play the question of the "what" of that which appears in favor of the question of the "how" of its appearing. In so doing, Husserl eliminates the subject-object problem of the moderns, conceiving instead the primordiality of an irreducible relation.[10] The how of appearing is seized upon according to its eidetic core. The elimination of the what of that which appears in the reduction gives phenomenology its descriptive (i.e., nonmetaphysical, nonspeculative) character. The invariant that composes the theme of reflection is the noematic core of what is signified in lived-experience. The noematic core performs a predelineating function vis-à-vis the "how" of the appearing of what appears. Husserl writes:

> Perception, for example, has its noema, most basically its perceptual sense, i.e., the *perceived as perceived* . . . In every case the noematic correlate, which is called a "sense" here (in its extended signification) is to be taken *precisely* as it inheres "immanently" in the lived-experience of perception, of judging, of liking, and so forth; that is, just as it is offered to us when we *inquire purely into this lived-experience itself*. (Hua III, 182/214)

This is significant. To the extent that we understand the noema as an invariant found already there in lived-experience, the formal content of reflection may genuinely claim to be based on a deformalized, concrete instantiation of the form. Reflection is thus seizing upon the already there, where the content of the already there is conceived in its invariant and predelineating function. In reflection, the Eidos is lifted out of the concrete.

For static phenomenology, the noematic core of thematic reflection is the locus of the problem of constitution. Yet the noema is only rendered to a first level reflection. The first level of reflection manifests, among other things, a necessity for a second level reflection by way of the already implicit work of the second level in the first level. The noema points to a noesis, as the two are an irreducible correlation. Just as the first level of reflection reveals the noema as what constitutes the synthetic identity of what appears, the second level of reflection reveals the noema to be itself already constituted by the higher level noetic intentions. The noema is not self-sufficient. Noesis and noema belong together in a correlation bound by eidetic law (Hua III, 206/241). The noesis is composed of a multiplicity of "higher forms" that are constitutive of the simple unity of the noema (Hua III, 206–208/241–243). But, the noesis is not a reflective construction. Rather, the noesis is a "really inherent component part" of lived-experience (Hua III, 202/237) that "runs through" the noema and into the predelineated flow of *Erlebnis* (Hua III, 212/247). Further, the noetic intentions are themselves constituted. The reflective unfolding of the intentional complex first signaled in lived-experience finds its constitutive terminus in the transcendental ego. Husserl writes:

> Every positing begins with a *point of initiation,* with a *positional point of origin* . . . This initiation belongs precisely to the positing as positing qua distinctive mode of original actionality. It is, perchance, like the *fiat,* like the initiating point of willing and acting . . . [E]very act of no matter what species can begin in the *mode of spontaneity pertaining, so to speak, to its creative beginning* in which the pure Ego makes its appearance as the subject of the spontaneity. (Hua III, 253/291)

The transcendentally pure ego is the singular pole of genesis—creative, original, and spontaneous.[11] By identifying genesis with a spontaneous ego, Husserl privileges the actional and the positional. Such privilege aims ultimately at making explicit the constituting function of the actional-positional in the presence of the subject to world.

On the basis of this reflective unfolding of the horizon of intentions already at work in the phenomenological point of departure, Husserl concludes that world-sense is constituted by the transcendental ego. Every intentionality is already noetic, and the noetic is always already caught in the creative productions of the transcendental ego. Husserl notes:

> Owing to its noetic moments, every intentive lived-experience is precisely noetic; it is of its essence to include in itself something such as a "sense" (*Sinn*) and possibly a manifold of sense on the basis of this sense-bestowal (*Sinngebung*) and, in unity with that, to effect further productions which become "senseful" (*sinnvolle*) precisely by this sense-bestowal. Such noetic moments are, e.g., directions of the regard of the pure Ego to the objects "meant" by

it owing to sense-bestowal, to the object which is "inherent" in
the sense. (Hua III, 181/213–214)

Husserl's is an idealism rooted in the claim that all reality is existent
by way of *Sinngebung*. This sense-bestowal, however, does not lead
to a subjective idealism (Hua III, 106ff/128ff). Instead, as Levinas
himself notes, this regressive unfolding leads back to the original phenomenon that makes the subject-object problem in modern philosophy possible. Even the transcendence of the world—i.e., the world *as*
transcendent—is constituted in the performances of the transcendental ego (TIPH, 50/25). Husserl's idealism is not the idealism of a Berkeley (TIPH, 68ff/39ff, 109/71), for, regarding their respective
conceptions of "consciousness," Levinas notes that Husserl and British Empiricism "have nothing in common but the name" (TIPH, 64/
35–36). One could say in Husserl's name what Heidegger said of the
moderns: the scandal is not that the modern problematic was never
solved, but that it was ever even a problem. Phenomenology jettisons
the very abstractions that fated the moderns to scandal. Thus, in
Husserl's hands idealism is able to retain its claim to concretion to the
extent that its structures are found already operative in lived-experience. The *Sinn* that concerns phenomenological idealism is the *Sinn*
limited to what appears within the juridical boundaries of noematic
unity. If the noema is the unbreakable core of lived-experience, a core
only exceeded by the noetic intentions, then the field of transcendental phenomenology may be said to be limited to and exhausted by
idealism.

However, as we have already remarked, the Husserl of *Ideas I* is
explicit regarding the privilege given to the positional and the actional.
This calls for an obvious question: What of the pre-positional and the
pre-actional intentionalities that play a constituting function? These
intentions compose horizons forgotten by Husserl's turn to idealism
and, at least as a point of departure, the horizons recollected by Levinas.
We should here hesitate before the term "horizon," mindful of Levinas's
identification of horizon with ocularity in *Totality and Infinity*—an identification that makes the horizonal encounter with the beyond being
impossible (TeI, 166/191). For Levinas, the forgotten horizons of
Husserlian phenomenology are forgotten modalities of relation. They
are forgotten because they are not reducible to the economy of vision.
The notion of a lost horizon is therefore not, for Levinas, a seeing that

has become obscured. Rather, the forgotten horizons recollected in the thought of alterity are relations that lie outside of the very boundaries of the ocular.

Rethinking the Reduction

What troubles Levinas about Husserl's delimiting of *Erlebnis*? Clearly, the critical focus will be on the character of Husserl's idealism and the horizons that his analysis of lived-experience marginalizes. In *Theory of Intuition*, we do not see so much a sustained criticism of Husserl, as much as a set of concerns that points the way to Levinas's critical work in the 1940s and 1950s. These concerns reduce to one basic problem: the problem of transcendence. How can transcendence be thought otherwise than as constituted by the ego? For Levinas, the necessity of thinking through the sense of this transcendence is demanded by Husserl's own phenomenology. Indeed, as he remarks in the concluding chapter of the *Theory of Intuition*, the entirety of the 1930 book is dedicated to showing how concrete intentionality is necessarily a transcendent intentionality—an intentionality without a predelineated, theoretical constitution. To begin explicating this transcendence without egoic constitution, Levinas must first break with the Husserlian logic of the noema, which Levinas interprets as performing the theoretical function of representation in its synthetic work. But Levinas is a phenomenologist. So, this break will only be possible within the phenomenological field. Phenomenology must be subjected to an immanent critique.

The central point of contention in *Theory of Intuition* is the primacy accorded to theory in Husserl's phenomenology, that is, the notion that "the theoretical thesis" plays the founding role in "conscious life" (TIPH, 91/57). This primacy of theory is betrayed in the privileged role played by representation in intentional analysis. Or more precisely and in the Husserlian lexicon, the location of the noema as the constituting core of identity in lived-experience reveals a kind of representation at the center of Husserl's work. Once the primary position of the noema is established, the noetic functions and the sense-bestowing spontaneity of the ego are justified as necessary theoretical structures. The justification derives from their status as implicit within the noematic core. Intentional analysis, on Husserl's account, takes place in acts of reflection.

Is reflection able to legitimate the domination of the noema? What do reflection and the method that makes it possible (viz., the reduction) tell us about the possibilities and limitations of a reflective method? To the extent that it claims to render the sense of lived-experience to the reflective regard in the figure of the noema, phenomenological reflection is the locus of the legitimation of the primacy of theory. It is therefore the site of Levinas's critical remarks.

The aim of reflection, as seizing upon the already there in the turn of consciousness to itself, is to render the reflected and the reflecting coincident. That is to say, what is lived in lived-experience (the reflected) must be immanent to and coincident with acts of reflection (the reflecting). As Levinas notes, "[t]he whole philosophical value of reflection consists in allowing us to grasp our life, and the world in our life, such as they are prior to reflection," otherwise what is revealed in reflection would only be modified states of consciousness and not life itself (TIPH, 196/136). Representation as noema aims at securing this coincidence. If the noema is understood as already operative in straightforward experience, and the properly directed ray of reflection regards the noema in a mode of neutrality, then this neutralization renders the one and same noema. The pre-reflective noema and the reflective noema are identical and coincident in *Sinn*. Thus, representation is not here understood as a formal copy of the given, but rather and more substantially must be understood as the representability of the core of what is straightforwardly given to reflection. The presentation-again, this re-presentation, is for Husserl the presentation of an identical sense. When Husserl says that what is seized upon in reflection is absolutely coincident with, and a nonmodified representation of, what emerges in lived-experience, the doctrine of the noema is not all that is at stake. It is also a question of the integrity of idealism. If the noema cannot hold to this identical sense and the coincidence of the reflected and reflecting is split, then the idealist claim to a first position is put in question. The primacy of theory is clearly a strategic move (and perhaps fateful decision) aimed at securing this coincidence.

But an internal disruption of this primacy emerges within Husserl's own work. The theoretical endeavor of reflection does not immediately exhaust the structure of intentionality. At the moment Levinas identifies this coincidence, he also identifies what he calls a "wavering in Husserl's conception of consciousness" (TIPH, 213–214/150).[12] Is all intentional life reducible to the immanence of theory? Is transcendence possible outside of representation? Affectivity would appear to be a candidate for a pre-reflective, nontheoretical transcendent intention. Affectivity adds a passive dimension to one's presence to world, which adds a quite decisive ambiguity to the matter. In a brief set of remarks, Levinas points the way to the affective life that will constitute his break with Husserlian idealism. Regarding this possibility of a concrete, nontheoretical transcendence, Levinas writes that

> [w]e now see that concrete life must be captured in all its forms and not merely in the theoretical form. Correlatively, the real world is not simply a world of things correlative to perceptive acts (purely theoretical acts); the real world is a world of objects of practical use and values. (TIPH, 74/44)

This constituted world of value and practice is not given over to representation. Nonetheless, it still has a sense, a sense signified otherwise than theory. This other signification arises from the nonrepresentational stratum of the concrete. Levinas writes:

> Let it be well understood: the fact that the attributes "valuable," "useful," or "being wanted" belong to the sphere of objectivity does not mean that they are given in a theoretical representation . . . [This extension of intentionality] expresses only the very general fact that consciousness transcends itself, that it directs itself toward something other than itself, that it has a sense. But "to have a sense" does not mean the same as "to represent" . . . [For example], the characteristic of the loved object is precisely to be given in a love intention, an intention that is irreducible to a purely theoretical representation. (TIPH, 74–75/44–45)

The intentionality constitutive of affective life—the world of affectivity—is not reducible to the neutrality of representation. The affective relation "is not an 'indifferent' medium of pure representations" (TIPH, 75/45). This is the first hint Levinas gives of the critical function of affective life. Its critical function lies in the nonindifference of the practical relation, and so the question of how affective intentions produce sense otherwise than via the noema serve to subvert the first position of representation. If such a relation, and hence such a sense, is possible, then we can begin to puzzle over the first position of idealism in phenomenology and the power of the transcendental ego. These other, affective relations comprise what will come to be called the "forgotten and unsuspected horizons" of phenomenology. Indeed, Levinas closes *Theory of Intuition* by noting the tension between concrete life and the primacy of theory. He ends with a question: "But is there not the possibility of overcoming this difficulty or fluctuation in Husserl's thought given with the affirmation of the intentional character of practical and axiological life?" (TIPH, /158). The tension does not subvert Husserl's phenomenology, but rather only requires that another horizon be taken up, a horizon adequate to the task of the *sui generis* character of practical-axiological objects. Therein lies the break with Husserlian idealism, both in terms of the matters themselves and the method of explicating those matters.

But there is something deeper in this account of the possibility of nontheoretical and nonrepresentational transcendencies than simply naming another modality of relation. It also raises serious questions about the scope and legitimacy of the reduction. The nonindifference of affectivity already implicitly calls into question the scope of the life rendered in reflection through Husserl's reduction. Does the notion of life say more than Husserl's account of the reduction makes manifest? In his first critical treatment of Husserl's idealism in *Theory of Intuition*, Levinas joins both Fink and Landgrebe in wondering about the legitimacy and motivations for the *epoché* and reduction. Given the fact that Fink's well-known *Kant-Studien* article appeared only three years following the publication of Levinas's *Theory of Intuition*, the debate about both the motivation and end result of the reduction is both historically and philosophically important. The question posed is fundamental: On what basis is the reduction motivated? And, on the basis of the answer to that question, what does the motivation for the reduction tell us about what it offers to reflection?[13] That is, in what way is the life rendered in reflection modified and compromised by the motives for the performance of the reduction? For Levinas, this question is not adequately answered by Husserl. Levinas writes that

> [f]or Husserl, philosophical intuition is a reflection on life considered in all its concrete fullness and wealth, a life which is considered but no longer lived. Reflection on life is divorced from life itself . . . The natural attitude is not purely contemplative; the world is not purely an object of scientific investigation. Yet it seems

that man *suddenly* accomplishes the phenomenological reduction by a purely theoretical act of reflection on life. Husserl offers no explanation for this change of attitude and does not even consider it a problem. Husserl does not raise the metaphysical problem of the situation of the *Homo philosophus*. (TIPH, 203/142)

The suddenness of the performance of the reduction and the purely theoretical interest that directs reflection legitimately opens up the question: What life is offered to reflection? For Levinas, it is quite clearly the theoretical life of the subject in the natural attitude.

Yet, we cannot truthfully say that the natural attitude is purely scientific and contemplative. Theory is only an aspect of the natural attitude and thus only an aspect of pre-reflective life. As Levinas will ask a decade later in "L'oeuvre d'Edmond Husserl," am I not something other than my theoretical life? For both Fink and Levinas, the path into phenomenology is determined by the performance of the reduction. The aim of that reduction is to account for the sense (and, ultimately, the origin of sense) of the life of the subject. Fink and Levinas have something in common in reading Husserl's treatment of the reduction, but there are also significant differences. A brief excursus into the relation between Fink and Levinas would be fruitful here, for in pausing to note these similarities and differences, important methodological aspects of Levinas's reflections may be brought into relief.

As Fink notes, the *Aufhebung* of the natural attitude that begins the reduction makes what is manifest to the reflecting regard foreign, strange, or unfamiliar *(Unbekannt)* to the life of the natural attitude.[14] For Levinas too, the suddenness of the reduction draws a strict line between life as it is in pre-reflective living and life as the already lived object of philosophical intuition. The unfamiliarity marked by this line, for Levinas, expressly concerns the incompatibility of the content of theory and the content of concrete life, where the latter is said to overdetermine the former. The difference between what is yielded to reflection and what is living in pre-reflective life is brought into relief in the practice of the reduction. This difference revealed in and through the reduction is, for both Levinas and Fink, not just an alteration of content: It is also the passage to the absolute, the passage to the true subject. "With the reduction," Fink writes, "the transcendental, absolute . . . comes to experience."[15] Levinas makes the identical claim when he writes that the reduction ". . . is the passage to an absolute viewpoint" (TIPH, 137/91–92). The absolute is not a content, but subjectivity itself. Fink calls this subjectivity given in the reduction the "true subject" *(wahre subjekt)*[16] and Levinas calls the same the "genuine self" *(véritable moi)* (TIPH, 213/149). This coincidence of terms is not incidental. It is germane to the matter itself of the reduction and subjectivity. The reduction is the passage to the absolute and true subject, and this destiny of the reduction establishes the grounds of phenomenology's claim to self-legitimacy. The reduction does not leave the world, but rather renders explicit the absolute of the world. Although we must understand that the reduction transcends mere worldliness in the passage to the absolute and true subject, and that this passage draws a line between the reflective and the pre-reflective, the absolute and the pre-reflective are not two worlds. Phenomenology is not subject to the problems of ontologism. The true subject of the absolute is simultaneously with, even in its distinction from, the pre-reflective.

The precise character of this absolute and the subjectivity manifest across the passage of the reduction mark the point where Levinas and Fink go their separate ways. Fink's understanding, the reduction gives access to the totality of concrete flowing life and not just to an abstraction from that life.[17] The problem of motivation derives from the complications involved in the shift from the naïve imprisonment of the natural attitude to the concrete flowing of true subjective life. For Levinas, this true or genuine subjective life cannot be understood in terms of the absoluteness of the flow of life. Rather, the life of the *véritable moi* can only be understood in terms of the standpoint from which this life is seen. The absolute standpoint taken by Husserl's interrogation of the transcendental ego limits the scope of what appears and therefore how life is rendered to reflection. So, for Levinas, the issue of motivation is answered by questioning, or putting into question, the standpoint taken by the reflecting ego. Fink's claim is that the passage from the inauthentic to the authentic subject is unmotivated and takes place, as it were, by fiat. This claim is unaffected by the discussion of the absolute and the true subject. Levinas's claim that the reduction betrays a theoretical interest, and is thereby motivated by the same, is justified when his reading takes into account not just the content of the absolute and the true subject, but also the standpoint from which that absolute may be disclosed. For Levinas, we must be attentive to the position taken prior to, within, and subsequent to the passage to the absolute. This position is a specific kind of relation to the concrete. The "theoretical thesis," Levinas writes, "has . . . a primacy in conscious life" (TIPH, 91/57). The theoretical thesis describes the way in which the absolute and the concrete, in Husserl's account, is set out from a particular viewpoint: The absolute is inseparable from the absolute viewpoint. On this point, Fink and Levinas part ways and the phenomenological stakes could not be higher. It is a question of the scope and legitimacy of Husserl's conception of the absolute and subjectivity.

In short, then, we might say that the reduction reveals the true subject for both Fink and Levinas. Only with Levinas do we see how the true subject is always the subject of a certain kind of truth. That is to say, the *veritas* character of the *wahre subjekt* or *véritable moi* is revealed by the reduction only when we, with Levinas, consider the absolute *and* the standpoint from which the absolute is seen. This *veritas* character betrays the privileged position of theory and representation in Husserl's analysis, as well as revealing for Levinas a hidden motivating interest behind the putative *Unmotiviertheit*[18] of Husserl's practice of the reduction.

The purchase of this reading of Husserl's limitation of the scope of the reduction lies in the question of the possibility of recovering those aspects of pre-reflective life "forgotten" and "unsuspected" by that reduction. What Husserl's reduction, with its theoretical motivation, reveals is only the theoretical content latent in the pre-reflective. The other aspects of pre-reflective life—viz., the aspects of affective and practical life—yield nontheoretical modalities of relation and thus produce a sense otherwise than by way of the noema. This other sense is hidden from Husserl's reduction, as he simply posits the primacy of theory. In this un- or de-legitimated positing, Husserl's phenomenology subsequently forgets other horizons constitutive of the life of *homo philosophus*. Levinas writes further that

> [t]he reduction is an act by which a philosopher reflects upon himself and, so to speak, "neutralizes" in himself the man living in the world, the man positing the world as existing, the man taking part in the world. The reduction consists in regarding one's own life in reflection. But by virtue of the primacy of theory, Husserl does not wonder how this "neutralization" of our life, which nevertheless is still an act of our life, has its foundation in life. (TIPH, 221–22/157)

The phenomenological results culled from the Husserlian reduction are therefore only possible by positing the primacy of theory. "Despite the revolutionary character of the phenomenological reduction," Levinas writes, "the revolution which it accomplishes is, in Husserl's philosophy, possible only to the extent that the natural attitude is theoretical" (TIPH, 222/157). In wondering about the motivation for the reduction, Levinas will not simply posit the spontaneity of an unmotivated reduction, as Fink will three years after the publication of *Theory of Intuition*. The spontaneity of the reduction merely points out the fact that "Husserl gives himself the freedom of theory just as he gives himself theory" (TIPH, 222/157). As we have seen above, Levinas wonders about the recovery of structures of the subject's presence to world prior to and outside of theory. To recover such unsuspected horizons amounts, in the end, to a surmounting of the freedom and theory of the reduction. Levinas's task is not to justify the reduction through a description of its paradoxes, but rather to exhibit modalities of relation that question the scope of what is revealed to a theoretically interested reduction. Levinas's early criticisms of Husserl therefore look to the transcendencies latent in the straightforward life of the subject, a life hidden from the reduction, in order to stage a departure from idealism. Only on the basis of pre-theoretical modalities of relation within a life prior to a theoretically motivated reduction is it possible to speak of a transcendence irreducible to immanence.

Now, as we noted above, Levinas is not engaged in an external critique of phenomenology in *Theory of Intuition*. He is, rather, attempting to surmount the theoretical compromising of the Husserlian program from within the phenomenological field itself. This strategy of critique makes it necessary for Levinas not only to point out the limits of the Husserlian practice of a theoretically prejudiced reduction, but also to recover the positive horizons of the reduction. "Philosophy," Levinas writes, "begins with the reduction" (TIPH, 219/153). How can one still philosophize within the positive horizons forgotten by the theoretically interested reduction? In 1930, Levinas has not yet posed the question of the relation between philosophy and nonphilosophy or philosophical experience and nonphilosophical experience.[19] So, in the *Theory of Intuition* it is simply a question of how to think the reduction without the prejudice of theory.[20] And, because the reduction is the very introduction into phenomenology (TIPH, 193/135), an immanent critique requires a reconsideration or rephrasing of the reduction itself.

For the phenomenological program, the reduction *aims* at rendering manifest concrete life and its structural composition. Husserl's *interpretation* of the reduction fails to adequately render the concrete. This failure does not call for a jettisoning of the method of reduction, but only points to the necessity of another reduction. That is, the failure of Husserl's account of the reduction is not a failure of the reduction itself. It is a failure to practice the reduction radically enough. Levinas writes,

> Concrete life is not the solipsist's life of a consciousness closed upon itself. Concrete being is not what exists for only one consciousness. In the very idea of concrete being is contained the idea of an intersubjective world. If we limit ourselves to describing the constitution of objects in an individual consciousness, in an *ego*, we will never reach objects as they are in concrete life but will reach only an abstraction. The reduction to an *ego*, the *egological reduction*, can only be a first step toward phenomenology. We must also discover "others" and the intersubjective world. A phenomenological intuition of the life of others, a reflection by *Einfühlung* opens the field of transcendental intersubjectivity and completes the work of the philosophical intuition of subjectivity. (TIPH, 214–215/150–151)

The egological reduction—the reduction to the subject of truth—fails to fully recover the life of the concrete subject. In its failure, the egological calls for a nonegological reduction. The intersubjective reduction is here announced as the possibility of phenomenological *and* philosophical access to concretion. So, while it at first appears that Levinas simply drops the problem of the reduction, further reflection reveals that his criticisms are aimed at recovering a more *successful* practice of the reduction. The question of "success" is determined by the ability of the reduction to disclose the fullness of concrete life. Although Levinas will not return to the term "intersubjective reduction" with sustained attention until "La philosophie et l'éveil" in 1976, we do want to suggest here that Levinas's exploration of the myriad structures of affective life are motivated by this call to an adequate practice of the reduction. The call to a reduction that returns us to the concrete is a call to an unmediated relation to the world. Thus, despite the fact that this intersubjective reduction is mentioned in 1930 with regard to the problem of *Einfühlung* and the intersubjective *world*, Levinas is not bound to the Husserlian treatment or posing of these problems. Levinas must free himself from Husserl's treatments, for he will ultimately contend that both projects are contaminated by representation: the representation of the other to me *(Einfühlung)* or of the other in the context of the shared world (intersubjectivity). What Levinas is bound to, however, is the necessity of fidelity to the concrete, to the forgotten, unsuspected horizons of idealism, and therefore to the relations constitutive of the sense of affective life. At this point, then, it is perhaps best to make this tentative methodological claim regarding the rubric under which Levinas's work after 1930 proceeds: The reduction is the very opening upon the phenomenological possibility of access to the concrete.

The concrete returns us to those horizons forgotten by Husserl's interpretation of the reduction, horizons not given over to theoretical interest. What are the other horizons of relation not given over to theory? Levinas's descriptions of these horizons and the new conceptions of subjectivity and sense emergent from those descriptions are made possible in his appeal to the pre-reflective life revealed by the reduction in absence of the idealist's prerogative. Affectivity, only indicated in *Theory of Intuition*, is the locus of these nontheoretical relations. In *Theory of Intuition*, Levinas does not tell us much more about the possibilities nascently at work within the pre-reflective life of the subject. Thus he tells us very little about the consequences of those possibilities for the problem of sense. We only have his hints. This explicit positive work awaits the analyses of the 1940s and 1950s. Nevertheless, the critical remarks in *Theory of Intuition* do point us toward the horizons to be introduced, if only negatively, via those horizons concealed by the reduction performed in the name of theory. With these methodological considerations in view, let us turn to Levinas's concrete work on transcendence and sensibility.

Two

The Subject outside Itself

Transcendence and Materiality
in the 1940s and 1950s

What possibilities lie hidden in intentionality once the privilege of theory is exposed? In what manner is it possible to think about relationality other than in terms of idealist intentions? These questions remain open at the close of *Theory of Intuition*, announced but not yet explored. When Levinas writes *Totality and Infinity*, he will think of relationality in terms of a sense-bestowal set out from absolute difference. But for that sense-bestowal to be possible, Levinas must first exhibit the concrete break with the idealist's account of intentionality. Idealism must be confronted from the inside, not simply opposed. Thus, Levinas's route to this sense-bestowal necessarily requires a concrete extension of Husserl's phenomenology. This route moves from idealism to transcendence and materiality to, in the end, a sense-bestowal from the outside—a sense set out from the Other. The present chapter reads Levinas's essays on Husserl from the 1940s and 1950s in terms of his account of the passage from idealism to transcendence and materiality. The terminus of Levinas's passage is a reversed sense-bestowal, and the final purchase of this reversal is the ethics of the facing face in *Totality and Infinity*. In the 1940s and 1950s, however, Levinas works through the necessary phenomenological ground propaedeutic to the ethics of the face. A reading of these essays is therefore structurally necessary.

We will read Levinas's account of phenomenological passage to transcendence and materiality in the following stages:

1. the structural opening of the system of idealism in "L'œuvre d'Edmond Husserl";

2. descriptions of subjectivity *as* transcendence in *De l'existence à l'existant* and *Time and the Other;*

3. the anarchical function of the sensible in "La ruine de la représentation."

It should be said that the works from this period do not give a treatment of the issue of sense. What they do treat is the problem of relation. But it is only from the relation of transcendence set out from the sensible that Levinas is able to forge a logic of sense that works otherwise than idealism. Thus, in treating these essays, we anticipate the logic of sense-bestowal from the outside, not just by identifying parallel structures, but by explicating the intentionality necessary for such a sense-bestowal. We are preparing the ground for *Totality and Infinity* via an inquiry into the structural opening of idealism.

This structural opening requires an alteration of the configuration of intentionality. The phenomenon of relation warrants such an alteration. As Husserl notes, intentionality is at once the most evident structure and the most complicated. He writes that " 'consciousness of something' is therefore something obviously understandable of itself and, at the same time, highly enigmatic" (Hua III, 169/200). If intentionality is obviously understandable of itself, an understanding most clearly attested to in Husserl's work on the transcendental subject, then what of the enigmatic appearance of intentionality? What form might this enigma take? For Husserl, the enigma is bound up with the "paradox of human subjectivity"[1] or "wonder of wonders"[2] that he names the transcendental subject. By contrast, for Levinas the enigma of Husserl is that at the concrete basis of this paradoxical wonder of wonders there lies another "foundation" that can only show itself outside the boundaries of idealism. The purpose of the present chapter is begin to unravel how intentionality already finds itself bound up with this second sense of the enigma, the modality of intention that is opposed to identity, yet is not a difference subsumed under identity. That is to say, we will begin to ask what structures are necessary to articulate a transcendence that is irreducible to the immanent appearance of the "how" of transcendence.

With this problematic in view, Levinas's essays on Husserl from the late 1950s, most notably the 1959 "La ruine de la représentation," will be our chief concern. We will anticipate our reading of "La ruine de la représentation" through a focused reflection on the 1940 essay "L'œuvre d'Edmond Husserl" and an account of the phenomenological significance of *Time and the Other* and *De l'existence à l'existant*. These characterizations aim at showing the shifting concerns of Levinas's confrontation with phenomenology, which ultimately reveals a shift from the problem of transcendence to the problem of the exterior.

Toward a Transcendent Intention

First, what are the issues that lead Levinas to Husserl after *Theory of Intuition*? On the basis of the findings of *Theory of Intuition*, two basic structures demand articulation: the relation of transcendence and the structure of the sensible. Affective intentionality *is* the interweaving of these two structures. "L'œuvre d'Edmond Husserl" is important because it provides us with an account of the methodological opening in the system of idealism, indicating the latent possibilities of affective life. *De l'existence à l'existant* and *Time and the Other,* on the other hand, both sketch out concrete modalities of the subject as transcendence. This "subject as transcendence" is not one that moves toward the world, but rather is a subject determined as transcendence by the object of its intentionality. This is a relation figured as fecundity, eros, emotion, etc., relations that relate in ways other than idealism. The sensibility that animates this transcendence is given its transcendental due in "La ruine de la représentation." Let us note again that the structures discovered in Levinas's rereading of Husserl will make possible the account of sense that is developed in *Totality and Infinity,* as well as make clear how, in affective life, the freedom and spontaneity of the ego is called into question.

Second, let us pause and consider both the context of Levinas's turn to Husserl—his starting point—and the endpoint toward which our reading of these essays is directed—his destination. In the *Theory of Intuition*, Levinas makes the thetic appearance of intentionality in Husserl's transcendental idealism his critical target. In opposition to that appearance of intentionality, Levinas proposes, in a programmatic fashion, the model of transcendence—an intentionality that moves outside of the representational boundaries of immanence. This leads Levinas to reject, not the idea of intentionality as relation, but only the representational limitation of that intention in Husserl's idealism. Husserl's interpretation of intentionality exhibits transcendence, in Levinas's view, only in the theoretically interested movement toward the intentional object. Transcendence is here only a modification of

immanence. This transcendence is neutralized in the reflective characterization of its structure, a methodological turnabout that reveals the
primacy of theory in Husserl's understanding of phenomenology
(TIPH, 99/63). Thus, in *Theory of Intuition*, Levinas undertakes preparatory work toward founding the theoretical intentionality of representation on the worldly intentionality of transcendence. In this regard,
Levinas will assert that ". . . every act of consciousness is an act of
transcendence" (TIPH, 181/125). This transcendence, as the founding
mode of intentional life, indicates ". . . other modes of existence than
that of the theoretical object" (TIPH, 99/63). In *Theory of Intuition*, it
should be noted that Levinas maintains a somewhat Heideggerian
concern[3]—viz., that the conception of representation lying at the basis
of Husserl's reflective method is inadequate to our first contact with
being (TIPH, 180/124). Transcendence, as a peculiar intention, names
this immediate relation.

Now that we have a sense of Levinas's starting point, some remarks concerning his destination are in order. The concern in 1930 with
immediate contact with being will fall from grace in *Totality and Infinity*. In *Totality and Infinity*, Levinas will fully thematize the structure of
the manifestation of exteriority, and it is the infinity of that exterior
which, as the undoing of form in the relation of transcendence, will
come to be the founding relation (TeI, xv–xvi/27). Levinas will consider
the methodological point of access to the exteriority of the face to be
the transcendent-intention, a sense of relation adequate to the task of
describing the ethical relation. Paradoxically, as we shall see, this intention is only adequate in its nonadequation. The transcendent-
intention will make it possible to speak of experience *par excellence*, the
"site" in which the idea of infinity overflows my powers. This overflow will come, not from a dogmatically metaphysical beyond, but from
and through a relation concretely produced in the facing relation (TeI,
170/196). This "break up of the formal structure of thought" is made
possible by intentional analysis, which "is the search for the concrete"
(TeI, xvi/28). This concrete relation (and the sense of this "concrete" will
be explicated below) is nothing other than the ethical relation. Another
kind of phenomenology is needed.

Thus, the guiding thread of the essays leading to and clustering
around the publication of *Totality and Infinity* is precisely how intentionality can be modified, starting from a transcendence concerned with
immediacy to being to a transcendence that puts subjectivity in ques-

tion. As Levinas remarks in the "Preface" to *Totality and Infinity*, "the essential of ethics is in its transcendent intention, and not every transcendent intention has the noesis-noema structure" (TeI, xvii/29). This intention is Levinas's destination even in the 1940s and 1950s. But, what remains unclear in *Theory of Intuition* is exactly how a transcendence immediately present to being undoes the structure of the noema. The meditations on intentionality in the transitional essays, however, articulate precisely this undoing. Further, this undoing is shown by Levinas to have its resources in the hidden horizons of Husserl's own thought, thereby preparing us for the note in *Totality and Infinity* that Husserlian phenomenology is the very passage to metaphysical exteriority (TeI, xvii/29).

The significance of the transitional essays therefore lies in their treatment of the precise terms of Levinas's modification of the structural possibilities of intentionality. The somewhat historico-genetic picture of Levinas's work that follows aims at showing that his reversal of sense described at the end of "La ruine de la représentation" (and elaborated in *Totality and Infinity*) has its roots in his self-described "long frequenting of Husserlian labors" (RR, 128). In the following sections we will witness three essential thematic movements: first, in the 1940 essay "L'œuvre d'Edmond Husserl," we will see how Levinas rethinks the possibilities of intentionality by way of the phenomenological notion of the concrete. This notion of the concrete—provisionally outlined in 1940—will allow us to conceive of relationality in terms of immediacy and materiality. These terms set the itinerary for Levinas's fully developed reading of Husserlian phenomenology in the 1959 essay "La ruine de la représentation" (and, indeed, up through *Otherwise than Being*). Second, we will characterize how *De l'existence à l'existant* and *Time and the Other*, despite their apparent critical concern with Heideggerian ontology, work as thematic extensions of the formal implications uncovered in the 1940 essay. Third and finally, we will see the explicit extension of the "forgotten horizon" in Husserl's phenomenology through a reading of "La ruine de la représentation." This essay gathers together the force of the work that precedes it, as it rehabilitates the transcendental function of sensibility. This rehabilitation justifies talk of a bestowal of sense from the outside. This bestowal of sense from the outside—*une Sinngebung éthique,* as Levinas will call it—provides the formal indicators of the transcendent intention. This intention is adequate to the logic of exteriority and the reversal of intentionality in the facing relation—our key to a phenomenology proper to the problem of alterity.

Unworking Husserl

The 1940 essay "L'œuvre d'Edmond Husserl" aims at cataloging basic Husserlian themes and thus, as such, promises only a glimpse (however important that glimpse) into what Levinas sees as most radical in Husserl's phenomenology. Indeed, the exposition betrays a somewhat partisan hermeneutic disposition when Levinas praises the "revolutionary" character of Heidegger's work in phenomenology (ŒH, 39). This revolutionary character will begin to show itself in *De l'existence à l'existant* and *Time and the Other*, but in "L'œuvre d'Edmond Husserl" Levinas takes up this innovation exclusively within Husserlian themes. These themes, as we shall see, open upon a new set of possibilities for phenomenology, possibilities truncated in *Theory of Intuition*.

There is very little actual extension of Husserl's phenomenology in the 1940 essay; the essay appears encyclopedic, a mere listing and summary of a doctrine of phenomenology. Nevertheless, a close reading of this effort witnesses a gathering—under the title of the single thinker "Husserl"—of a set of themes that forms the basis for Levinas's explosion of phenomenology through the rupture and decay of representation. So, this apparent exercise in summary reveals more than one may usually anticipate from such an endeavor. The fact that Levinas collects these themes—themes both conservative and radical—under a single author already tells us that in Levinas's hands phenomenology will become more than the explicit letter of its founder. To indicate both the work and significance of the already present tensions in the 1940 essay, we should confess to reading "L'œuvre d'Edmond Husserl" with the work of the late 1950s in view. Such a reading will allow us to see the clandestine emergence of "another phenomenology" and thus the hidden radicality in what may first appear to be Levinas's summary of another thinker. Such a forward-looking reading may give us a glimpse of the "experience" of phenomenology enacted in the collecting of these sometimes fractured and disparate Husserlian themes. Indeed, Levinas himself claims that "L'œuvre d'Edmond Husserl" is not an exercise in doxography, but rather an attempt to bring out the ". . . unity of phenomenological inspiration, its appearance and its message" (ŒH, 9). Paradoxically, this inspirational unity testifies to the profound *disunity* that lies at the very heart of the phenomenological project.

Levinas's critical account of the basic features of Husserl's positive and fully developed phenomenology begins with the problem of phenomenological idealism. Here he repeats the orientation of *Theory of Intuition*: the first position of theory in Husserl's doctrine. This first position of theory is most clearly seen at that moment when Husserl situates all particularity under the rubric of the eidetic, i.e., under the synthetic work of constitution, thematized in the intuition of its accomplishments. The accomplished synthetic work of the subject and what it offers to intuition gives Husserl's phenomenology the character of what Levinas calls a "Platonic realism" (ŒH, 51). This realism recasts the authentic motifs of Platonism in the phenomenological notion of the Eidos (ŒH, 19, 49).[4] To be sure, when considered within the specific reflective context of Husserl's method, this authentic Platonism squares with Husserl's own "reproach of Platonism" in §22 of *Ideas I*. The Platonic realism of Husserl's work is only a realism of the Eidos in terms of the function of the eidetic stratum in the process of constitution, a process that, as Husserl says, must be understood without being "driven to metaphysical hypostatizations" (Hua III, 41/41). This recovery of eidetic insight without the temptation of metaphysical hypostatizations—i.e., without the pitfalls of ontologism—motivates Husserl's turn to idealism.

The rejection of metaphysical hypostatization, made explicit as early as the *Logical Investigations*,[5] alters the character of the problem of reflection and the problem of world. Reflection and world are traditionally conceived (e.g., in British empiricism) in terms of the opposition of the inner and outer. In Husserl's hands, however, idealism transforms the very notions of interior and exterior—reflective consciousness and world—through the reduction of the "what" of that which appears to the "how" of its appearing. Such a reduction, key to the phenomenological turn, renders the problem of interiority and exteriority an evidential problem. It is therefore not a question of the relation between the inner sphere of the psyche and the hypothesized external world. Indeed, Husserl has shown how such an endeavor rests on a dogmatic metaphysical foundation. This reduction to the "how" of the appearing of that which appears renders interior and exterior modalities of the strata of the lived-experience of sense. Levinas writes that "the interiority of thought and the exteriority of the object are abstractions drawn from the concrete fact of the spirituality (*spiritualité*) which is sense" (ŒH, 26). The primary strata of sense[6] both animates and founds the interior/exterior modes of appearance, which in turn renders both inner and outer as modalities within one and the same intentional life.

This state of affairs commences the reflective ascent of the transcendental subject. The motivations for idealism lie in the phenomenological reduction itself: Interior and exterior emerge within the flow of the lived-experience of a subject. Hence, this motivation generates an idealism for which the world is decidedly not ". . . absolutely strange to the subject" (ŒH, 32). This lived-experience that admits no foreignness is, of course, intentionally structured. Intentionality does not signify, for Husserl, a singular and straightforward relation of a subject to an object, but rather a complex of structures that perform a synthetic function of ideal identification across multiplicity. "The act of seizing upon an object—the objectivating act—is," Levinas writes, "a synthesis of identification" (ŒH, 22). The synthesis of identification excludes all that is strange and foreign, assembling all difference under the rubric of the constituting acts of the subject. The strata of sense, then, manifests the original basis for the reflective context. This strata of sense is immediately interpreted by Husserl according to the act(s) of identification performed by the ego. This is a fateful move. Identification, on Husserl's account, renders ideality within intentionality, which in turn reveals that the intentional relation ". . . is essentially the act of bestowing a sense (*Sinngebung*)" (ŒH, 22). The world revealed after the reduction is ". . . a world constituted by thought" (ŒH, 38). This no doubt hearkens back to Levinas's concerns about the theoretical character of the reduction in *Theory of Intuition*.

Husserl's explication of lived-experience implicates the sense-bestowing function of the transcendental ego. The genesis of the sense that is initially reflectively uncovered by the phenomenological reduction emanates from the transcendental ego. Phenomenology, taking its clue from the strata of sense itself, asks the genetic question: Whence sense? According to Levinas, Husserl's turn to genetic phenomenology uncovers nothing less ". . . than a process of *Sinngebung* and of identification of moments by thought" (ŒH, 34). The bestowal of sense from the subject as transcendental ego indicates, for Levinas, that Husserl's conception of transcendental subjectivity presupposes a notion of freedom. Levinas writes that

> [t]he *Sinngebung,* the fact of thinking and bestowing a sense, intellection—is not an engagement with an other. It is freedom. Every engagement is . . . in principle reducible to a sense and by way of this sense, the fact of bestowing a sense is freedom and origin. (ŒH, 39)

The turn to sense-bestowal liberates consciousness from the situatedness of engagement with the world, and thus in this turn consciousness regains and solidifies its freedom. "The total possession of self in reflection," Levinas writes, "is only the reverse side of freedom" (ŒH, 38). Freedom and the reflective securing of evidence are coextensive.

The meaning of the freedom of the subject is made clear in this context. The freedom that Levinas attributes to phenomenology is here revealed as a methodological freedom—i.e., the freedom to capture all sense and evidence within the boundaries of the constituted. "The evidence of the given world" is, Levinas notes, nothing other than ". . . the positive accomplishment of freedom" (ŒH, 24). Levinas's identification of freedom with the sense-bestowing function of the Ego is no doubt justified. Consider the following passage from *Ideas I* that bears directly on the issue at hand. It comes from the concluding sections on the problems of noetic-noematic structures. Husserl writes that

> [a] synthesis . . . becomes [or] arises in *original production* . . . The positing, the positing-thereupon, positing antecedently and consequently, etc., is its [the Ego's] *free spontaneity and activity*; the Ego does not live in the positings as passively dwelling in them; the positings are instead radiations from the pure Ego as from a primal source of generations. Every positing begins with a *point of initiation*, with a *positional point of origin.*[7] (Hua III, 253/291)

The boundaries of the constituted refer, in the end, to the genetically prior moment of sense-bestowal. This original production of sense upsurges in free spontaneity and activity. The spontaneity of the Ego initiates the origin of the sense. The stratum of sense underpins the positing of something as something. Freedom, then, is to be understood in terms of the Ego's being unconstrained by materiality in general and so unrestricted by the object of the intention. Indeed, the object as a constituted unity, appearing under the phenomenological reduction, bears already within it its debt to this freely spontaneous, original production. Freedom is a freedom from the sensual. This is not a metaphysical claim about the subject, but rather a structural feature resulting from Husserl's methodological solipsism and the consequent delimitation of sense and its genesis. To call freedom into question, then, is not simply an issue of questioning the freedom of the will; it is, rather, a questioning of the directionality of the flow of sense, a questioning of the very genetic source of sense itself.[8] It is, we might say, a transcendental question.

At this point, we may again be led to repeat the formulations of *Theory of Intuition* and conceive Husserl's phenomenology as an intellectualism. The linking of idealism and freedom indicates that, above all, the boundaries marked by Husserl restrict phenomenology to the evidential function of intuition and therefore the free play of constituting consciousness, a consciousness not constrained by materiality. This method of intuition, as has already been remarked in the *Theory of Intuition*, claims as its boundaries the play of intuiting and intuited in the lived-experience of the reflective subject. However, the 1940 essay marks its progress with the following question, no doubt inspired by Heidegger: "Spiritual life (*la vie spirituelle*) is the fact of bestowing a sense. But, am I not something other than this act?" (ŒH, 35).[9] Does Husserl's phenomenology indicate paths that propose a positive answer this question? To answer this question in the affirmative, Levinas must find resources in Husserl that break with the primacy of intellection.

To this end, Levinas will claim in "L'œuvre d'Edmond Husserl" that, despite the idealism and correlative notion of freedom, it is "perhaps incorrect to characterize Husserl's phenomenology as an intellectualism" (ŒH, 23). With this remark, Levinas has already come a long way with regard to the possibilities of Husserl's phenomenology, for in 1930 Levinas had written that ". . . one can reproach Husserl for his intellectualism" (TIPH, 174/119) and had taken note of the "profoundly intellectualist" character of his intuitionism (TIPH, 219/155). What provokes this revision of Levinas's understanding of phenomenology? Levinas's remark in 1940 on the fundamental mistake of the intellectualist characterization *might* be seen as a reversal of the judgment of Husserl in 1930—a reversal perhaps motivated by the availability of new texts.[10] Indeed, in 1940 Levinas adds *Formal and Transcendental Logic*, *Cartesian Meditations*, *The Crisis of European Sciences*, and *Experience and Judgment*, as well as a few short articles, to his list of consulted texts.[11] Given the fact that these texts (especially *Experience and Judgment*) explode the horizons of axiology and the problem of materiality, coupled with the fact that Levinas's rereading of Husserl's phenomenology focuses on the radicality of the notions of practical intentionality and passivity, we may initially be persuaded that such texts provoke another reading of phenomenology and its possibilities.

However, this is shortsighted. Such an account of the altered reading and judgment of Husserl fails to take into account the fact that in 1930 Levinas already had on hand the *Jahrbuch* edition of the *Zeitbewußtsein* text (which in part motivates his rereading of Husserl in 1940), as it is cited on eleven occasions in the *Theory of Intuition* text.[12] That is, the very text that provides the site of new possibilities for phenomenology in 1940 passes through the 1930 text without threatening the integrity of the intellectualist characterization of Husserl's work. We may better view this shift in Levinas's characterization of the possibilities of phenomenology in terms of his announcement at the end of the *Theory of Intuition*, where he ways that, in addition to justifying intellectualism, Husserl is also "seeking the place of being in concrete life" (TIPH, 223/158). Seeking the place of being in concrete life—which, for Levinas, will come to be the problem of sensibility in 1959—introduces a difficult ambiguity in Husserl's phenomenology: the problematic interplay between the theoretical and the concrete.[13] Thus, in closing the 1930 text, Levinas wonders if the difficulty of the interplay between the theoretical and the concrete may be exceeded ". . . with the affirmation of the intentional character of practical and axiological life" (TIPH, 223/158). This query also hearkens back to the "Introduction" to the same text, wherein Levinas remarks that, like Bergson said of himself, "Husserl had an intuition of his philosophy before he made it a philosophy of intuition" (TIPH, 12/xxxii). The intuition of phenomenology intuits the place of abstraction in the concrete flow of life (cf., Hua III, §19), whereas phenomenology's intuition neutralizes the stratum of the concrete in eidetic analysis (cf., Hua III, §109). This poses the question of the relation between the concreteness that inspires phenomenology to the intuitionism that underpins the method. How is this juxtaposition to be exceeded? If we take both the reflections of 1940 and Levinas's own anecdotal testimony[14] seriously, the answer is quite direct. The turn to axiological intentionality in Husserl's work overturns phenomenology's problematic reliance on theoretical modes of the intention and presents a return to the concrete *as* concrete. Such a claim, when made in 1930, requires a critique of *Theory of Intuition* on the basis of the text itself: the critique of Husserl in *Theory of Intuition* must be rewritten on the basis of the matters disclosed in that critique. Levinas is led, subsequent to the study of the problems of Husserl's intellectualism, to confirm the hidden resources of intentional analysis, resources that exceed intellectualism. Hence, there are philosophical motivations already in the 1930 text that lead Levinas to reread Husserl's phenomenology with a view to the radical possibilities latent within the method itself.

It is therefore certainly unjust to characterize Husserl's phenomenology as intellectualism. As we have just suggested, this claim is justified by Levinas when he turns to the notion of the "concrete." Levinas conceives the concrete thusly: that within which the intellectual itself is always already caught and that to which Husserl necessarily turns to ground phenomenological abstraction (ŒH, 29). In his treatment of Husserl's "turn to the concrete," Levinas conceives the concrete as the site or source of the distinction between the interior of the eidetic and the exterior of the sensation or material. For Husserl, the concrete will be philosophically rendered primarily in terms of sense—i.e., the synthetic work of the eidetic stratum of lived-experience, in turn intuited in its palpable actuality as pure possibility free from factual conditions. Initially, then, it would appear that all sensation will have to be interpreted in terms of the *faculty* of affectivity, which is already structured from within the subject and will therefore remain, in the phenomenological sense, interior (ŒH, 32f). Idealism of necessity imposes this reflective logic on the analysis. Idealism demands that what is presented in the field of lived-experience be rendered in terms of the noesis through which the original presentation is (or has already been) secured and made possible. It is precisely this privileged application of methodological solipsism to what is presented in the concrete that problematizes the relation between the concrete and the theoretical.

Nevertheless, Levinas identifies another possibility at work in the appeal to the concrete. But for this possibility to emerge, the concrete must be construed in terms of practical intentionality and passivity. This other intentionality breaks with the dominant appeal to phenomenological interiority or immanence. To bring this possibility into relief, it is first necessary to pause and consider both the initial context of the phenomenal appeal to the concrete in Husserl's phenomenology and how this notion of the concrete reveals an *opening* in the system of pure phenomenology. From the *Logical Investigations* forward, Husserl is quite explicit about the juxtaposition of the intellectual to the concrete. In the

Logical Investigations, the concrete is distinguished in terms of its immediacy. This immediacy is both phenomenally differentiated from the formal or abstract appearance of the eidetic and can further be said to generate the same. "A concrete object," Husserl writes "is immediate and is independent in its not needing to be based on other [i.e., eidetic] presentations *(Vorstellens)*," which is to say, the concrete *is* the immediate in the fullness of its implications and that from which the abstract or formal "... *must* be based" (Hua XIX/1, 252/453). Though the term has not been developed by Husserl in the *Logical Investigations*, the concrete signifies the immediacy of the *pre-reflective* strata that serve as the phenomenological ground of all that is won through reflection. Therefore, the concrete is a mode of presentation in immediacy without the predelineating function of the constituting subject. This is the notion of the concrete Levinas evokes in his "Fribourg, Husserl, et phénoménologie," what Levinas calls, in a series of important synonyms, the "individual, the immediate, the concrete" (FHP, 98; also 96, 99–100). In the *Phenomenological Psychology* lectures from 1925, Husserl claims that the literal presentation of concrete individuals precedes the very notion of a "thing," in the sense that the meaning of "concrete" is to be individual and self-sufficient (Hua IX, 100–1/75–76). To precede the work of the subject in constitution is to be concrete, to present without prior presentations. On this account, the phenomenological notion of the concrete offers, in principle, the possibility of a presentation that is not itself mediated by the prior work of constitution by the subject. Thus, the fact that Husserl embraces an idealism that will ultimately posit transcendental subjectivity as "the one absolute existent" (Hua XVII, 277/271) might tempt one to forget that there remains this other "absolute" in phenomenology. Indeed, the concrete warrants the descriptive term "absolute" for the very reason that it shows itself without the prior workings or presentations of the perceiving subject, and hence has an absolute purity, as it were, *in its impurity*.

In "L'œuvre d'Edmond Husserl," Levinas has his own particular use for the notion of the concrete and its possibilities for extending phenomenology. His concern is awakened in asking the question of the signification of that which "... has nothing of the intellectual" (ŒH, 24). This is of course another way of questioning the peculiar signification of the immediacy of the concrete. Levinas's thematic concern with this signification in 1940 is two-fold: the appearance of the concrete in axiological modalities of intentionality and the materiality of the concrete in time-consciousness. Following Husserl's suggestions, the significance for Levinas of this two-part turn to the concrete lies in the identification of immediacy and the way in which immediacy transforms the possibilities of an intentionality freed from intellectualism.

First, some notes on the axiological mode of intentionality. The axiological mode of intentionality indicates a mode of relationality that does not, in the strict sense of the term, objectivate the object to which the subject is related. The object of the axiological intention is peculiar; it derives its peculiarity from its decidedly nontheoretical status. The object of theoretical intentionality, the object of the intellectualist disposition *par excellence*, is subsumed under reflective judgment and reflective determination. The concrete axiological intention, however, appears otherwise than this reflective judgment and determination. Indeed, in §117 of *Ideas I*, Husserl notes that valuation and the axiological object demand "a 'being' of a new region" (Hua III, 244/282).[15] In order to present this presentation, Husserl will characterize the axiological object as "pre-given," which is to say, given prior to the reflective seizing upon by the sense-bestowing subject. Husserl writes:

> As possibilities running parallel to the theoretical attitude, there are the axiological and practical attitudes. Valuing acts . . . can relate to pre-given objectivities . . . These are not simply objectivities founded in general and in *this* sense objectivities of a higher level, but they are precisely objectivities originally constituted as spontaneous products and which only as such come to possible originary givenness . . . Thus we arrive in each case at pre-given objectivities which do not spring from theoretical acts but are constituted in intentional lived-experience imparting to them nothing of logico-categorial formations. (Hua IV, 7/9)

The objective content of the intentionality of the axiological attitude thus gives itself originarily as *not* springing from the spontaneous theoretical acts of constituting consciousness. Rather, it gives itself in its immediacy. The content of *this* intentionality is an "other spontaneous act" and its pre-givenness is prior to the reflective rendering of its sense. Axiological intentionality and its object are concrete and thus the immediacy of its original givenness resists, in its very sense, the intellectualist's reflective grasp.

This "other side" of phenomenology constitutes Levinas's first break with the anti-intellectualist critique of phenomenology in the

Theory of Intuition. Immediately following his remark that it is incorrect to characterize Husserlian phenomenology as an intellectualism, Levinas will go on to claim that the intentionality of desire or sentiment offers a nonobjective sense. In Levinas's words,

> The intention of desire, or of sentiment—considered as desire or sentiment—contains an original sense which is not objective in the narrow sense of the term. It is Husserl who has introduced into philosophy the idea that thought is able to have a sense . . . in which the object is absolutely undetermined, a quasi-absence of an object.[16] (ŒH, 24).

The qualification "considered as" is significant. What it signifies is the necessity of what Husserl called an "axiological intuition" in *Ideas II* (cf., Hua IV, 9/10). This peculiar sort of intuition grasps desire or sentiment as the feeling itself, and therefore does not grasp such modalities under the reflective activity of judgment. Reflective judgment is improper; it compromises the living immediacy of desire or sentiment. The reflective disposition fails to consider desire as desire, sentiment as sentiment. Considered as axiological, the sense of the presented intention breaks with the intellectualist construal of objectivity insofar as its sense of givenness does not spring from the relation of knowledge. The sense given is only objective in the sense that it evokes the positivity of the transcendence of the subject and marks its "objective" movement. In looking back at the significance of axiological intentionality, Levinas notes in an interview that

> [t]he character of value [the quasi-absent object of axiological intentionality] does not fasten itself to beings consequent to the modification by *knowledge*, but comes from a specific attitude of consciousness, of a non-theoretical intentionality, straightoff irreducible to knowledge. There is here a Husserlian possibility which can be developed beyond what Husserl himself said. . . . (EeI, 22/32)

Here Levinas has established the notion that the quasi-absent object of axiological intentionality breaks with the relation of knowing. This is of course tantamount to breaking with the intellectualism attributed to Husserl in the *Theory of Intuition*. This object is described by Levinas as quasi-absent precisely because it is not objective in the reflective sense of objectivity. That is to say, the axiological object is not fully present and immanent to the subject, but instead transcendent in its concrete presentation. As such, this object demands a mode of exposition other than the phenomenological tracing of the genesis of sense in transcendental subjectivity. Because the axiological object is an intentional object and therefore manifests itself as a relation, it signifies a relation of transcendence. In its signification, concrete axiological intentionality transcends otherwise than the play of transcendence/immanence in reflection.

The second aspect of the concrete that concerns Levinas in 1940 is the problematic relation of materiality to consciousness—specifically the relation articulated in Husserl's reflections on time-consciousness. The problem of materiality and time is borne by Husserl's conception of the *Ur-impression,* that first "moment" constitutive of the constituted play of retention and protention. Husserl considers time almost exclusively as already constituted. Hence, his exposition is primarily that of "the time of theoretical thought, of formal time, only qualified by those contents which fill in and participate in time's rhythm without creating it" (ŒH, 42). Constituted time, then, remains a self-enclosed flux that, in the end, is generated by the freedom of the subject (ŒH, 41). There is no creation, properly speaking, outside of this flux, and thus the subject remains unconstrained in its generation and explication of sense. Nothing in constituted time threatens the methodological freedom of the subject.

But the notion of the *Ur-impression* halts this sequence. The *Ur-impression* may also be said to offer an original passivity that cannot be explicated or recuperated within the play of retention and protention. The play of retention and protention is a play within the free subject, the constituting subject of constituted time. The *Ur-impression,* however, claims itself as the origin of every consciousness; it proposes to constitute that which, in constituted time, is the source of constituting. Levinas writes that

> The origin of every consciousness is the first impression, the "*Ur-impression.*" But this original passivity is at the same time an initial spontaneity. The first intentionality where consciousness constitutes itself is the present. The present is the very surging up of the mind, its presence to itself, a presence that does not enchain consciousness: the impression passes. (ŒH, 41)

At its origin, which surges across or through time,[17] consciousness finds itself enchained to the materiality of the impression in passivity in its first intention. Still, the impression passes. Consciousness is thereby able to gain or regain its status as free inside the play of constituted time. Levinas, however, emphasizes the sense in which impressional consciousness, at its concrete origin in time, precedes the space within which an intellectualism remains viable. The impression marks the first constituting from "outside" of time of what becomes, in constituted time, a constituting from "inside" of time. This movement from impressional consciousness to the free constituting subject is found in the original passivity of the concrete. This passivity is also a spontaneity. Passivity is the generative source of what becomes the free subject, but at its concrete origin consciousness is already other than the relation knowing. To be sure, Levinas conceives the relation enacted in this original passivity to be a "first intentionality"—a characterization he will modify in the 1960s—but it is important here that this intentionality implicates a relation of original transcendence. This is a transcendence much different than the reflectively uncovered appearance of the immanence/transcendence distinction. In its concrete signification, materiality transcends otherwise than the play of transcendence/immanence in reflection.

Now, we have just seen that the freedom Levinas attributes to the transcendental subject defines itself in terms of its being unconstrained in *Sinngebung*. To the extent that this conception of subjectivity dominates the letter of phenomenology, Husserl may be considered an intellectualist. However, "L'œuvre d'Edmond Husserl" exhibits quite clearly the extent to which Husserl's phenomenology opens upon horizons decidedly other than those recuperable within an intellectualism. To show this, we have considered Levinas's turn—with Husserl—to the immediacy of the concrete. The axiological and material modalities of the concrete disclose horizons of intentionality that signify otherwise than epistemic relations. These horizons question the very primacy of the free subject. The sense of this questioning lies in the ability of axiology and materiality to constrain or limit the powers of the epistemic relation, or, perhaps better put, the powers of the relation of intentions revealed to and in reflection. Turning to the concrete, Levinas has, in the sense outlined above, put freedom into question.

The full implications of this questioning remain to be seen. Our reading of "L'œuvre d'Edmond Husserl" endeavors only to show the latent possibilities of intentionality covered over by the 1930 judgment of phenomenology. In the remainder of the present chapter, we will witness Levinas's deployment of these latent possibilities first in *De l'existence à l'existant* and *Time and the Other*—texts which rethink subjectivity—and then with more detail in the 1959 essay "La ruine de la représentation"—a text which rethinks intentionality and materiality. If we have been successful in the present exposition, then those analyses will be seen as inextricably linked to the project of 1940 in terms of their methodological possibility. This link is cashed out in the further elaboration of concrete subjectivity appearing in the descriptions of transcendence in *De l'existence à l'existant* and *Time and the Other*, as well as the appeal to the subject's presence to the world in "La ruine de la représentation." Transcendence and presence to the world signify, in this context, nothing less than the development of the structure of the immediacy of the concrete first described in "L'œuvre d'Edmond Husserl." How can the concrete signify otherwise than as predelineated? The studies found in *De l'existence à l'existant* and *Time and the Other* begin to develop this signification.

Subjectivity as Transcendence

The work accomplished in 1940 consists primarily in the indication of the forgotten possibilities in Husserl's phenomenology—possibilities that are forgotten by both Husserl himself and Levinas's interpretative stance in the *Theory of Intuition*. These possibilities lack a fully explicated structure of transcendence. In the 1940s, the texts *De l'existence à l'existant* and *Time and the Other* draw out some of those implications through sustained phenomenological analysis. It should be noted that Levinas's concern in these texts is not explicitly with Husserlian phenomenology, but rather with a certain critical reworking of Heidegger's notions of ecstatic temporality and the care structure of the existential analytic. Such a preoccupation has already been expressed in Levinas's emphasis on the "revolutionary character" of Heidegger's work on time (ŒH, 39). To this extent, Husserl's phenomenology, it must be admitted, takes a backseat to the problem of overcoming both ontology and ecstatic temporality. (One might still argue for a continuity between the ecstatic notion of time and Husserl's notion of constituted time). Nevertheless, the general character of both *De l'existence à l'existant* and *Time and the Other* reflects an ongoing concern with issues raised in "L'œuvre d'Edmond Husserl." The present thematic summary and characterization of *De l'existence à l'existant* and *Time and the Other* aims at capturing the essence of the relevant analyses and so at exhibiting a certain continuity of concern. In these analyses, Levinas describes the subject *as* transcendence. This makes subjectivity, *l'existant*, concrete. Transcendence is here not conceived as a property of the subject; the subject *is* its being outside itself. Levinas's descriptions are indispensable as preparatory work toward the reversal of intentionality in *Totality and Infinity* to the extent that they are, in some sense, *evidence* for the legitimacy of a nonmediated transcendence. As Levinas puts it in his "Preface" to *De l'existence a l'existant*, "our exposition cannot however hide the perspectives within which it is situated, and it constantly anticipates developments reserved for a subsequent work" (DEE, 10/15).

The primary task of *De l'existence a l'existant* is to articulate a notion of subjectivity that departs from being and its descriptive categories. Levinas calls this "an ex-cendence" (DEE, 10/15) of the categories of Being. Such an endeavor consists in articulating a transcendence that is not bound by being; thus, the task of the text already opposes Heidegger. In confronting the problems of Heidegger's fundamental ontology, Levinas turns to the problem of time—specifically the defense of the instant against the existential phenomenological notion of ecstatic temporality. The notion of the instant provokes Levinas to rethink subjectivity, against the ecstatic stretch of care, in terms of hypostasis.

But, these concerns, while they form the central issue of the text itself, lie outside our present theme. Of interest for our project is how Levinas extends the notion of axiology in his descriptions of transcendence. The emergence of transcendence as a necessary structure of the subjectivity related to the beyond being—the explicit task of the text— articulates the notion of the concrete in a developed descriptive, and not merely methodological, context. The descriptions in *De l'existence à l'existant* function, according to Levinas, as an *anti*phenomenology. They are antiphenomenological because the transcendence rendered by Levinas determines itself as transcending at the moment it leaves the boundaries of intuition and intuition's presupposition of a certain position and modality of ego (DEE, 112/66). The sense of this "anti" is understood in terms of its break with thought and the "sphere of light." The movement beyond intuition is ultimately accomplished as the movement toward alterity (DEE, 146/85), which is an alterity only insofar as it does not appear to the cogito and its powers of illumination. We can therefore see how *De l'existence à l'existant* builds on the antiintellectualist thesis of *Theory of Intuition*. What is interesting about Levinas's strategy in *De l'existence à l'existant* is that he does not contest Husserl's intellectualism with another method. Rather, intellectualism is contested in the descriptions themselves. Levinas's task is thus to bring into relief, in some manner unassisted by light, modalities of subjective life that oppose intellectualist phenomenology from within the matters themselves. It is, in short, to practice phenomenology otherwise than Husserl.

Levinas's studies that describe the subject in a relation or modality of transcendence are exemplary of the possibilities opened up by the recovery of axiology. So, these studies aim at what is at once beyond phenomenological description (as it is beyond the relation of knowing) and within the scope of the concretization of axiological intentionality (as this transcendence is still maintained in a relation and is in some manner described). Take for example the chapter on hypostasis. Levinas remarks there that emotion—a central axiological concern—is "a way of holding on while losing one's base" (DEE, 121/71). This losing of one's base is a modality of transcendence that, while the subject remains an item in the relation, is an extension of the subject outside itself. The relation proper to emotion is thus not an ecstatic relation emanating from the subject. Instead it is a relation already determined by the object of emotion itself. Thus, Levinas will describe emotion as a rupture of the subject's equilibrium—in a word, vertigo. He writes:

> Emotion puts into question not the existence, but the subjectivity of the subject; it prevents the subject from gathering itself up, reacting, being someone. What is positive in the subject sinks away into a nowhere. Emotion is a way of holding on while losing one's base. All emotion is fundamentally vertigo, that vertigo one feels insinuating itself, that *finding oneself over a void.* (DEE, 121/70–71)

Emotion is determined, not by the position of the subject, but from the object of emotion. The vertigo comes from the lack of balance such a reversed determination imposes.

Levinas's descriptions of the transcendence of the erotic already foreshadows the account of metaphysical desire in *Totality and Infinity*. In *De l'existence à l'existant*, eros articulates something of this same sense of dispossession in relation described in the account of emotion. Eros is a "transcendence that can be conceived as something radical," precisely because it does not inevitably return to itself as both origin and telos (DEE, 164/96). What does not return the subject to itself may be found in the asymmetrical relation of the interhuman, an erotic relation of love without reciprocity. Eros, when thought outside the categories of knowing and possessing, expels the subject outside itself. Levinas writes:

> It [the asymmetrical] is brought about by Eros, where in the proximity of another the distance is wholly maintained, a distance whose pathos is made up of this proximity and this duality of beings. What is presented as the failure of communication in love in fact constitutes the positive character of the relationship; this absence of the other is precisely his presence qua other. The other is the neighbor(but proximity is not a degradation of, or a stage on the way to, fusion. (DEE163/95)

This radical transcendence leads Levinas to the social relation, which here is characterized as an "asymmetrical intersubjectivity" that ". . . is the locus of transcendence in which the subject, while preserving its subject, has the possibility of not inevitably returning to itself, the possibility of being fecund" (DEE, 164/96). Reciprocity is refused. A relation that does not return to itself, a relation fated to exile, replaces the intimacy of fair exchanges. Eros is fecund—but the meaning of this fecundity awaits, at the time of *De l'existence à l'existant*, its full examination.

Time and the Other makes good on Levinas's promissory note regarding fecundity. The transcendence in fecundity preserves the subjectivity of the subject, yet demands an exposition that dispossesses the subject of its first position. In other words, the implication is that of an intentionality—a relation—that is not reducible to the positionality of the subject and its acts, in a word, a *practical* intentionality. The significance of this transcendence emerges in the studies of the subject in relation to what is beyond being. The relation to the beyond being demands just such a logic: transcendence precedes the first position of the I.

> How, in the alterity of a you, can I remain I, without being ab-
> sorbed or losing myself in that you? How can the ego that I am
> remain myself in a you, without being nonetheless the ego that
> I am in my present—that is to say, an ego that inevitably returns
> to itself? How can the ego become other to itself? (TA, 85/91)

Determination of relation from the outside indicates that the origin of
sense produced in the relation lies beyond the productive powers of
the ego. The ego is given over to something other than itself. "This
situation," Levinas writes, "cannot be qualified as power" (TA, 85/91).
And, because this sense must be produced in a relation, the determination of transcendence by the axiological object, not the I, is necessary.
This reversal makes it possible for intentionality to sustain sense otherwise than what is produced by the ego. Dispossession is one manner
of describing this conception of sense and relationality. The full development of this notion is, in Levinas's own words, "reserved for subsequent work" that would extend the provisional descriptions in *De
l'existence à l'existant*. *Time and the Other* is a significant contribution to
this extension.

Levinas notes in his 1979 preface to its republication that the
primary task of *Time and the Other* is the recovery of the genuine fecundity that ". . . puts into question the very idea of power, such as it
is embodied in transcendental subjectivity, the center and source of
intentional acts" (TA, 15/37). Putting power into question is easily
transposed onto the questioning of freedom in "L'œuvre d'Edmond
Husserl," insofar as the questioning of both power and freedom consists in problematizing the constituting spontaneity of the Ego. To put
power in question is not just the positivity of ethics. It is also to question the primacy of knowing and Being. The fruit of questioning epistemology and ontology is borne when Levinas forges, across the
remains of a ruined transcendental subjectivity, a sense of a relation to
the other ". . . where the *Other* (*autrui*) takes the place of the other
(*autre*)" (TA, 89/94).

If this is his goal, then Levinas has put the precondition bluntly:
he must first conceive transcendence in a manner that exceeds the
power of the subject as constituting. The myriad analyses of feminin-
ity, eros, enjoyment, the voluptuous, the caress, paternity and other
manifestations of radical transcendence accomplish this aim. The structures opened up in *Time and the Other* may be legitimately character-

ized as "radical" transcendencies. They are modalities of the subject's extension beyond itself in relation to an alterity. The relation to alterity alters the traditional sense of transcendence at its root. This makes Levinas's sense of transcendence radical. And further, this transcendent relation puts the subject in contact with a genuine sense of alterity. This alterity maintains its integrity, its genuine otherness, by way of the fact that it is not "grasped," "possessed," or "known." Grasping, possessing, knowing are all synonyms of power (TA, 83/90). The point of access to this relation lies in the immediacy of the subject to its relation, unmediated by the reflective prerogative. Immediacy here signifies the concretion of intentionality, which allows transcendence to appear not as a relation of correlation, but rather as a relation of the subject to a "fundamental disorder" (TA, 82/89). This is why, for example, Levinas will describe the caress as ". . . a mode of the subject's being, where the subject who is in contact with another goes beyond this contact" (TA, 82/84). The immediacy of the concrete signifies beyond what might be rendered as present in this relation: in *Time and the Other*, this immediacy opens upon an infinite future.

> This "not knowing," this fundamental disorder, is the essential. It is like a game with something slipping away, a game absolutely without project or plan, not with what can become ours or us, but with something other, always other, always inaccessible, and always still to come. (82/89)

The erotic relation, specifically the carnality of the caress, is exemplary of this contact with alterity. In the caress, Eros becomes a relation with an Other that does not return to the Ego in satisfaction. Rather, in the lover's caress, which "goes beyond contact" and is ". . . the anticipation of the pure future without content" (TA, 82/89), the erotic relation ". . . furnishes us with the basis of an analysis of this relationship with mystery—provided that it is set forth in terms entirely different from those of the Platonism that is a world of light" (TA, 64/76). This is a movement without return. In characterizing the temporality of this movement, Levinas will speak of an "absence in a horizon of the future, an absence that is time" (TA, 83/90). *Avenir*, the future, is always *à venir*, always "to come." The radicality of this transcendence is not comprised by the ego precisely because the subject is outside itself. The object "always to come" determines the subject, in its futurity, as transcending.

These descriptions of transcendence sound a sort of structural echo of the "quasi-absent object" (and the transcendent relation it implicates) methodologically described in "L'œuvre d'Edmond Husserl." The immediacy toward which the 1940 essay gestures finds its descriptive content, its deformalization, in the transcendence of Eros. Levinas's attempt to find ". . . the temporal transcendence of the present toward the mystery of the future" (TA, 89/94) functions in this context as nothing other than the activation and fulfillment of the methodological possibilities opened up by axiological intentionality and quasi-object materiality.

What emerges from the studies of *De l'existence à l'existant* and *Time and the Other,* then, is a conception of subjectivity that in its relationality is dispossessed of itself. The dispossession of subjectivity emerges within that relationality in which the freedom and power of the subject no longer hold a first position. Dispossession, in this context, is nothing other than the elaboration of the phenomenological possibilities formally present in what "L'œuvre d'Edmond Husserl" calls either the enchainment of subjectivity to the impression or the transcendence that outstrips the epistemic relation. What remained unfulfilled in 1940 was actualization of the language with which to articulate the transcendence of the concrete. That is to say, the 1940 essay makes possible the inscription of a genuine transcendence into relationality, but it remains unclear how this transcendence might be articulated. The temporality of transcendence described in *Time and the Other*—the opening upon the future in the contact that goes beyond contact, descriptively fulfills the methodological promise of the (re)turn to the concrete.

If this transcendence is a relation set out from alterity, then we have covered quite a distance toward the notion of a production of sense out of absolute difference. Despite the provisional nature of many analyses in *De l'existence à l'existant* and *Time and the Other*, they do begin to fill out the descriptive possibilities of intentionality indicated in "L'œuvre d'Edmond Husserl." The structures exhibited in these analyses will show up again in the account of Desire and Enjoyment in *Totality and Infinity*, where the secret transcendental character of the analyses in *De l'existence a l'existant* and *Time and the Other* will be made explicit.

For the most part, this description of transcendence builds on the possibilities of axiological intentionality. When we arrive at *Totality and Infinity,* these relations will have a transcendental twist not yet elaborated in the work of the 1940s. It remains the task of "La ruine de la représentation"—published some dozen years after *Time and the Other*—to articulate precisely how practical intentionality gains transcendental purchase. Let us turn to that essay.

Decaying Representation

In the 1954 essay "The Ego and the Totality," Levinas notes that, despite Husserl's repeated critiques, there remains a "basic truth" of the sensualist philosophies, a truth which "survives the criticism" of transcendental phenomenology (MT, 24/26). In the context of this 1954 essay, such a survival of sensualism sounds a critical note on Husserl, as this surviving sensualism is understood by Levinas to offer a notion of exteriority adequate, in its non-adequation, to the language of alterity as excessive phenomenality. As such, it presents a surmounting of Husserl's phenomenologically motivated idealism. This excessive exteriority, of course, will provide the context of the alterity of the face that faces in *Totality and Infinity*. The site of this facing and its exceeding of thought lies in sensibility, that wherein "this sense, this plenitude of meaning anterior to any *Sinngebung*" (LC, 45/22) may be said to rupture the boundaries of phenomenological possibility. Sensibility, already at issue for Levinas in the 1950s, will provide the general scene for the logic of the anteriority of the posterior that structures the analyses of *Totality and Infinity*.

Our concern with Levinas's treatment of Husserl may lead us to conclude that in the early 1950s Levinas has turned away from and rejected the possibilities of Husserl's phenomenology in favor of a rehabilitated sensualism modeled, perhaps, on the notion of transcendence that was described in the *Theory of Intuition* in 1930. Indeed, Levinas's various characterizations of Husserl's work after "L'œuvre d'Edmond Husserl" up to and through *Totality and Infinity* tends to portray phenomenology as opposed to the metaphysics of exteriority. For the most part, Husserl appears as a foil. The present reading, however, proposes to overturn such an understanding of Levinas's relation to Husserl's phenomenology. As we shall see, quite a different picture of Husserl emerges when we turn to Levinas's work on intentionality in the 1959 essay "La ruine de la représentation." In this essay we see Levinas make good on the promissory note from 1940 regarding materiality. This essay will provide us with the precise analyses that underpin the language of alterity developed in *Totality and Infinity*. It will also make it possible for us to make sense of Levinas's (surprising) claim in the "Preface" to that text that Husserlian phenomenology makes possible the passage to metaphysical exteriority (TeI, xvii/29). Further, it will allow us to begin to understand the positivity of Levinas's relation to phenomenology and the way in which his treatment of Husserl is indispensable for and inseparable from the logic of exteriority developed in *Totality and Infinity*.

First, a brief word must be said regarding the sort of reading of Husserl that Levinas offers in "La ruine de la représentation." Levinas's return to Husserl in the late 1950s marks a rehabilitation of what Levinas calls the "forgotten horizon" of sensibility in Husserl's phenomenology. The aim of this rehabilitation is the establishment of the way in which phenomenology calls itself into question when the transcendental function of this forgotten horizon is given its due. Indeed, Levinas will say in "Lévy-Bruhl et la philosophy contemporaine"—appearing in 1957, two years before publishing "La ruine de la représentation" in commemoration of Husserl's birth—that the *Logical Investigations* itself already prepares *"la ruine de la réprésentation* (LB, 55). The ruining is already part of the phenomenological project. In this way, it must be said that Levinas does not strictly offer the reader a double reading of Husserl. That is to say, the explication of the precise terms of the inadequacy and subsequent decay of representation in "La ruine de la représentation" does not simply aim at exposing the tension between the de facto descriptions of phenomenology and its juridical constraining of evidence—though such a tension is no doubt indicated. Rather, the exposition of the forgotten horizon of sensibility yields the locus of Levinas's extension of phenomenology through phenomenology itself and therefore fundamentally conceiving of phenomenology as engaged in constant self-critique and transgression of its established boundaries.[18]

In the 1940 essay "L'œuvre d'Edmond Husserl" this peculiar notion of phenomenological self-critique and self-transgression is already announced in a somewhat clandestine manner as the necessary return of analysis to the concrete (ŒH, 29f, 42). And, as in the 1940 essay, the movement to the concrete in 1959 entails nothing less than the reorientation of the phenomenological notion of the transcendental away from the horizon of subjective idealism and toward the forgotten horizon of the sensible, this "other" transcendental. This movement from a forgetting to a remembering suggests that the reading may be simply characterized as a retrieval. That may be the case, but we must remark that it is a retrieval with a price to be paid. The price to be paid lies in the loss of the evidential comfort of an idealism, as what is retrieved makes requisite the rupturing transgression of the boundaries of a phenomenology delimited as an idealism. Furthermore, this method of reading renders Levinas's work in "La ruine de la représentation," as well as the deformalization of the structure of intentionality exposed in that essay in *Totality and Infinity*, eminently phenomenological even in its movement away from the letter of Husserlian methodological eidetics. Indeed, we are led to conclude that Levinas recognizes transgression—herein, the transgression of the phenomenologically sound notion of representation in sensibility—as written into the very matter of transcendental phenomenology. It is this conception of phenomenology that composes the positivity of Levinas's relation to Husserl.

Thus, our explicit task in the present section concerns the clarification of the peculiar relation Levinas holds to phenomenology in the late 1950's and how that relation manifests itself in the reading of Husserl in "La ruine de la représentation." There are a pair of overlapping tensions that comprise the motivation for the following reflections, tensions that lie at the enigmatic basis of Levinas's transformation of phenomenology. The first tension: It is quite peculiar, on the one hand, to discover the claim by Levinas in his essay "Réflexions sur la 'technique' phénoménologique" that "[p]henomenology is a destruction of representation and of the theoretical object" (RTP, 114) and then, on the other hand and in direct opposition to this characterization of phenomenology, to consider Levinas's comments regarding Husserl's "obsession" with representation (TeI, 95/122).[19] Phenomenology, then, is at once the destructor of representation *and* its most profound guarantor. The second tension: Levinas will consistently claim phenomenology to be inseparable from intentionality (cf., RR, 126) and consider that intentionality inseparable from the noesis-noema relation sustained by the activity of *Sinngebung*, yet will come to characterize his own position as a "phenomenology" that make possible an "ethical *Sinngebung*" (RR, 135). Phenomenology is simultaneously the sovereign security of the objective *and* the abrupt ethical awakening by the enigmatic.

The tension manifest in these two instances will be understandable on the basis of the two-fold sense of representation and the two-fold sense of intentionality emergent from Levinas's self-described "long frequenting of Husserlian labors" (RR, 128). This two-fold sense reflects the deployment of the strategy of reading outlined above. What we will discover in this frequenting of Husserl's labor is the sense of representation overcome by phenomenology in the return to the things themselves and the sense of representation reinstituted in the accomplishment(s) of intentional analysis. Intentionality will be shown in its two-fold sense—that is, the sense in which it may be said to rehabilitate representation in the phenomenological notion of essence and the sense in which the movement of intentionality implicates the forgotten horizon that has already decayed the representation discovered in reflection. Thus, through phenomenology's overcoming of the problem of representation, a method of analysis is discovered that is able both to sustain the phenomenological reinstatement of representation as noema and indicate co-implicated horizons that destruct that reinstatement. In other words, intentionality becomes, on Levinas's excavation of its structures, both the totalitarian point of access for the philosophy of the Same and the movement toward the enigma, the Other not deduced on the basis of the Same, and ultimately the ethical bestowal of sense. Liberated from its idealistic constraints, intentionality will introduce a two-fold sense of the transcendental. From this two-fold sense of the transcendental, there will emerge the two-fold sense in which intentionality exceeds itself. In each of these doubled structures, we will simultaneously find the constrained conservatism of Husserl's method and the radicality of the unsuspected horizons already implicated in the conservative moment. Further, on the basis of this series of two-fold appearances, we will see how intentionality, lodged within philosophy, comes to invert the philosophical eros (RR, 127–128).

The essay "La ruine de la représentation" holds a distinctive place in Levinas's considerations leading up to *Totality and Infinity*. Because Levinas will insist on the necessity of Husserl's phenomenology for the passage to exteriority, it is necessary to see precisely how this necessity works itself out concretely. This concrete work is the work of intentionality in sensibility, a work that establishes a sense of relationality that is able to sustain the relation to the enigma, the Other, and therefore ultimately the ethical relation. The essay itself has not yet arrived at the ethics of the facing face. To be sure, the very idea of the ethical relation occupies only the concluding remarks. Nevertheless, the *passage* to ethics must be navigated by way of intentional analysis and it is exactly this navigation that "La ruine de la représentation" performs. The analyses in this essay are not yet ethical, but rather, so to speak, "proto"-ethical. The sense of this "proto"-ethical lies in the initial phenomenological necessity of formalizing the structure that, in its concrete deployment, will open upon the structure of the ethical relation. Hence, the intentionality sought must exhibit a genuine, sustainable sense of alterity, an alterity not set out from the Same, and therefore an alterity in intentionality that functions otherwise than representation. Though this alterity is not yet named the human other of the ethical relation, this institution of the Other in the Same—or alternatively the Other at the basis of the Same—manifests the transcendence necessary for ethics to be articulated as an experience *par excellence*.

Phenomenology, according to Levinas, inaugurates a "new style in philosophy" (RR, 127–128). For Levinas, we first encounter the force of this new style in the "renewal of the very concept of the transcendental," a concept which appears as the "essential property of phenomenology" (RR, 127). As a renewed and renovated transcendental philosophy, Husserl's phenomenology takes *structure* as its essential theme. As a transcendental philosophy concerned with structure, phenomenology is a return to a description of consciousness—viz., consciousness understood, not as possessing the property "intentional," but rather as intentionality itself. Although intentionality may at first appear as an innocuous observation regarding subjective life, the theory of consciousness and subjectivity emergent from this conception of experience as *Erlebnis* will come to mark the end of the modern problematic. Husserl ends this problematic in the return to intentional consciousness as the evidential boundary of philosophical research.

The return to intentional consciousness as the locus of philosophical exposition is not, however, the return to a representational theory of mind. Representation, taken in its classical form, implicates that beings "support themselves by themselves," as if they were "substances" of some peculiar sort (RR, 127). Representation, on this account, is manifest in the comfort of disinterestedness, a comfort that comes to be the condition of the being of representation itself. The new style of phenomenology, the style of intentional analysis, contests the legitimacy of the notion that our presence to the world is a presence to a self-standing and self-manifesting objectivity of which the mind forms representations *subsequent* to this straightforward presence. This contestation has two aspects. The first aspect regards the appearance of the world as an objective correlate of the subject. On the representational account, there is a comfortable distance and that which appears is manifest directly and immanently. As Levinas notes, however, for Husserl this characterization is transformed by the turn to intentional analysis, an analysis that is adequate to the "how" of the appearance of the world, bracketing the "what" of that which becomes manifest. Representation, in its classical form, is inadequate to this mode of presence and runs up against a peculiar sort of *aporia* in the face of transcendence. Levinas writes that

> "the in itself of the object to be represented and possessed in consciousness, that is, to become subjective in the final account" would be . . . problematic in a philosophy that poses the subject as an immanent sphere, enclosed in itself; this problem is advanced beyond with the idea of the intentionality of consciousness, since the presence of the subject before the transcendent things is the very definition of consciousness. (RR, 129)

The classical formulation of representation, then, cannot account for its original presence to the world. To the extent that this classical formulation is predicated on the comfortable distance it claims to take from the world, it can only conceive consciousness as self-enclosed. As self-enclosed and immanent, the transcendence of the world is forgotten.

In remembering this transcendence, Husserl's phenomenology revolutionizes the philosophical conception of consciousness or subjectivity. The recognition and structural priority of the movement of intentionality toward the world and the correlate presence of the subject before the world as transcendent exhibits the transcendent intentionality that is constitutive of the primordial subject. Husserl's subject, for Levinas, is not self-enclosed and does not repeat the problematic formulation of subjectivity characteristic of the tradition. Nevertheless, the straightforward subject-object correlation characteristic of intentionality, even in its transcendent manifestation, conceals the "other dynamism" (RR, 129) that animates intentionality. This animation, which enigmatically hides itself and is concealed in its straightforward labor, yields the transcendental clue for Husserl. The clue, of course, is that our immediate presence to things "does not yet comprehend the sense (*sens*) of things" (RR, 127), though the world does signify this meaning through the straightforward manifestation of transcendence.

Husserlian phenomenology, taking precisely this signification as its clue, recognizes the "new possibilities of the philosopher" in the necessity of philosophical exposition to surpass (*dépasser*), in intentional analysis, the immediate presence of consciousness to the world and the immediate presence of things. The immediacy of things conceals the complex of intentions implicit in the straightforward presence of the world and the naive attitude that lives in that presence. In other words, the natural attitude must be overcome, and the motivational basis of this overcoming is the recognition of the structures that, in their constitutional function, underpin the given. The "given" is the explicit presence that bears within it the implicit sense. Levinas notes that

> . . . intentionality designates a relation with the object, but a relation such that it bears within it, essentially, an implicit sense. Presence before things implicates an other presence before it, which this initial presence is not aware of, a presence of other correlative horizons of these implicit intentions and horizons which . . . the consideration of the object given in the naive attitude would not discover. (RR, 130)

This is the first glimpse of the sense proper to the phenomenological trope that the transcendental subject is "more objective than objectivity." The implicit is not a simple deficiency of the explicit, but rather is the "forgotten landscape" (RR, 130) of that which thought holds in its immediate grasp. In Husserl's words,

> [this is] a form of *reflection* which has the remarkable property that what is seized upon perceptually in reflection is characterized fundamentally not only as something which exists and endures while it is being regarded perceptually but also as something which *already existed before* this regard was turned to it. (Hua III, 83/98)

Thought first finds itself present to the transcendence of the world, but exceeds itself by manifesting, in the explicitness of the transcendent given, the implicit horizon of sense—a horizon that forms a "background" which is *ready to be perceived*" (Hua III, 84/99). Thus, in the recognition of this internal horizon, thought exceeds itself in its first presence.

At this point, though something methodologically radical is glimpsed, the explicit priority given to this internal horizon bespeaks a certain conservatism in Husserl's phenomenology. This conservatism brings to the fore a new sense of representation in Husserl's exposition of the transcendental field—the internal horizon of the implicit—as a complex of noetic-noematic correlations. This schema, which guides the task of transcendental exposition, issues in a new sense of representation understood in its constitutive role, immanent to transcendence, and therefore not representation from a comfortable distance. Despite the fact that Husserl notes "another horizon" at the transcendent source of subjective life—a horizon Levinas will soon exploit—we find Husserl seduced by this new sense of representation. This seduction shows itself in the fact that he extends the noesis-noema correlation to ". . . all kinds of intentive lived-experience" (Hua III, 188/221). As a result of this methodological extension, all transcendence may be accounted for by way of the exposition of the internal horizon of the implicit. The noesis-noema correlation—where the noema is understood as the phenomenologically sound conception of representation—extends to all intentionalities. The exceeding of thought by thought itself, delimited by this correlation, becomes an exceeding which is eminently and immanently exhaustible.

Husserl's conception of the exceeding of the present by the implicit intentions of the transcendentally ideal runs its course in the exposition of the subjectivity more objective that objectivity. This exceeding is implicated in the movement toward the world, a movement which is underpinned and structured by the transcendental apparatus. The ideal intentions that form the field of explication for the transcendentally ideal task of Husserl's phenomenology are implicated in this movement and thus the motivational basis for the reflective turn to the noetic-noematic—the phenomenologically sound version of representation—is legitimated by the natural attitude itself. However, the very movement that justifies the phenomenological notion of representation also bears within it a horizon that is decidedly nonrepresentational: the forgotten horizon of sensibility. The horizon of sensibility, as Levinas will make clear, implicates an intentionality of transcendence that exceeds otherwise than the transcendental field of the ideal. It implicates a transcendence that decays representation, even representation in its phenomenological form.

Levinas notes that this other horizon is not foreign to Husserl. Rather, and quite to the contrary, Husserl himself recognizes a second transcendental item at the very source of the content of reflection. In Husserl's hands, the movement of intentionality toward the world is considered as structured by the noematic core of this movement, i.e., the core of the sense signified in the presence to the world. Nevertheless, there is a second horizon that surrounds this movement and which may be said to structure its very possibility. Levinas writes that

> [w]hat Husserl illustrates in his concrete analyses is that the thought which goes toward its object *surrounds* the thoughts which open upon the noematic horizons, this thought already supports the subject in its movement toward the object, supporting . . . the work of the subject, and plays a transcendental role: sensibility and sensible qualities are not . . . [factual instances] of the categorial form or ideal essence, but the situation where the subject already takes up its position in order to accomplish a categorial intuition . . . [It is] the condition that the subject requires for its perception. (RR, 131–32)

The sensible surrounds and structures the movement toward the object and thereby structures the very possibility of the noematic horizons that form the field of transcendental exposition for Husserl. The sensible is transcendental, not in the sense that it is already an ideality, but rather that it is a presupposed condition of all reflective life. The transcendental function of the sensible is an "original experience" and not a "fruit borne of experience"; rather, it signifies the anteriority of sensible qualities forgotten in Husserl's rehabilitation of representation in the concept of the noema (RR, 133).

In remembering this horizon of sensibility, a memory that will again be taken up in *Totality and Infinity* (cf., TeI, 108ff/135ff), Levinas recalls the Heideggerian prerogative which places the situation of the subject at the original basis of the reflective attitude. To be sure, Levinas recalls this prerogative with a hint of positivity, but the context of his discussion and the content of his findings indicate a state of affairs immanently within the Husserlian problematic of intentionality. The situation of the subject, in Levinas's treatment, resembles Heidegger's formal insistence on the primacy of worldly being, but Levinas's analysis opens upon the transcendence of sensibility and the intentionality proper to this exceeding of thought. It does not open upon the formal considerations of the existential analytic. In order to destruct the reha- bilitated representation of Husserl's noema, Levinas returns to the original materiality of the situation in which consciousness finds itself present to the world. However, in this return we find that coextensive with the *Sinngebung* of the idealist subject is the constituting function of that which is constituted. The sensible, that upon which sense is bestowed, is not just constituted, but constituting (RR, 133). Husserl himself had identified this two-fold transcendental. Indeed, as Levinas notes, Husserl himself "wavered between the disengagement of tran- scendental idealism and the engagement in the world," and this wa- vering is, in Levinas's view, not his weakness but his strength (RR, 133). Such a wavering may be seen as a weakness, insofar as it indicates a contamination of the purity of representation, yet Levinas commends Husserl for illuminating this "double perspective" (RR, 133) regarding intentionality and its structure. Ultimately, we would contend, Levinas commends Husserl for this illumination precisely because such a discovery allows for the formal possibility and necessity of the ethical, although Husserl's allegiance to the principle of evidence and conse- quent disingenuosness regarding his descriptive radicality cover over such horizons.

This mixture of the ideal and the sensible in Husserl indicates a two-fold sense of the transcendental, and also a two-fold sense of the way in which thought exceeds itself. Husserl's transcendental idealism exhibits how thought exceeds itself in terms of its internal horizon of noetic and noematic correlations. Husserl's transcendental sensualism, on the other hand, exhibits how thought exceeds itself in this "other horizon," the horizon of the sensible—the "other side" of the transcen- dence of those things immediately present to the subject. The first exceeding, the internal horizon, was safe for the Husserlian project. This second exceeding, however, renders the very terms of the reflective prerogative unstable and introduces a danger that cannot be smoothed over by the rhythms of reflection.

The rhythms of reflection are driven by what Levinas calls the philosophical eros. The philosophical eros marks as its essential task the reduction of the other to the same, which allows thought, despite its exceeding of itself, to remain sovereign. Husserl, in accordance with the evidential principle that regulates phenomenology, succumbs to the philosophical eros in spite of disclosing precisely that which would betray it. The exceeding of thought by thought, of thought at its very generative source, has a two-fold appearance in Husserl. The exceeding of the sensible is the exceeding of thought by way of the forgotten horizon of phenomenology. To be sure, this horizon is not forgotten innocently and without a certain plot or conspiracy. The horizon of the sensible, Levinas writes, "... takes us outside of the categories of subject-object and ruins the sovereignty of representation" (RR, 133). To be sure, the exceeding of thought by the internal horizon of sense takes us outside the categories of subject-object by illuminating the constitutive function of the implicit intentions. Still, this exceeding remains conservative, insofar as it repairs the content as well as the *telos* of the representation it initially ruins. Husserl's noema preserves this remnant of the old world. Husserl's conservatism evinces the reinstatement of the philosophical eros, that eros wherein consciousness is "... an instant of full possession of self where nothing of the strange, nothing of the other comes to limit the glorious identification of the Same in thought" (RR, 134–35).

Sensibility ruins the sovereignty of representation. It ruins representation because it does not exceed in such a way as to allow its essential difference to be recovered in the identity of the noema. Its exceeding refuses to follow rules. Thought is generated out of sensibility, but thought as a system of correlations is inadequate to the exceeding of the sensible. In 1959, the sensible is still an intentionality for Levinas and does not yet institute the relation of radical separation,[20] but it is still an intentionality that demands a wholly other structure than that structure which would recuperate all things strange and exterior within the boundaries of the familiar, thereby reconciling difference in identity. The sensible cannot be ignored by phenomenology, for it is established, by Husserl himself, as a transcendental condition of thought itself. The transcendence of the intentionality of the sensible is not the transcendence of the world rendered immanent in reflection, nor is it the transcendence of the projections of the Same. This transcendence is not the transcendence of Husserl or Heidegger. An unsuspected turn of events awakens phenomenology from a certain dogmatic slumber: Sensibility introduces an alterity within the boundaries of the identical, which, under the rubric of another transcendental, warrants the trope "an Other constitutive of the Same." Alterity reclaims its role as sense-bestower in the transcendental function of sensibility. The catch here is that such an awakening is not imposed on phenomenology from outside; rather, it was always already there, a forgotten horizon, waiting to interrupt again phenomenology's dream of wakeful consciousness.

Levinas's concluding remarks to the essay "La ruine de la représentation" give us some essential clues regarding the ultimate significance of this discovery of thought exceeding itself in the sensible—viz., the sense of alterity over to which thought passes and which is the sense of alterity constitutive of the formal structure of intentionality deformalized in the analyses of *Totality and Infinity*. As we have seen, the transcendental function of the sensible is such that thought is exceeded at its generative source. This is the "other" transcendental that takes us outside idealism and decays the phenomenologically sound conception of representation as noema. Solidifying the analysis, Levinas writes that

> [t]hought directed toward the object in every sincerity of its intention, does not touch being in its naive sincerity, thinks more than it thinks and otherwise than it actually thinks and, in this sense, is not immanent to itself, even if, by way of its regard, it grasps the object at which it aims "in flesh and bone." We are otherwise than idealism, since being is neither in thought, nor outside thought, but rather thought itself is outside itself (*la pensée elle-même est hors d'elle-même*). (RR, 135)

The term "being" here designates the transcendental function of the sensible. The sensible marks the expulsion of thought out of the boundaries of Same, and this expulsion out of the Same is constitutive of the very identity of intentionality: thought itself is outside itself. The totalizing function of representation is shown, when taken back to the sensible—to being—as its transcendental condition, to be already placed within forgotten horizons, horizons to which the logic of the noema is wholly inadequate.

It is according to this model that we should begin to understand the formal structure of the transcendent-intention deformalized in *Totality and Infinity*. The formalization of the structure of intentionality takes place in what must be called the *transcendental* analyses of "La ruine de la représentation" and these analyses indicate an intentionality that is the destructor of representation. As the destructor of representation—that is, as that which ruins the dream of a purely homological thought—this transcendent-intention understands itself as the movement toward the sensible, determined by the sensible, and therefore a movement without return. This movement without return recovers an original sense of a transcendence that is able to sustain the thought of alterity without interpreting that alterity as "... deducible out of the same plan or out of the plan of the Same" (RR, 135). This transcendence is excessive and it transforms the very idea of phenomenality by way of the exceeding of thought within thought itself. Phenomenality can now begin to characterize the economy of exteriority.

But this is still an intentionality. It is an intentionality of sensible transcendence, and thus an intentionality conditioned by a sensibility that is strange and other. Precisely because this movement of excessive manifestation is intentional—which is to say, it maintains its essential quality of relationality—Levinas's ruining of the phenomenologically sound representation is still a phenomenology. What sort of phenomenology? Levinas is brief yet explicit on this matter. Phenomenology for Husserl, despite his own descriptive findings, is always a *Sinngebung* issued from a sovereign ego that absorbs otherness in identity. Still, Levinas writes,

> in a phenomenology where the activity of totalizing and totalitarian representation is already exceeded in its own intention, where representation finds itself already placed in horizons which, in some manner, it has not wanted, but of which it cannot dispense—an ethical *Sinngebung* becomes possible, that is to say, a *Sinngebung* essentially respectful of the Other. (RR, 135)

The transcendence disclosed in sensibility makes possible—as a formal possibility—the bestowal of sense from the outside. Within the boundaries of the present analysis, this bestowal of sense issues from the transcendental function of sensibility. To be sure, it is too formal of an alterity to yet be the human other. Nevertheless, it is exactly within this conception of intentionality in which an ethics becomes possible. An ethical *Sinngebung* is, as Levinas himself says, a bestowal of sense which is essentially respectful of the Other and this respectfulness of alterity is accomplished in an intentionality transcendentally conditioned by sensibility. Respect is accomplished and maintained to the extent that an intentionality set out from sensibility does not impose the conditions of the Same on the Other. Rather, if and when considered within the logic of the Same, such an intentionality is seen as separated from its origin and condition. Constituted by the alterity of sensibility, the Same is essentially separated from the Other, but maintains, across this gap, the irreducible fact of relation. What, then, is this distance, other than the space of the ethical? If this distance is formally rendered possible within Husserl's phenomenology, then we have come a long way in understanding exactly how, recalling the "Preface" to *Totality and Infinity*," phenomenology makes possible the passage into ethics and metaphysical exteriority.

This reading of Levinas's "La ruine de la représentation" indicates the significance of Levinas's essay for his own work up through *Totality and Infinity* and, indeed, for phenomenology itself. The significance of "La ruine de la représentation" essay lies in the peculiar relation to Husserl it establishes. This relation, though it insists on a transgression and rupture of the first position of idealism in phenomenology, nevertheless takes up the horizon of phenomenology itself through the structure of sensibility. Levinas returns to Husserl in this regard precisely because it is Husserl who can provide a sensualism that retains the claim of the transcendental. This is why, despite the characterization of sensualism cited above from "The Ego and the Totality," it is necessary for Levinas to move beyond Husserl only through the opening of the boundaries of idealism disclosed by Husserl himself. Though Levinas's insistence that intentionality is constituted by sensibility—i.e., constituted from the outside—may at first glance seem critical of Husserl, we must also insist that this shift in the idea of sense-bestowal and constitution initiated by Levinas is legitimated, perhaps even demanded, by phenomenology itself. To this end, the exposition of the transcendental function of sensibility elaborates and extends the methodological implications and suggestions regarding materiality in 1940. *De l'existence à l'existant* and *Time and the Other*, as we have seen, take up the problem of axiology. This leaves the second sense of the concrete in "L'œuvre d'Edmond Husserl" undeveloped. The descriptive content of *De l'existence à l'existant* and *Time and the Other* is concerned with providing figures of the transcendence of the subject. "La ruine de la représentation" establishes how materiality signifies without being rendered a predelineated structural item.

Further, and in a strictly Levinasian vein, by retaining the constitutive efficacy of the transcendental in remembering the horizon of the sensible, Levinas is able to forge a conception of alterity through sensibility that is not a return to a strictly or merely nonphilosophical empiricism. The sensibility to which he appeals is, rather, justified by both the boundaries and lack thereof disclosed by the original field of transcendental phenomenology. And, finally, it is this relation to phenomenology that allows us to begin to understand Levinas's claim in "Trace of the Other" that the problem of alterity and its mode of signification must be understood ". . . by situating it with respect to the phenomenology it interrupts" (TrA, 199/356). Or, perhaps more pressing for our present concerns, Levinas's rethinking of both axiology and materiality/sensibility allows us to begin to understand his claim in the "Preface" to *Totality and Infinity* that through the search for the concrete in intentional analysis, Husserlian phenomenology makes possible the passage to metaphysical exteriority.

Three

The Subject in Question

Relation and Sense in *Totality and Infinity*

A face is pure, conceptless experience.

—Levinas

We concluded the previous chapter with Levinas's account of an ethical sense-bestowal, a *Sinngebung* made possible and necessary in Levinas's transformation of the structure of intentionality through sensibility. The significance of this transformation lies in his identification of a modality of relation between the oneself and the other instituted prior to the accomplishments of constituting consciousness. The constitutive function of sensibility, what Levinas calls a transcendental sensualism, opens us to a description of just such a relation.

The constitutive function of sensibility is our first clue to what Levinas calls an "experience without concept"—the face, in a word. In the 1950s, Levinas's recovery of this forgotten transcendental horizon establishes a general logic of materiality within the movement of transcendental genesis, the genesis of the subject from the other. This general logic of the sense-bestowing function of materiality will undergo a kind of individuation in the ethics of the face-to-face. In the face-to-face, the bestowal of sense signifies the singularity of the face. *Totality and Infinity* will show us how the singularity of the face, signifying in its facing position, deformalizes the general logic materiality. Thus, we will here read *Totality and Infinity* in terms of its having moved from thinking the function of materiality in general to the specification of materiality as the exteriority of the face. In a microhistorical context: Having asked the question of the logic of materiality in general in 1959, Levinas is then able to specify the analysis in the concrete signification of the facing face in the ethical relation of separation in *Totality and Infinity*, 1961.

Our reading of *Totality and Infinity* will therefore insist on situating the question of ethics within the problem of sense. This insistence will help clarify the meaning of Levinas's remark to Philippe Nemo that he does not seek a construction of an ethics, but rather seeks its sense *(sens)* (EeI, 85/90).

Objectivity and Transcendence

Some preliminary notes on our reading of *Totality and Infinity*. It is perhaps trivial to note that the structural problem of transcendence animates the method and descriptive analyses of *Totality and Infinity*. Such a claim is a common starting point for reading *Totality and Infinity*. But it is nevertheless fruitful to rehearse this problematic in a phenomenological context, for it opens up significant new issues. Early in *Totality and Infinity*, Levinas makes the following remark regarding transcendence and the structure of the transcendent-intention the text attempts to expose:

> The "intentionality" of transcendence is unique in its kind. *The difference between objectivity and transcendence will serve as a general guideline for all the analyses of this work.* (TeI, 20/49; emphasis in original)

The quotation marks put around the term intentionality are significant and part of the present task will be to determine why it is necessary for Levinas to qualify his use of that term. The problem of transcendence is explicated by Levinas both in terms of the problem of what signifies as transcendent and the correlative problem of intentionality or relationality. How Levinas articulates transcendence as radically transcendent, wholly other, and yet retains a sense of relationality is, in a nutshell, the primary phenomenological project of *Totality and Infinity*. How one is to render the structural composition of that articulation remains an importantly difficult task. And so the central problem of our reading here is that of making explicit this implicit structural composition. The paradox of relation in radical transcendence is the site at which the question of the structure of alterity in *Totality and Infinity* is to be asked and answered. Thus, the present reflections may be considered a prolonged meditation on the meaning of the phrases "intentionality of transcendence" and "transcendent intention" that recur throughout *Totality and Infinity.*

We should also not fail to note that in the passage quoted above, Levinas emphasizes the *difference* between objectivity and transcendence as the clue to his exposition. This suggests that there is a kind of juxtapositional necessity of objectivity for the appearance of the genuine sense of transcendence. Indeed, this directs us back to Levinas's remarks in the "Preface" to *Totality and Infinity* regarding Husserl's phenomenology as a *passage* to the metaphysics of exteriority (TeI, xvii/ 29). This notion of passage implicates phenomenology in its own interruption, in the opening of its *de jure* closed system. In order to make the work of this context and passage evident, the present chapter will firstly consider the problem of *Sinngebung* in both phenomenology and *Totality and Infinity.* The issue of *Sinngebung* is an indispensable problematic for our reading of *Totality and Infinity* for two reasons: one negative, one positive. The negative relevance of the problem of *Sinngebung* is that, in securing the boundaries of the objective, Husserl explicitly links the problem of constitution with thematization. This link brings into relief both what is at issue and what is at stake in *conceiving transcendence radically.* Levinas's conception of transcendence insists on transcendence as such and so not on transcendence as a modification of immanence. The nonmodified status of transcendence *qua* transcendence makes it "radical." Radicality emanates from Levinas's transcendence having separated itself from a prior, phenomenologically conservative, notion at its root: the logic of immanence. The negative function of the problem of *Sinngebung* therefore outlines the boundaries of the philosophy of the Same, as well as the logical necessities for any thought that would propose to think beyond it.

But the problem of sense-bestowal is not merely one of marking limits. The positive relevance of the problem of *Sinngebung* lies in Levinas's recasting of sense-genesis. Though Husserl conceives this generation primarily in terms of the transcendental ego, Levinas shows us in *Totality and Infinity* how the general logic of *Sinngebung* remains in place in the reversal of intentionality: This is the *sens* of the face-to-face. Thus the issue of the generation of sense, though it flows otherwise than idealism, is a necessary methodological precondition of both our understanding of the phenomenological status of transcendence in *Totality and Infinity* and the modality of relation such a transcendence— *l'autrui*—sustains with the I.

We will therefore take the problem of sense-bestowal as the context for our reading of *Totality and Infinity*. From that initial account of *Sinngebung*, we will turn attention to the "Preface" to *Totality and Infinity*. The "Preface" warrants special attention because it sets out the basic, formal underpinnings of the text. A close reading of the "Preface" prepares us for the concrete problem of articulating a structure of transcendence that resists the traditional phenomenological problem of sense-bestowal and constitution. The problem of transcendence will be taken up with two aspects in view: the problem of manifestation and the problem of relation. The problem of manifestation will treat the function of *expression* and *kath auto* as modalities of *manifestation* that are not reducible to *thematization* (and we employ these terms rigorously).[1] This exposition will speak to the issue of the peculiar signification demanded by a radical conception of transcendence. The problem of relation will treat the modality of relation implicit in manifestations found in Levinas's studies of Enjoyment and Desire. Enjoyment and Desire in *Totality and Infinity*, as we shall see, make explicit and concrete the relation the I holds to transcendence. Levinas thereby makes the subject as transcending explicit—i.e., as a (provisionally characterized) transcendent intention. His accounts of Enjoyment and Desire will also make good on his promissory notes on affective intentionality in the 1940 "L'œuvre d'Edmond Husserl," insofar as Enjoyment and Desire, as modalities of relation, pertain to the axiological life of the subject anterior to the work of thematization. The identification of manifestation and relation as the fundamental components of the transcendent intention give us an important first glimpse into the radical phenomenology at work in *Totality and Infinity*.

However, the possibilities latent within the axiological mode of relation run up against their limit in the face-to-face. Our penultimate section will take up the reversal of intentionality implicated in the ethical relation. Enjoyment and Desire are indispensable for articulating this reversal; Levinas's analyses constitute a preliminary break with the thematization and thus accomplish much of the work demanded by the thought of transcendence. Ethics, however, demands another step and the logic of *Sinngebung* is our key. The reversal of intentionality in the ethical relation takes up the positivity of the logic of sense-bestowal, as our reading of the transcendence of the face-to-face will begin to build upon Levinas's remarks at the end of "La ruine de la réprésentation" on "*une Sinngebung éthique*." The bestowal of sense from the outside, the constitution of the sense of the ethical set out from the Other, will guide our exposition of the formal structure of this reversal of the flow of sense. The concluding section will identify what may be called the general economy of exteriority operative in the text of *Totality and Infinity*, an economy that the face-to-face relation manifests *par excellence*. This general economy of exteriority will bring us full circle to the "Preface," answering the question of how, for Levinas, Husserl's phenomenology makes possible the passage to ethics.

A final note on Levinas's reworking of Husserl in *Totality and Infinity:* It is our basic contention that *Totality and Infinity* must be read as a phenomenological rethinking of sense and transcendentality, but one that first must break with the nucleus of meaning constituted by the free subject. Levinas accomplishes this break in part by situating the founding condition of experience in the sensible. This move produces a reorientation of the notion of the transcendental such that it ceases to resemble what the tradition, dominated by the turn to the spontaneous performances of subjectivity, has called "the condition of possibility." This new, postsubjectivistic transcendental is an enigmatic "condition" precisely because this transcendental intertwines (and so does not bifurcate) the language of the transcendental and the empirical.[2] To this end, the methodological work of *Totality and Infinity* continues and extends the discovery of a transcendental sensualism in "La ruine de la répresentation," a sensualism which recollected the forgotten transcendental horizon of sensibility. The language of empiricism is therein co-opted, but with a twist of the transcendental. With regard to the language of the transcendental, Levinas will *reject* the traditional appendage of ego (viz., the *cogito* of Kant and Husserl) to the condition that conditions all experience, thereby jettisoning any stable notion of foundation.[3] The first position of the "I think" will have to be contested. The subject is not self-certain, but *mise en question*. What Levinas will want to *retain* in the notion of the transcendental is the constitutive function of the structural item that bears the designation "transcendental." In the case of the language of empiricism, Levinas will *reject* the Aristotelian notion of the *tode ti* (TeI, 30, 90, 265/59, 118, 290), for it is "situated on the same plane as the concept" (TeI, 90/118) and— according to eidetic law (see Hua III, 28f/27f)—it subsumes the particularity of the sensible under the rubric of the universal. The second position of materiality will be contested. What Levinas will want to *retain* in the notion of the sensible is the secret alterity nascent in naming

the essential difference between the sensible as exterior and the universal as interior.[4] The maintenance of this difference necessitates a logic
". . . pursued beyond the *tode ti*" (TeI, 265/290). The empirical beyond
the *tode ti* is nothing other than the logic of the exterior, which is nothing
other than the absurd logic of the anteriority of the posterior (e.g., TeI,
144/170). The "absurdity" and sense of this anteriority is properly seen
when it is restored to its constitutive function.

Levinas will therefore rethink sense by intertwining (and not
without some paradoxical difficulties) the transcendental and the
empirical. The sense of alterity must be understood as constituted from
out of the generative function of exteriority. This exteriority, despite the
fact that it signifies wholly otherwise than the signification of immanence, must be described in terms of its relation to the I. The possibility of relationality brings us to the kernel of our study: How is the
wholly other, transcendence, to be related to the subject without reduction to the form of the Same? The flow of sense in sense-bestowal holds
the key to this enigma. The problem of signification sustains the difference between the exterior and the I, and, on the basis of this difference, we can understand the space of the interval traversed in "*une
Sinngebung éthique.*" But, we must first see what is entailed in the very
idea of sense-bestowal. We therefore begin our reading with an exposition of phenomenological problem of the constitution of sense within
which Levinas operates.

The Problem of Sinngebung

Let us begin with an overview of the general problem of *Sinngebung*
in both phenomenology and the text of *Totality and Infinity*. In our
account of Levinas's work in the 1940s and 1950s, we saw how Levinas
negotiated a path from transcendence to what he terms a *Sinngebung
éthique* in "La ruine de la répresentation": the transformation of intentionality through the structure of sensibility. Levinas will, in the polemi-
cal aspects of *Totality and Infinity*, set aside his confidence in the
positivity of *Sinngebung* in 1959 in favor of the juxtaposition of
the metaphysics of exteriority to the idealist model of sense-bestowal.
The Husserlian notion of sense-bestowal that Levinas juxtaposes to
exteriority is, of course, the account of the genesis of meaning wherein
meaning, according to the Levinasian lexicon, is issued from the Same

and imposed on the Other. Indeed, as Levinas relates in his preface to the 1987 German translation of *Totality and Infinity*, the overall aim of *Totality and Infinity* is to dispute "that the synthesis of knowledge, the totality of being embraced by the *transcendental ego*, [and] the presence captured in representation . . . may be the ultimate instances of sense" (PEA, 232). In other words, *Totality and Infinity* is a book about sense and perhaps about another sort of presence, but not a book about the sense and presence set out from the transcendental ego. Rather, it is a book about the "forgotten and unsuspected horizons" that, despite being forgotten and obscured, do themselves endow sense *(prêtent un sens)* (TeI, xvi/28). And yet, these horizons are not constrained by and cannot be legitimately construed within the boundaries of idealism. Further, Levinas's evocation of the transcendental ego directly implicates the problem of *Sinngebung* as both a necessary backdrop to the text and the principle problem to be exceeded. This testimony, in addition to the frequent juxtapositions of *Sinngebung* to the logic of exteriority found in the text itself, warrants our treatment of the methodological problem of sense-bestowal.

The issue of *Sinngebung* manifests itself in Husserl's conception of the constitution of meaning, as Levinas implies in his prefatory remarks to the German edition. As Landgrebe[5] and Fink[6] have noted, there is a double meaning of sense-bestowal at work in Husserl's transcendental phenomenology: the problem of "sense-formation" (Fink) or "apperception" (Landgrebe) and the problem of "creation." The constitutional problematic of sense-formation or apperception is implicit in the movement of thematization—the shift of the reflective regard from pregiven unities toward the levels of constitutional work that have already produced these unities. This aspect of the sense-bestowal problematic, set within the boundaries of static explication, emerges at the moment of *accomplished* genesis. Static explication sets out on the basis of this pregiven structure. The term "constitution" names the implicit work of consciousness on that world pregiven as a unity to experience, though such work is covered over in our straightforward dealings with the world. The problem of creation, on the other hand, turns to what Husserl terms the "primal *logos*" (Hua XVII, 280/274) or the "primally institutive" mode of consciousness (Hua XVII, 317/317) and takes us to a more primordial site of genesis. Creation turns to the generative source of the "sphere of being of absolute origins *[Seinssphäre absoluter Ursprünge]*" (Hua III, 107/129). Husserl's (re)turn to primally institutive consciousness—the transcendental ego and absolute subjectivity—is concerned exclusively with the genetic problem *qua* active genesis. Active genesis is nothing other than the original creation or birth of sense within and from the ego itself.

There are, therefore, two senses of sense-bestowal in Husserl's work. The first sense (sense-formation or apperception) labors within the boundaries of static analysis. Static analysis, which "... is guided by the unity of the supposed object" (Hua XVII, 316/316), discovers sense-bestowal by starting with the actual presentation of a straight-forward perceptual unity or object-sense and, by regressive reflection, ultimately discovers conditions of possibility for that unity. That is to say, pre-given unities in lived-experience provide "transcendental clues" upon which an explication (*Auslegung*) is based; static exposition searches for the implicit structures that structure the explicit (Hua III, §150; also, Hua XVII, 252/245). In the *Cartesian Meditations*, Husserl writes that

> ... the intentional object ... plays, for reasons easily understood, the role of "transcendental clue" to the typical infinite multiplici-ties of possible *cogitationes* that, in a possible synthesis, bear the intentional object within them ... as the same meant object. Necessarily the point of departure is the object given "straight-forwardly" at the particular time. From it reflection goes back to the mode of consciousness at that time and to the potential modes of consciousness included horizonally in that mode. . . . (Hua I, 87/50)

The shift of the regard from what is straightforwardly given to the implicit structures of experience amounts to the shift from what is constituted to the structures that performed the constituting. This shifting of the regard operates within the boundaries of what has already been accomplished by consciousness. As Husserl notes in *Formal and Transcendental Logic,* the exposition is static precisely because

> [s]tatic analysis takes the object-sense and, starting from its man-ners of givenness, follows up and explicates the "proper and actual" sense, consulting those manners of givenness as intentional references to the possible "It Itself." (Hua XVII, 318/318)

The very sense "object" presupposes the synthetic activity of the transcendental subject and thus the apperception or sense-formation problem of sense-bestowal legitimates itself, in the end, in its appeal to the object of perception—a pregiven unity.[7] In reflection on the implicit buried in the *Leitfaden* of the explicit, a subsequently described sense is discovered to have predelineated the pregiven state of affairs. This hidden yet accomplished predelineation marks the static sense of bestowal—a bestowal both presupposed in the pregiven unity of mundane egoic life and rendered in reflection to the life of the transcendental subject.

Explication within the boundaries of static constitution takes the phenomenologist to the primal activity of genesis in absolute consciousness, and so ultimately to the transcendental ego. Husserl writes that "the static constitution of objects, which relates to an already "developed" subjectivity, has its counterpart in an inquiry into *apriori genetic constitution*" and in this inquiry "lies the sedimented 'history'" of the sense disclosed in static analysis (Hua XVII, 257/250). That is to say, the problem of creation—i.e., of *Urstiftung* in the field of the sedimented "history" of reflectively uncovered sense—builds upon the static account of the bestowal of sense. The field of static constitution necessarily points back to the creative activity of subjectivity (Hua XVII, 317/317).[8] This creative activity is the presupposition that underpins and structures the static aspect of the *Sinngebung* problematic. Thus Husserl claims that disclosure of sense in reflection already points back to a prior creative act. In the *Phenomenological Psychology* lectures, Husserl remarks that

> [t]he genesis of spiritualized realities manifestly refers back to activities of a creative subjectivity. The sense refers back to a sense-forming subjectivity which creates. . . . (Hua IX, 112/85)

This creative subjectivity or transcendental ego is the "primitive basis for everything that I accept as existent" (Hua XVII, 246/239), for this active ego provides "the primitive intentional basis for my world" (Hua XVII, 243/237).

As the intentional basis of world-sense, the primitive mode of consciousness cannot be dependent upon the world for its generative functioning. Husserl will claim that the transcendental ego "precedes the being of the world" (Hua XVII, 235/228), not because it performs an act of abstraction, but precisely because it is the primal, genera-tive source of the sense of the lived-world.[9] On this, Husserl writes that

> . . . no mode of non-original consciousness of objects belonging to a fundamental sort is essentially possible, unless there has previously occurred, in the synthetic unity of immanent tempo-rality, the corresponding mode of original consciousness of the Same—as, genetically, the "primally institutive" mode of con-sciousness, back to which every mode of non-original conscious-ness points genetically. (Hua XVII, 317/317)

Sense is born from the creative activity of the primal ego; absolute consciousness, the primal *logos*, gives birth to meaning. Husserl invokes this cluster of maternal imagery when he writes that

> [p]henomenology in our sense is the science of "origins," of the "mothers" of all cognition; and it is the maternal ground [*Mutterboden*] of all philosophical method: to this ground and to the work in it, everything leads back.[10] (Hua V, 80/69)

This maternal ground is the generative origin of sense—sense that finds itself instituted in the constitutive work of the ego in the world, but which is not itself of the world. As a product of active genesis, sense is bestowed from the active ego.

This aspect of the problem of sense-bestowal brings us to what Husserl calls the "double genetic after-effect." The double after-effect addresses the scope of the problem of *Sinngebung*—viz., the boundaries of its effect and the claustrophobic limitations it puts on a thought that would seek to exceed it. Husserl writes

> . . . every manner of original givenness has a *double genetic after-effect. Firstly,* its after-effect in the form of possible recollective reproductions, *via* retentions that attach themselves to it quite immediately by a process of original genesis; and, *secondly,* its "apperceptional" after-effect, which is such that anything (no matter how it is already constituted) that is present in a similar new situation will be apperceived in a similar manner. (Hua XVII, 317/317)

So, the double effect of the genesis of sense sets the boundaries of possibility established in that sense-bestowal. The bestowal of sense, in its original active genetic moment, determines a unified seam of eidetic work across the field of temporal possibility. The transcendental field is delimited by the determination of time manifest in the effect of original sense-genesis. The recollective after-effect implements an uncontaminated pastness of the "history" of sense, preserved in retention. The purity of the protentional horizon is assured in terms of the apperceptive work of sense on the world—and every possible world—of perception. The creative work of the maternal ground claims to eliminate possibilities outside the already constituted. The seamlessness of time, the after-effect of genesis, insures such a limitation of possibility.

Here we must postpone a temporal consideration of materiality and passivity—the other pole of genesis—for, in *Totality and Infinity*, Levinas is not yet concerned with the temporal notion of absence implicated in the problem of sensation. In *Totality and Infinity*, the issue of passivity is connected with patience.[11] Patience renders passivity within the general problem of death and suffering (cf., TeI, 139, 212, 215ff/165, 235, 238ff). Now, to be sure, the problem of *Sinngebung*—on either the positivity of Levinas's alteration of Husserl or the unsympathetic identification of idealism with the totalitarian thought of the Same—is nothing other than the problem of the function of sense and its genesis. The genetic problematic implicates the structure of time in the question of genesis. But, in 1961, Levinas is taken with the problem of signification, especially how signification manifests in a manner that confounds the boundaries of Husserl's sense-bestowal problematic. This approach to the problem postpones consideration of the latent radicality in Husserl's work on passivity and materiality in favor of an account of what might be called the superlative *activity* of sense in its genesis from the outside. Indeed, Levinas writes that ". . . the term welcome of the Other expresses a simultaneity of activity and passivity," which is a simultaneity that situates the relation with the Other "outside of the dichotomies valid for things" (TeI, 62/89).

For Levinas, the full accomplishment of objectivity—that from which he will differentiate transcendence—is found in Husserl's idealist conception of sense-bestowal. This full accomplishment is won through Husserl's subtle linking of luminosity to autopresentation, a link Levinas thinks concludes the realism of sense implicit in the whole of Western philosophy (TeI, 68/95). In *Totality and Infinity*, the face will of course serve as the exemplary instance of exteriority, as it is the face that ". . . brings us to a notion of sense prior to my *Sinngebung* and thus independent of my initiative and my power" (TeI, 22/51). This pleni-tude of sense is sought beyond or outside the "adequate idea" that is the "result of *Sinngebung*" (TeI, 271/295; also, TeI, 96/123). The *force* of the exteriority of the face will issue from the fact that "the face signi-fies by itself; its signification precedes *Sinngebung*" (TeI, 239/261). This intertwining of the problem of sense with *Sinngebung* is made explicit in Levinas's essay "Freedom and Commandment" from 1953:

> If a face is not *known*, that is not because it does not have sense; it is not known because its relationship with us does not refer to its constitution and, to use Husserl's term, is anterior to every *Sinngebung*. This sense, this plenitude of sense prior to any *Sinngebung*, but which is nonetheless a relationship enacted by understanding, a nonviolent relationship, describes the very struc-ture of a created being. (LC, 45/22)

Levinas makes it clear in this passage how the break with objectivity—enacted in a fully developed notion of transcendence—reorients our thinking through the problem of creation. The passage from objectiv-ity to transcendence structurally juxtaposes signification to *Sinngebung*. Signification of transcendence is a "signification [of what] precedes *Sinngebung*, and rather than justifying idealism, marks its limit" (TeI, 182/207). Transcendence, then, marks the limit of the idealist construal of sense-bestowal. The effect of this marking is two-fold: Transcen-dence marks the limit of the extension of egoic constitution, as well as the conditions necessary for thinking beyond the constitutional framework.

Interrupting Phenomenology

Let us now turn to the "Preface" to *Totality and Infinity*. In his conclud-ing remarks to the "Preface," Levinas tells us quite famously that the concrete descriptions in the text itself should be read as "unsaying the said" of the "Preface" (TeI, xviii/30). "Unsaying the said" indicates that the formal considerations of Levinas's prefatory remarks undergo (or perhaps have arisen from) deformalized analyses in the body of the text.

As such, the formalizations are precisely that: formal considerations that emerge within concrete "life." In other words, the formal structures outlined in the "Preface" are already parasitic on the notions explicated as concrete, notions unmediated by form in the descriptive accounts of signification, manifestation, Desire, Enjoyment, and the Face. Nevertheless, it also must be said that the formal structure of the transcendent intention, the central issue of the "Preface," is of utmost *methodological* importance. That is, the Said is indispensable for the Unsaying insofar as it gives us direct access to the method through which the structures of signification, et al. come to be understood.

With this understanding of the nature of the "Preface," our reading will focus on two formal aspects of Levinas's remarks. First, the question of transcendence: the question of both access to transcendence (the methodological problematic) and the status accorded to the structures described (the philosophical purchase of the exposition). Second, and interwoven with the issue of transcendence, is the function of Husserl's phenomenology as a passage to metaphysical exteriority. To both ends, the central issue of the "Preface" is that of accounting for intentionality and its radical modification when placed in contact with sensibility.

The "Preface" clearly announces the issue of transcendence—its possibility and consequences for the structure of intentionality—as the central problem of *Totality and Infinity*. The "Preface" begins with a figure: Levinas wants to ". . . oppose to the objectivism of war a subjectivity borne from the eschatological vision" (TeI, xiv/25), a vision which ". . . institutes a relation with being beyond the totality" (TeI, xi/22). Transcendence names the structural item leading to this relation beyond the totality. Our access to this transcendence, the path to its manifestation, takes us ". . . from the experience of totality *back* to a situation where the totality breaks up, a situation that conditions the totality itself" (TeI, xiii/24; emphasis mine). This method of exposition is a counterpart to Levinas's remark that *Totality and Infinity* emphasizes the difference between objectivity and transcendence. This difference must be thought, not by simple opposition of the infinite to the totality, but rather in the *passage* from objectivity to transcendence. And our movement through this passage is a movement *back* to the original situation out of which totality arises; it is a movement toward what is "first philosophy," to anticipate the language of the later Levinas. But Levinas wavers in *Totality and Infinity*. Though the passageway is a movement "backward," Levinas will also say that the concept of infinity—the rigorously developed logic of transcendence (TeI, xiii/24–25)—is ". . . as primordial as totality" (TeI, xi/23). Transcendence is already implicated within the logic of totality and thus is "reflected within the totality and history, within experience" (TeI, xi/23).[12] The movement beyond the totality departs from and within the experience of totality, confronting identity with difference, the familiar with the strange, or, as Levinas puts it, the Same with the Other. We might add here that it is phenomenologically important that Levinas's analysis does not work within ontologism—the positing of two opposed worlds—and all of its impossible paradoxes. We begin with experience and trace it back to its point of rupture. Further, this issue reminds us of why it was important for us to commence our reading by rehearsing the problem of *Sinngebung;* it is *within* the experience of the totalizing function of the constituting ego that the genuine possibility of radical transcendence comes into relief. It is only within "asking back" *(Rückfrage)* to the confrontation of objectivity and difference, to the site at which totality breaks up, that the logic of a legitimate thought of the Other is made evidently possible.

This passage from totality to transcendence traces the constitutional work of representation, objectivity, evidence, totality, etc., back to the source from which the work itself must draw. Levinas's work in *Totality and Infinity* attempts to trace the constitut*ing* back to the moment in which it is determined as constitut*ed*, a simple yet severe reversal of priority. The logic of constitution is overturned by and through that source which conditions the totalizing work of synthesis. This source is still maintained as a relation. But relationality must be rethought. The break up of totality institutes a relation with "a surplus always exterior to the totality" (TeI, xi/22), which is precisely the relation with the plenitude of sense noted above in "Freedom and Commandment." The methodological point of access for this tracing back—a tracing back that aims at contact with exteriority—is what Husserl's phenomenology calls intentional analysis. Intentional analysis in contact with exteriority describes "a relation or an intentionality of a wholly different type" (TeI, xii/23). In taking up Husserl's phenomenology as the living source for disruption of totality, Levinas renews the reading of Husserl already at work in both "L'œuvre d'Edmond Husserl" and "La ruine de la représentation." That is to say, it is in turning to the radicality implicit in phenomenology, despite the fact that the Husserlian prerogative forgets the radical horizons that Levinas is able to implicate the philosophy of totality in its own interruption.

This implication is two-fold: First, phenomenology is the methodological access to what ultimately contests the rules laid down by Husserl; second, phenomenology, as a philosophy of totality in Husserl's hands, will be taken back to the source of its content. On this first problematic, Levinas writes that

> [i]ntentional analysis is the search for the concrete. Notions held under the direct gaze of the thought that defines them are nevertheless, unbeknown to this naive thought, revealed to be implanted in horizons unsuspected by this thought; these horizons endow them with a sense—such is the essential teaching of Husserl. What does it matter if in the Husserlian phenomenology taken literally these unsuspected horizons are in their turn interpreted as thoughts aiming at objects. (TeI, xvi/28)

The search for the concrete is the locus of the positivity that Levinas claims for Husserl's phenomenology. This positivity, however, is not a positivity of an adopted doctrine. Rather, the turn to the concrete takes up the methodological possibilities of intentionality hidden by Husserl's privileging of the theoretical attitude, awakening the forgotten horizons. As we saw above, the concretion that guides Husserl's phenomenology, within his logic of sense, is in large part the concrete activity of the creative subject. The search for the concrete undertaken by Levinas, of course, does not turn to this creative activity. Levinas's rehabilitation of the concrete in the intentional analysis of *Totality and Infinity* turns to the immediacy of the sensible, which is a return to the unmediated exteriority of the plenitude of sense lying "behind"—on the other side, beyond, outside—the idealist *Sinngebung*. The concrete is contact with the exterior. Further, the method is intentional insofar as it insists on the primacy of relation, with all due qualifications regarding that term. Levinas will think relation in terms of transcendence and therefore as a relation across an absolute interval (TeI, 210, 260/233, 283). The *experience* of another modality of relation, described here within the problem of the production of sense, leads Levinas to qualify his use of the term relation. Levinas will quite famously call the relation with the Other a "relation without relation" (TeI, 271/295).

The method of exposition and the character of the findings, however, remain focused on the structure of relation. Levinas is quickly compelled to qualify his use of the term intentionality on the basis of the matter itself, viz., the interval across which the relation must be maintained. This interval, as we shall see, displaces the subject from its origin, separates it from the point of its birth. Despite the fact that intentionality has been understood primarily on the model of the thematic, the method at work in *Totality and Infinity* proceeds by way of the structure of intention—the relationality of the subject and the production of sense from out of the relation. Its findings therefore discover an intentionality. To this end, then, Levinas's relation to Husserl's method must be understood as recovering what Levinas has called phenomenological inspiration (ŒH, 9), which is the *experience* of phenomenology as concrete possibility and hence not the recitation of and adherence to its rules. Phenomenological inspiration explodes the possibilities of intentionality as a relation beyond those relations of cognition and representation. This experience of phenomenology provokes Levinas to note that ". . . not every transcendent intention has the noesis-noema structure" (TeI, xvii/29). The relation across the absolute interval of separation demonstrates the possibility of an intentionality of transcendence that relates without the noesis-noema structure, without the mediation of representation.

There is a second aspect to Levinas's implication of phenomenology in its own interruption. This second aspect takes up the issue of the transcendental function of those forgotten horizons which, despite their being forgotten, still endow phenomenology with a sense. In the passage just quoted, Levinas notes that these forgotten horizons are not already constituted horizons awaiting explication, but are rather horizons that themselves actively bestow sense. Already, then, we have seen the implication of the transcendental function of what interrupts the continuity of phenomenological idealism. And this forgetting is not without reason. The forgotten horizons are suppressed by idealism precisely because they do not fall under the rubric of the constituted. The activity of the creative subject cannot be adequate to these horizons; the constitution of the subject by long forgotten horizons points to a failure of representation, to a failure of the activity of the ego, and to a passivity of a subject separated from its origin. Put bluntly, and in a purely Levinasian register, the constitutional function of forgotten horizons conditions the boundaries of thought that would seek to keep totality safe from the anarchic signification of infinity. Thus, Levinas's interruption of the totality does not simply juxtapose the thought of exteriority to the thought of totality. Instead, the thought of the exterior conditions the thought of totality. Levinas therefore seeks to

> . . . proceed from the experience of totality back to a situation where totality breaks up, a situation that conditions the totality itself. Such a situation is the gleam of exteriority or of transcendence in the face of the Other. The rigorously developed concept of this transcendence is expressed by the term infinity . . . [T]he way we are describing to work back and remain this side of objective certitude resembles what has come to be called the transcendental method (in which the technical procedures of transcendental idealism need not necessarily be comprised). (TeI, xiii/25)

Levinas's hesitation before the term "transcendental" is quite significant. What provokes Levinas's hesitation is the procedural techniques of idealism. Indeed, the aim of *Totality and Infinity* is to exhibit that and how the intentionality of knowing—the sense of the thematic object in idealism's intentionality—already presupposes the essential nonadequation of the idea of infinity (TeI, xv/27). Exhibiting this presupposition and purging the intentional method of such a prejudice, Levinas shows, by way of this conditioning moment of exteriority, how we may justifiably employ the well-known trope "the other in me" (TeI, 21/50).

With these two aspects of the "Preface" in place, we can see more precisely the relation Levinas holds to Husserl in *Totality and Infinity*. The alteration of intentional analysis Levinas initiates necessitates reawakening forgotten horizons in Husserl's phenomenology. The notion of "forgotten" is decisive here and it also indicates the somewhat ambiguous place of Husserl in *Totality and Infinity*. That is to say, the structure of forgetting implies that what is forgotten is already lodged, in some manner or another, within *die Sachen* of phenomenology; the horizon must have been somehow previously present and effective in order for that horizon to have the status "forgotten." Forgetting is therefore something like a modification of presence. Lodging the forgotten horizon of the exterior within the boundaries of representation is an occasion of Levinas's more general claims about the insertion of the infinite in the finite, the Other in the Same. The exterior is in this manner *immanent* to phenomenology, even in phenomenology's forgetfulness.

But it is also the case that the horizon of exteriority introduces a logic wholly foreign to the evidential principle of phenomenology. Indeed, exteriority is destructive of the very methodological centerpiece of transcendental explication: the noema, which Levinas interprets as representation. The forgotten horizon is thus necessarily on the margins of phenomenology, insofar as its recollection calls into question the very methodological compass of the transcendental project. As we saw above, the transcendentality of the exterior completely reorients the notion of the transcendental as located within egoic "space," as exteriority shifts the acts constituting away from the height of the inside and toward the height of the outside. The marginal status of the exterior in phenomenology, coupled with the destructive effect its recollection has on thematic intentionality, inscribes the overturning of phenomenology within the very horizon of phenomenology. The overturning, this fundamental alteration, of Husserl's phenomenology does not come from without. Rather, it is already made necessary in the project of intentional analysis. It is according to this logic of overturning or alteration[13] that we ought to see how Levinas's work is within, even while on the margins of, phenomenology, as well as how that work is destructive of that delimitation of intentionality which dominates the Husserlian tradition.

Manifestation and Signification

With these formal considerations in view, we are prepared to turn to the question of signification and the structure of transcendence that concretizes the logic of alteration. The question of how to articulate transcendence outside the boundaries of the transcendental ego must first ask this question: How can alterity signify without the constitutional apparatus? How can appearance be thought without the structures of the subject to whom something appears? Our exposition of the Husserlian doctrine of sense-bestowal has made evident both the scope and ground of this doctrine. It is important to keep this scope and ground in view, as it makes clear precisely what Levinas must accomplish in order to preserve the integrity of alterity. The first and foremost task is that of breaking with the notion of a pregiven unity, for, as we saw in the opening remarks above, the notion of pregiven unity provides the necessary clue to Husserl's analysis. To break with this sense of unity will already be to contest the first position of generative, creative subjectivity. The question that follows from this rupture of unity is how this transcendence may be said to signify without form, and therefore "how" this plenitude of sense that precedes the work of *Sinngebung* may be articulated. The question of what Levinas calls manifestation answers both issues: how the pregiven unity is to be broken up and how what lies outside of this unity may show itself. And, if we proceed with this cluster of problems in view, then we will arrive again at the problem of alterity as the problem of sense—both the signification of sense and the locus of its genesis. In other words, our question is not simply how the unicity of the subject is to be interrupted, but rather, more acutely, how the sense that constitutes the content of subjectivity *as intentional, as already in a relation constitutive of its being and substantiality*, may be said to already interrupt the wakeful life of the ego.

Thus we begin with the question of signification in terms of manifestation as expression and *kath auto*. Levinas employs the terms expression and *kath auto* as variants on the term manifestation in order to oppose thematization. For, as we have seen, the propositional rendering of what appears as a theme already implicates the constitutional structures emanating from the transcendental ego. Expression and *kath auto*, for Levinas, designate modalities of manifestation that manifest without the imposition of the formal structures of perceiving subjectivity on what becomes manifest. In other words, manifestation denotes the appearance of the exterior *as concrete*, where the term concrete indicates an appearance in its immediacy. First, the question of expression.

The function of expression is that of complicating the predelineating work of form. Form, in the philosophy of the Same, is that of which the theme is an exemplar. Expression, however, consists in nothing less than questioning the priority of form. For Levinas, the lived-presence of the face of the Other manifests a phenomenal excess which, by way of what will come to be called its transcendence, outstrips the possibility of conceptual grasp and therefore the possibility of securing the strictly formal aspects of its enigmatic meaning. The face, which is expression *par excellence*, manifests as nonadequation. Expression presents the face in and as its refusal to be contained, and so expression cannot be encompassed nor can it be understood as the object of an epistemic relation (TeI, 168/194). Levinas writes:

> Thus, signification or expression is contrasted to every intuitive given (*donnée intuitive*), precisely because to signify is not to give. Signification is not an ideal essence nor is it a relation presented to intellectual intuition, which would still be analogous to the sensation presented to the eye. It is the presence of exteriority *par excellence* . . . It is the production of sense. (TeI, 37–38/66)

The face, exteriority in its preeminent manifestation, is the production of sense, but is a production of sense that does not offer itself to intuition as construed in an act of intellection. It should be noted here that, though expression manifests without the supporting apparatus of ideality, it is not the expression of non-sense. Rather, expression produces sense that is excessive of form and therefore a sense that is not anchored in the synthetic work of form. The production of sense in or as expression makes form insecure.

This production of sense, then, must come to pass within a notion of experience that cannot be understood on the model of the constituting subject. This notion of experience, which Levinas will at times call a "radical empiricism" (TeI, 170/196), is experience as concrete—that is, experience of the immediate (TeI, 22/51–52), which, in its nonmediated immediacy, warrants the characterization "absolute." Experience of the absolute, which is happens through the unraveling of form by the expressive manifestation of the exterior, is that lived-experience which allows for the revelation of the face as expression without and outside of the life of the disclosive subject. In the experience of the absolute, the Other expresses qua Other. The absolute is a coincidence of expression with what is expressed—not the coincidence of the theme with an ideal kernal. This latter coincidence would be an epistemic or ontological coincidence, traceable back to an originary generation of meaning in the ego. Expression, however, manifests outside the economies of knowing and being (if such a distinction is even tenable). Levinas writes:

> *Absolute experience is not disclosure but revelation:* the coincidence of the expressed with that which expresses, which is the privileged manifestation of the Other, the manifestation of a face over and

beyond form. Form incessantly betrays its own manifestation—congealing into a plastic form, as this form is adequate to the Same, alienates the exteriority of the other. The face is a living-presence, it is expression. The life of expression consists in undoing (*défaire*) the form in which the being, laid bare as a theme, hides itself from the same . . . At each instant it [the being] undoes the form that it presents. (TeI, 37/65–66)

The life of expression leads Levinas to remark that, in its expressive manifestation, the Other ". . . is not *present*, does not attend his own manifestation," but rather is ". . . a being who is manifested precisely as absent from his manifestation: a manifestation in the absence of being—a phenomenon" (TeI, 152–153/178). Levinas's attribution of productivity of sense to expression thus makes good on the methodological note in "L'œuvre d'Edmond Husserl" that ". . . thought is able to have a sense . . . in which the object is absolutely undetermined, a quasi-absence of an object" (ŒH, 24). In not attending its manifestation, yet producing sense, alterity signifies independent of the initiative of the idealist's *Sinngebung* (TeI, 22/51). The expressive manifestation of the Other is manifestation of a quasi-object. The Other is not an object precisely because its expressive life consists in undoing precisely what would make it an object.

If alterity signifies in manifestation, then how are we to understand the sign-face that signifies? Expression finds its locus in the speaking proper to the face. This speaking, which Levinas claims "proceeds from absolute difference" (TeI, 168/194), is not a speaking reducible to type-token correlations in written or spoken language. The sign at issue here is the face, and so the sign is not a mediating item, but expression itself. Signification, the sign, speaks in and from the face, the expression that issues from the Other in its approach, a speaking that speaks through the very materiality of the eyes. The symbolic relation between signs does not mediate the manifestation of the face in expression. Rather, the symbolic relation of language is preceded by the signification of the face. "[I]t is not the mediation of the sign that forms signification," Levinas says, "but signification (whose primordial event is the face to face) that makes the sign function possible" (TeI, 181/206). The proper function of language for Levinas is therefore to enact "the presentation of sense" (TeI, 181/206). The presentation of sense is the "speaking of the face"—expression. Levinas writes:

> This way of undoing the form adequate to the Same so as to present oneself as other is to signify or to have a meaning. To present oneself by signifying is to speak. This presence, affirmed in the presence of the image as the focus of the gaze that is fixed on you, is said . . . The eyes break through the mask—the language of the eyes, impossible to dissemble. The eye does not shine; it speaks. (TeI, 38/66)

The accomplishment of the signification of the face is its "breakthrough" or "divestiture" of both form and, more deeply, the very logic of form. Thus, the face that signifies refers not to a predelineating form but only to itself. The face, as Jill Robbins puts it, ". . . escapes the referrals inherent in sign systems."[14] The eyes that speak, the face that expresses—these manifestations do not "shine," and thus are not reducible to the economy or play of light. The light of the intellect that would illuminate a practical act is improper to the manifestation of the exteriority of the face. Still, another question arises: How is Levinas able to reconcile the positivity of signification, expression and manifestation, with the negative work of nonattendance, quasi-absence and nonthematization? This question is answered with his notion of *kath auto*.

Expression undoes, unravels, and thereby exceeds form. Expression exceeds the synthetic work of essence or ideality. Expression is manifestation and this modality of manifestation distinguishes itself from thematization by unraveling the form that supports the sense-structure of the movement of thematization. However, the question of manifestation without thematization still demands a further point of clarity: How may we more precisely articulate the expressive manifestation of exteriority, the expression of singularity without reference to acts of consciousness? Significative manifestation is given a negative characterization: It is the undoing of form in expression. If expression is not the productive work of synthesis, then how are we to understand the positivity of manifestation? How does exteriority signify without form? How can we understand signification on the model of a radical nonadequation—one that is not a *modification* of adequation, but rather outside, beyond, and otherwise than the adequate?

Levinas employs the Greek term *kath auto* to make this signification explicit. In Levinas's rendering, *kath auto* bears the sense of what signifies with reference only to itself. Signification with reference to itself designates the modality of manifestation that does not, of its very essence, refer to the subject as an apriori condition of its possibility. *Kath auto*, to hark back to the preceding chapter, is concrete signification, signification as expression without logically prior presentations. The sense of the term *kath auto* links with expression most directly when Levinas notes that the Other who breaks with the economy of thematization "does not manifest itself by these qualities [of the adequate idea], but *kath auto*. It *expresses itself*" (TeI, 21/51). Expression undoes form and the positivity that emerges from this undoing brings us to manifestation *kath auto*. Levinas writes that

> [t]he manifestation *kath auto* in which a being concerns us without slipping away and without betraying itself does not consist in its being disclosed, its being exposed to the gaze that would take it as a theme for interpretation, and would command an absolute position dominating the object. Manifestation *kath auto* consists in a being telling itself to us independently of every position we would have taken in its regard, expressing itself. (TeI, 37/65)

Manifestation without disclosure, which does not depend on the formal stratum imposed or discovered by the disclosive subject, does not refer back to the positionality of the subject to which the manifested, in its signification, stands in relation. Manifestation, in this account, signifies without reference to another logically prior constituting structure. Indeed, as Levinas writes, ". . . the Other enters into relation while remaining *kath auto*, where he expresses himself without our having to disclose him from a 'point of view,' in a borrowed light" (TeI, 39/67). Therefore the Other has "sense by itself" that ". . . signifies before we have projected light upon it" (TeI, 47/74). Insofar as the manifestation *kath auto* signifies without the light of disclosure, the Other who signifies is "wholly in relation to himself, *kath auto*, a being that stands beyond every attribute" (TeI, 46/74). Standing beyond every attribute, the signification of alterity situates itself outside of reflection and the cluster of attributions that reflective thematization would hope to discover. There is no form imposed on signification *kath auto*; the sense of the signification is self-constituting, not already constituted. Having unraveled form in expression, then, the exteriority of the face produces sense in and through its manifestation *kath auto*. Referring only to itself, manifestation *kath auto* signifies as a singularity, a genuinely radical signification of nonadequation. This modality of manifestation is not a theme. And its signification is radical to the extent that, because it only refers to itself when it manifests, it is not a lack of adequation (which could be captured in an eidetic intuition);[15] its very sense is beyond adequation and its modifications.

If manifestation does not necessarily refer back to the positionality of the subject, then *kath auto* signifies without implicating itself in the ego's ray of regard. Manifestation therefore does not submit itself to apperceptive constitution. Reflection does not discover what sustains manifestation, but rather, in the case of *kath auto*, is already conditioned by the anteriority of what manifests itself. If manifestation *kath auto* does not return to apperceptive constitution as the implicit condition of its appearance, then the work of the creative subject is not implicated in signification. In the signification or manifestation *kath auto*—i.e., in fully accomplished expression—Levinas will say that ". . . the manifestation and the manifested coincide" (TeI, 272/296). The sense of what is manifest does not coincide with the eidetic stratum; though this may be the case with the givenness of empirical objects, alterity demands another coincidence, and so a different relation to itself. The relation of the manifested to itself refuses thematization; thematization would render the sense of the manifested within the economy of form. The reflective uncovering of sense would thereby leave behind the originary manifestation. To borrow a temporal phrase from Levinas's post-*Totality and Infinity* work, reflection is *late* to what signifies *kath auto*. Further, and with great importance to Levinas's vocabulary, we can say that manifestation *kath auto* is the signification of an absolute *singularity*. Absolute singularity must be understood here as already having broken with the traditional notion of singularity as token or instance; *kath auto* is not *tode ti*. Expression, manifestation *kath auto*, is signification of a singularity without universality. Signification without universality, against the logic of sense-bestowal and on the other side of its limit, is manifestation without thematization and thus manifestation without necessary reference to the subject that would propose what signifies as a theme. As Robbins makes clear, the other ". . . does not even signify *as* himself; he signifies without the benefit of the 'as' structure."[16] One must imagine qualification quotations around the term "benefit"; the as structure obscures singularity and so is an act of violence.

It is important to note here that Levinas's position maintains a sort of "purity." The purity I have in mind inheres in the complete lack of mixture of the aims of the ego with the face itself. In facing, Levinas will write, that which emits the sign of signification manifests "without proposing himself as a theme" and manifests in this modality "despite the interposition of the sign" (TeI, 69/96). This purity will remain with Levinas for the most part throughout his philosophical itinerary, but it is most pronounced in this rethinking of manifestation as expression and *kath auto*. The problem of sense-bestowal in idealism, and what it demands of the thought that would exceed it, necessitates such a conception of manifestation. This conception of manifestation—in its purity—is necessary to the extent that even a trace of the thematic in manifestation would immediately refer us to the (co-)constitutive functioning of the subject. This functioning would no doubt contaminate the aim of Levinas's meditation. The possibility of thinking the plenitude of sense or the surplus exterior to totality requires a conception of manifestation that signifies without reference to anterior structures of the subject. Manifestation *kath auto* proposes the purity necessary for such a radical break with the signification aspect of the idealist *Sinngebung*. Manifestation opposed to thematization makes good on the promise in the "Preface" to produce a pure and absolute signification (what Levinas calls a "signification without context" (TeI, xii/23). As we shall see, the final justification for this purity—only provisionally indicated hitherto—lies in the reversal of the direction of the bestowal of sense in sensibility and the ethical relation. Before we unpack the ethical *Sinngebung*, we must first consider the problem of relation: in what modality is the subject related to manifestation *kath auto*?

Affectivity as Enjoyment and Desire

Though Levinas has articulated the structure of manifestation adequate (in its radical non-adequation) to the transcendence of alterity, a question still remains: how may the subject be in relation with transcendence, without the analysis falling back into the logic of positionality? This is a significant issue, for the positionality of the subject anchors the logic that underpins thematization, the logic that is the very point of departure for idealism. The relationality of affective life is the clue to this nonpositional mode of relation. Specifically, relations of Desire and Enjoyment provide Levinas with descriptive occasions to articulate the modality of relation proper to transcendence. The present section, then, will make these two affective relations clear. Clarity must be gained with regard to the status of those items—ego and object—maintained in relation. To this end, it is necessary for us to consider the issue of sensibility, as sensibility provides the structural site of the relations of Desire and Enjoyment.

Sensibility provides the structural item necessary for access to the relation of/to transcendence. Alphonso Lingis's observation is of great importance here. Lingis notes that that there are two sensibilities at work in *Totality and Infinity*: the sensibility of sensuous Enjoyment and the sensibility of the face.[17] However, we also want to mediate this distinction with the fact that the sensibility at work in both the sensual life of the subject (Desire and Enjoyment) and in the ethical relation (the face) occasion the same logic: the logic of sense-bestowal from the outside. This insistence on the same logic renders the distinction one of token and not of type; to be sure, though, the face does in some decisive manner alter the sense of transcendence thought in Desire/Enjoyment. In examining the structure of sensibility as such, as well as its specifications in Desire and Enjoyment, we can render explicit the modality of relation it implicates. This modality of relation brings an intentionality into relief that does not have the noesis-noema structure. Hence, our exposition will begin to see what Levinas means when he talks in the "Preface" of "another" intentionality outside the correlational structure of noesis-noema.

In rethinking sensibility, as Wyschogrod has pointed out, Levinas is attempting to detach the function of sensation from the cognitive aspects of representation and *Sinngebung*.[18] The detachment of sensation from representation and sense-bestowal necessarily entails a reversal of the Husserlian/Kantian conception of sensation (though the basic problem is at least as old as Jacobi's critique of Kant). By turning the concept of sensation on its head, it is possible to alter sensibility *from* the posterior status of the sensible as constituted *to* the sensible as a self-constituted signification (i.e., expression and *kath auto*). Levinas seeks in sensibility what is anterior to the work of the constituting subject on the world. The self-constituted signification *kath auto* is altered in sensibility from constituted content to constituting structural item. This gives the anteriority of the sensible a transcendental role. We should not overlook the importance of the findings of "La ruine de la représentation" in this context. Levinas writes in *Totality and Infinity* that

[r]ather than taking sensations to be contents destined to fill apriori forms of objectivity, a transcendental function *sui generis* must be recognized in them (and for each qualitative specificity in its own mode); apriori formal structures of the non-I are not necessarily structures of objectivity. The specificity of each sensation reduced precisely to that 'quality without support or extension' the sensualists sought in it designates a structure not necessarily reducible to the schema of an object endowed with qualities. *The senses have a sense that is not predetermined as objectification.* (TeI, 162/188; emphasis mine)

This quality without support or extension is a concrete object, the signification of which has been explicated as expression and *kath auto*. The concretion of sensation opens upon a transcendental conception of sensibility, specified in the modalities of Desire and Enjoyment. The transcendental function of sensation does not, of course, return to the I and representation as the source and support of its sense. Here Levinas in *Totality and Infinity* rehearses the general logic of the analysis of the sensible offered in "La ruine de la répresentation"; however, in the 1961 text he is concerned with fully explicating the *specificity* of sensualism. This is the importance of relations of Desire and Enjoyment. This *deformalization* of the formal notion of sensibility from "La ruine de la répresentation" has compelling consequences for the life of the subject subjected to the *transcendental* functioning of sensibility.

Sensibility, as Lingis has shown, is structurally determined in and by the moment of contact with alterity. Contact is not a consciousness of contact, but rather the very moment of the subjection of the subject to that with which one is in contact.[19] As such, sensibility does not designate a faculty through which the sensible is perceived. Rather, the sensible—purged of the inferior status accorded it by the idealist notion of *tode ti*—is alterity and thus constitutes our openness to the exterior. Levinas writes:

This situation is not reducible to a representation, not even an inarticulate representation. It is a question of the sensibility which is the *manner* of Enjoyment. It is when one interprets sensibility as representation and mutilated thought that one is compelled to invoke the finitude of our thought in order to account for these 'obscure' thoughts. The sensibility we are describing starting with

> Enjoyment of the element does not belong to the order of thought but to that of sentiment, that is, the affectivity wherein the egoism of the I pulsates. (TeI, 108/135)

Thus, sensibility does not indicate or display an insufficiency of thought to what is manifest as sensible. Levinas says that "its intention . . . does not go in the direction of representation" and so is not "situated on the plane of representation" (TeI, 109/136). Rather, sensibility is that out from which Enjoyment is set and this setting out from the sensible refuses any analysis that leads back to representation. *This* sensibility, Levinas notes, ". . . finds itself immediately at the term (*elle se trouve immédiatement au terme*)" (TeI, 109/136).

Sensibility is therefore nothing other than the signification outlined previously as expression and *kath auto,* but here rendered in terms of sensation and element. Sensibility in general, to the extent that it marks a relation before the work of representation, ". . . establishes a relation with a pure quality without support" (TeI, 109/136). This pure quality without support is the manifestation of that which expresses, that which signifies *kath auto,* that which signifies, in a word, *concretely.* The sensible being, Levinas writes, "*concretizes this manner of being,* which consists in finding a condition in what, in other respects, can appear as the object of thought, as simply constituted" (TeI, 109/136). The transcendental function of sensibility thus offers a condition that issues from the very item the thought of totality has always considered as conditioned. The structure of sensibility, then, institutes the general structure of relationality; this relation is pure, and so does not rest upon the work of constitution or representation. The specific modes of sensibility found in Desire and Enjoyment deploy or deformalize sensibility as particular manifestations of the general structure of the sensible. Desire and Enjoyment thus aim at exhibiting both the transcendence of the relation and the transcendental function of the axiological quasi-object (the Desired, the Enjoyed) of the relation. This specification institutes a concrete reversal of *animation.*

Let us turn to Desire. Levinas's analysis of what he terms "metaphysical" Desire does not, as Peperzak notes, immediately link itself with the specific figure of the face of the human other.[20] Rather, the movement of metaphysical Desire manifests a mode of relationality in which the I is not bound to itself, is not enchained, to hearken back to "L'œuvre d'Edmond Husserl." This decentered I is capable of transcending, in its relation to the world, the economy of representation, which opens up a mode of relationality that does not necessarily specify the human other as the "quasi-object." Desire moves toward the exteriority and alterity of otherness in general, where the alterity of the otherness is nonadequate to the idea of representation, yet has a sense (TeI, 4/34). So, the human other is not immediately the theme of the movement of Desire (though the human other will become the preeminent other of the relation). Instead, the structure the general logic of Desire, which is the Desire that aims at the alterity of the absolutely other, aims at describing a concrete relation of transcendence as such— transcendence without the specificity of the human other.

To make this general logic of the relation of transcendence evident, Levinas begins with his well-known juxtaposition of Desire to Need. When Desire is determined as Need, the intention revealed in the movement of that (nonmetaphysical) Desire remains tied to the boundaries of the self-sufficient, idealist subject, even when that subject is subjected to a lack. Desire as Need is a movement that is determined by a void or emptiness in the subject, which in turn determines the directionality of the movement of the Desiring intention as set out from the position of the subject. The Needed—the object of Need—is, at least teleologically, reducible to the subject of Need. The lack in the subject that desires as Need determines what it desires with regard to its position and interest. Therefore Need does not seek the foreign; Need seeks only what might satisfy the void opened in lack. Opposed to this movement, which remains anchored in the positionality of the subject, metaphysical Desire moves toward the absolutely other. In moving toward the absolutely other, metaphysical Desire does not return to egoic life as its animating origin. Levinas writes:

> The metaphysical Desire tends toward a wholly other matter, toward the absolutely other . . . The metaphysical Desire does not long to return, for it is Desire for a land not of our birth, for a land foreign to every nature, which has not been our fatherland and to which we shall never betake ourselves. Metaphysical Desire does not rest upon any prior kinship. It is a Desire that cannot be satisfied . . . The metaphysical Desire has another intention; it Desires the beyond of everything that can simply complete it. It is like goodness—the Desired does not fulfill it, but deepens it. (TeI, 3–4/33–34)

Desire already breaks with the philosophy of identity. The movement of Desire, which does not rest on prior kinship and thus does not derive the other from the interested constitutional work of the Same, sustains the radical, nonmodified difference of the absolutely other. This nonmodified difference is carried by the very movement of Desire; it does not seek completion, but only a deepening, transcendence.

Desire asks for another intention. Desire requires an intention adequate to the nonadequation of the radical difference metaphysical Desire introduces to relationality. The term "intention" here designates the modality of relation, and in articulating this modality, Levinas introduces the twin motifs of infinity and height. The infinite, on Levinas's account, is not the inadequate work of measure. It is, rather, the exterior, the very impossibility of measure. Introducing the motif of the infinite, Levinas here aims at invoking a sense of relation that exceeds the content of the relata—a thought that thinks more than it thinks, the object of relation that exceeds the boundaries of possible cognition. This exceeding warrants the name "height." Levinas evokes Plato: "I cannot think of any study as making the mind look upwards, except one which has to do with the unseen."[21] The relation to the infinite, then, is the relation of Desire to the exterior, the unseen, that which stands above or beyond the I who desires. Levinas's example *par excellence* is the face. Because the infinite distinguishes itself from objects of cognition, the relation of metaphysical Desire is set out from and structured by that which is Desired. This relation is not set out from an intention of the subject, which would ultimately be recuperable as a representation of the interest and position of the ego. On this, Levinas writes that

> [i]nfinity is not the "object" of a cognition . . . but is the Desirable, that which arouses Desire, that is, that which is approachable by a thought that at each instant *thinks more than it thinks*. The infinite is not thereby an immense object, exceeding the horizons of the look. It is Desire that measures the infinity of the infinite, for it is a measure through the very impossibility of measure. The excessiveness measured by Desire is the face. Thus we again meet with the distinction between Desire and Need. Desire is an aspiration that the Desirable animates; it originates from its "object," it is revelation. Whereas Need is a void of the Soul, it proceeds from the subject. (TeI, 33/62)

Origination from the Desirable institutes and concretizes the general logic of sensibility. That is, the transcendental function of the exterior is specified in the generative function of the Desirable in the intention of Desire. The decisive distinction between Desire and Need confirms this reversal in origin. The radical difference demanded by the relation of Desire is maintained in the reversal of the flow of sense in the constituting-constituted relation. The Desirable can only be constituted as what would fulfill the void in the subject if we determine Desire as Need. But that would be a perversion of the sense of Desire as metaphysical. Metaphysical Desire is constituted by the very exterior toward which it moves. Metaphysical Desire is animated by the Desirable. The intention of *this* Desire is set out from the "object," and thus the Desiring is constituted by the Desirable. The origin of metaphysical Desire, its birth, is not to be found in the desiring ego of Need. Need gives birth to itself. Metaphysical Desire is born, exiled, we might say, from its land of origin.

Desire is only part of the story of affective life in *Totality and Infinity*. "Sensibility," Levinas writes, "is Enjoyment" (TeI, 109/136). The fact that Enjoyment is sensibility *par excellence* derives its sense from the fact that, in the affective state of enjoying, the first position of the I is contested. This contestation or displacement of the first position of the I is what Levinas calls the "contraction" of the axiological structure of sentiment, a contraction captured in the figure of Enjoyment. Levinas writes that

> [w]hat is termed an affective state does not have the dull monotony of a state, but is a vibrant exaltation in which dawns the self. For the I is not the *support* of Enjoyment. The "intentional" structure is here wholly different; the I is the very contraction of sentiment, the pole of a spiral whose coiling and involution is drawn by Enjoyment. (TeI, 91/118)

The I is not the source of Enjoyment and thus does not originate from a need. The subject of Enjoyment does not return to itself in the satisfaction of representation or consumption. In the case of Enjoyment, we cannot conceive affectivity as a faculty situated within the constellation of consciousness. Rather, the quasi-object of affective life is that from which the subject originates. The I is *supported* by affectivity and thus cannot be said to contain affection. Like Desire, Enjoyment is born.

Enjoyment is born or dawns from within affectivity, and here, to reiterate, we must think affectivity as *concrete*.

Further, as concrete, the affective life of Enjoyment that gives birth to the subject is a life that holds itself in relation to the exterior. This is the relation of the sensual body to what is enjoyed. The sensual body in this modality of relation lives the very contestation of the idealist conception of meaning bestowal (TeI, 102/129). The locus of this contestation lies the sensual body's being caught in or by the object of its relation; the object of Enjoyment is not sustained by the interested position of the subject. This mode of relation to the exterior reverses the direction of sustenance, from the sustaining of the particular by the universal to the sustaining of the intention by that at which it aims. The site of the general is sustained by the singular. Enjoyment is an intention, however, insofar as it names a relation of the subject to the elemental. But this is an intention reversed. The direction of that intention must be understood as conditioned by the sensuality of that toward which it aims. Levinas writes that

> [t]he intentionality aiming at the exterior changes direction in the course of its very aim by becoming interior to the exteriority it constitutes, somehow comes from the point to which it goes, recognizing itself past in its future, lives from what it thinks. (TeI, 102/129)

If one tries to understand Enjoyment from the position of the interested subject, then one's understanding of it is late to the origin. That intentionality toward which the enjoying subject *may* be said to move is, at its origin, *already* set out from that toward which it moves. Enjoyment is animated by what is enjoyed, not vice versa. Enjoyment is produced in the subject by the elemental.

This understanding of the relation of Enjoyment leads Levinas to develop the logic of "living from," a logic that sets intentionality out from the elemental. "Living from" is sensibility proper, insofar as, in this case, sensibility is understood as the subject's being subjected to the elemental, subjected to the sensible and thereby liberated from the constraints of cognition. This subjection renders problematic the direction of constitution that would seek to ground the enjoyed in a consciousness of Enjoyment. Indeed, the direction of constitution, the direction and place of origination, is wholly reversed and without return to the free subject. Levinas writes that

> If the intentionality of "living-from" which is properly Enjoyment is not constituted, this is therefore not because an elusive, inconceivable content, inconvertible into a meaning of thought, irreducible to the present and consequently unrepresentible, would compromise the universality of representation and the transcendental method; it is the very movement of constitution the is reversed. (TeI, 102/129)

Enjoyment interrupts and compromises the transcendental method that would seek to capture sense in representation and anchor sense in the transcendental ego. Thus Levinas will write further that "[i]n 'living from . . . ,' the process of constitution which comes into play wherever there is representation is reversed" (TeI, 101/128). The reversal of constitution, then, is not just an insufficiency of cognition, but a resituating of generative origin. The sense of Enjoyment issues from and so is constituted by what is enjoyed. The production of the sense of Enjoyment has therefore displaced the boundaries of idealism. The sense of Enjoyment issues from the outside.

Enjoyment and Desire both capture modalities of relation where the sense of relation is generated from outside the boundaries of idealism. The signification made possible by these modalities of relation has been made evident: expression and *kath auto*. As modalities of relation, Enjoyment and Desire radicalize the axiological appearance of intentionality glimpsed in our reading of "L'œuvre d'Edmond Husserl." This radicalization happens via an immersion of the subject into elemental affective life. This immersion provides a first glance into the structure of radical transcendence, a transcendence that breaks with the idealist distinction between transcendence and immanence. Axiological intentionality, in Levinas's hands, transforms itself at the moment that the origin of the intention is identified with the axiological object. This modality of relation already reverses the work of representation on the sensible; the sensible conditions the sense of representation. Ethics further radicalizes this reversal. Now that we have established this relation to transcendence, we are properly poised to see the effect of the ethical relation on the affective mode of relationality.

The Birth of the Ethical Subject

Now, a turn to ethics. The ethics of the face-to-face is quite straightforwardly understood as the interruption of my egoic life by the vulnerability of the Other. Vulnerability punctures the rhythm of consciousness and its sense of self-responsibility. The interruption of self-responsibility opens to the subject as for-the-Other or the questioning of the Same by the Other. Interruption and questioning impose absolute obligation. The empirical descriptions of this interruption have, for the most part, dominated commentary on *Totality and Infinity*. The widow, the stranger, the orphan—these images have come both figuratively and literally to represent the aim and content of the ethics of *Totality and Infinity*.

Our concern here, however, is not with the straightforward sense of moral consciousness, but rather with how the peculiar sensibility of the face alters transcendental sensualism. In other words, our concern is with the alteration of the problem of sense in the sensibility of the face. How is an ethical *Sinngebung* different than the reversal of sense-bestowal in affective life? The key to this difference is the function of asymmetry and height in the interruptive effect of the face. The putting in question *(mise en question)* of freedom by the most high displaces origin in a way that will come to manifest the traumatic production of infinity. The interruptive effect of the face-to-face—the traumatic effect of the infinite on/in the finite—warrants the characterization Levinas gives it: "*Le face-à-face demeure situation ultime*" (TeI, 53/81). The ultimate situation of the face-to-face nuances the reversal of the transcendental we find in Desire and Enjoyment. Ethics is the production of sense as infinity and the institution of a relation of separation that is maintained across the "dead time" of the nothingness of the interval (TeI, 260/284). And, Levinas will conclude, it is *the human Other alone* who is capable of marking this absolute interval (TeI, 260/283). The present section aims at rendering explicit the terms of this interval and the structures of *human* alterity.

The interval, coupled with the face-to-face as the ultimate situation, shows us how the ethical relation introduces something more radical into the problem of sense than is provided by Desire and Enjoyment. Still, it was nevertheless necessary for us to uncover both the modality of the signification of alterity and the transcendental structure of sensibility in order to bring into relief the general logic of exteriority. The general logic of exteriority—the problem of the transcendental function of sensibility—will be altered in the ethical relation, but this alteration must be understood as moving within the horizon of this general logic. This method of reading the problem of ethics reinscribes the transcendental problematic into the scene of the face-to-face. Thus, we are seeking to recover the problem of primordial donation that has become buried in what commentators have, for the most part, come to understand as a straightforward set of descriptions. Further, this reading focuses on Levinas's claim that what is called ethics is nothing other than the "putting into question" of spontaneity (TeI, 13/43). Here we concur with Simon Critchley[22] that the very function or performance of exteriority warrants, to some degree, the status "ethics." But, part of the aim of the present section is to show how, for Levinas, only the exteriority of the facing face is capable of questioning spontaneity and freedom. Desire and Enjoyment do not put subjectivity in question. Therefore only the production of sense set out from the face may be called ethical.

The axiological modalities Levinas exploits in the studies of affective life run up against their structural limitations in the face-to-face relation. Limitation is appropriate here, for there is a limited ability of those structures to introduce a transcendence that radically breaks with idealism. Though Desire and Enjoyment certainly express a modality of relation that relates otherwise than the constituting ego, the precise position of the ego in this reversed constitution of sense remains unclear. Without a doubt, the analyses uncover the transcendental function of sensibility and therefore the first position of representation is contested. Nevertheless, Levinas will still write that "[t]he relation with the Other alone introduces a dimension of transcendence, and leads us to a relation totally different from experience in the sensible sense of the term, relative and egoist" (TeI, 167/193). It would seem, then, that the transcendence of Desire and Enjoyment, despite revealing the transcendental function of what is Desired or Enjoyed, leaves the relative and egoistic position of the subject clandestinely intact—albeit in a modified form. To be sure, the position of the subject is grounded in what is not subjective and thus the absolute position of the subject is problematized; however, there is a tranquil and untroubled character to the relations of Desire and Enjoyment.[23] This tranquillity fails to definitively secure the reversal of the intentionality and the reversal of the flow of sense. The reversal is insecure because the position of the subject is maintained concurrently with its transcendental condition. To anticipate the ethical language, the Desired and the Enjoyed fail to come from a position of height. These modalities of sensibility fail to sustain a relation to infinity; only the inscription of the infinite in the finite— captured in the ethical relation—testifies to the troubling and interruptive effect of alterity.

This much is evident when Levinas writes that, in Enjoyment, "the Same determines the Other while being determined by it" (TeI, 101/ 128). The double flow of sense implicit in affective life still lies open to dialogical analyses of hermeneutic and existential phenomenology. These conceptions of phenomenology ground sense in the interplay of passivity and activity.[24] Levinas will want to insist that the welcome of the Other in moral consciousness is not reducible to the intentionality of an "aiming at" or an "opening onto" (TeH, 64), both of which would have ethics commence with the (perhaps mediated) interest of the I (TeH, 73). The hermeneutic and existential conceptions of phenomenology (of which the dialogical is a variant) fail to access the unmediated sense of alterity—the infinite—that is the determining characteristic of the *complete* reversal of idealism. This reversal is the most radical task set out in *Totality and Infinity*. The clandestinely doubled determination of sense in the relation of Enjoyment (as well as perhaps Desire) maintains a double flow, thereby leaving a sort of quasi-constitutive function to the I.

This relation of doubled determination of sense does not yet adequately *put in question* the status of the I. Only in the *mise en question* can we call the relation to exteriority ethical (TeI, 13/43). This is not to say that the I disappears from Levinas's analysis of the face-to-face. Rather, it simply functions differently in ethics than it does in Desire and Enjoyment. Indeed, the question of relation in ethics is the question of the relation between a being separated from that to which it is vigilantly dedicated. In this relation, only "I" am summoned. Hence Levinas will insist on a peculiar sense of the unicity of the I (cf., TeI, 90f/117f).[25] The sense of the unicity of the I is issued in through the moral summons. Only I can answer. In relation across separation, the I, while unique, is also separated from itself, separated from whence the sense of relation originates. In the face-to-face, this separation not only reverses the position of the transcendental, but also calls into question both the freedom of positionality and its genetic privilege. In this context, Levinas will speak of freedom as "created" (cf., TeI, 54/ 83). In Desire and Enjoyment, the link between freedom and the ipseity of the I is not yet made fully evident; indeed, this is perhaps *the* limitation of the untroubled character of affective life. This is why it is necessary for Levinas to turn to the ethical relation, the relation of height. It is the structure of the sense of this relation that decisively transforms the traditional connection between freedom and subjectivity, a connection phenomenological idealism expresses as the sense-bestowing function of the primal ego. The ethical encounter, which establishes a different transcendence, is the only modality of relation that concretely places the security and freedom of the ego in question. In this questioning, we find the structural radicality of the facing relation. In this questioning, in this facing relation, we find Levinas's most decisive appropriation of the logic and generative function of sense-bestowal and employment of both against idealism.

The ethical encounter with the face ruptures the very idea of an intentionality rooted in the position of the Same. In this way, the encounter profoundly alters the transcendence of Desire and Enjoyment. In the moment of absolute command, the face comes as disruption of the naive and secure world of the sensibility, the worlds of Desire and Enjoyment that sustain the life of the subject despite dispossessing it of its first position.[26] The sensibility of the face introduces a difference or asymmetry that, while constituting the sense of the ethical relation, does not appear before the positional I without troubling it. Affective life, as life that flows through and sustains the subject, is interrupted by both the difference of asymmetry and the moral summons situated in this asymmetrical space. That is to say, it is not simply the asymmetry of the Other that enacts the structural reversal and interruption of intentionality. Rather, the structural reversal of interruption has its basis in the face-to-face relation, which is always the relation of *height*. Height is the relation in which the face of the Other expresses his or her eminence. The relation is *affective* (the face is a modality of sensibility) from the "... dimension of height from which he or she 'descends'" (TeI, 240/262). The relation of height, in turn, initiates a relation that does not present exteriority as a source toward which I move or from which I live. Rather, as the anterior generative source prior to the movement of the transcendent intention of Desire and Enjoyment, the ethical sense of relation in moral consciousness issues from the human Other. "The face," Levinas writes, "speaks to me and thereby invites me to a relation incommensurate with a power exercised, be it Enjoyment or knowledge" (TeI, 172/198).

When the facing face manifests difference, it is incommensurate with the powers of idealism. Freedom and spontaneity are called into question. The infinity of the human Other, the Other from which the movement of "ethical intentionality," ". . . exceeds my powers . . . by calling them into question" (TeI, 170/196). Levinas writes that the asymmetry of the Other introduced from the position of height produces a separation not restricted to the intentionality of "opening onto . . ." or an "aiming at . . ." (TeH, 63). Difference and separation puts freedom in question at a structural moment genetically prior to the boundaries within which freedom is exercised. That is, freedom is put in question before the I is present to itself and its content. The I is *created* as freedom. For Levinas,

> [i]t is an issue of putting consciousness into question and not a matter of the "consciousness of" putting in question. It is an issue of a movement oriented wholly otherwise than a grasp of consciousness and which, like Penelope at night, unravels in some manner at every instant that which was so gloriously woven in the daytime . . . Neither the notion of the greatest, nor that of the most mysterious accounts for it, but rather the notions of height and infinity. (TeH, 64)

Putting freedom and spontaneity into question, which is nothing other than the disturbance of both the reflective life of idealism and the pre-reflective tranquillity of elemental life, precedes the gaze that would capture its content. Consciousness is put in question in the face-to-face precisely because the position of height from which the human Other comes imposes a sense on the relation from outside the boundaries of the "consciousness of" that sense. And, freedom is put in question before it is capable of responding to this putting in question; passivity precedes the will. Levinas says that welcoming the Other puts my freedom into question (TeI, 58/85), which suggests the presence of the Other to a pre-formed subject. Yet, the first institution of the sense of the facing relation *already* displaces the subject. The displacement of the subject, the moment of putting in question genetically prior to the self-awareness of one's responsibility, is the condition of the welcome. Welcoming is, to be bluntly phenomenological, a mundanization of the transcendental moment of putting consciousness in question. This first institution of sense locates the origin of the subject outside itself. Thus, my welcome is a response to a moral summons and therefore a "commencement of moral consciousness" (TeI, 56/84), but we must be careful in conceiving this moral consciousness. It is already constituted in its primordially given sense at the moment of interruption of the Same by the Other.

The asymmetry of the Other, then, interrupts the life of the Same. This interruption calls freedom itself into question. What does it mean to interrogate the structure of that which precedes freedom? This interrogation takes us to the origin of consciousness, the subject, where origin precedes the creative, constitutive life of the subject. Interrogation of the origin that precedes creativity, spontaneity, and freedom brings us to the structure of a created being. To explicate such a subject means to trace the movement of a being ". . . back to what precedes its condition" (TeI, 56/84). Levinas writes that

> Freedom is not bare. To philosophize is to trace freedom back to what lies before it, to disclose the investiture that liberates freedom from the arbitrary. Knowledge as a critique, as a tracing back to what precedes freedom, can arise only in a being that has an origin prior to its origin—a being who is created. (TeI, 57/84–85)

The origin that precedes freedom comes from the outside. The origin of ethical subjectivity precedes the boundaries within which the origin may be recuperated. Therefore this conditioning from the outside, this origination, gives birth to the subject. The I is a born subject, a created subject, generated and named in and through the affect of the moral summons.

Levinas's invocation of the language of origin and creation hearkens back to the problem of the logic of sense. Creation is here displaced, of course; the subject is not creative, but created. Creation and origin from the outside, from the beyond, makes the structure of separation possible and seals its resistance to totality. Levinas writes further:

> The absolute gap of separation which transcendence implies could not be better expressed than by the term creation, in which the kinship of beings among themselves is affirmed, but at the same time their radical heterogeneity also, their reciprocal exteriority coming from nothingness. One may speak of creation to characterize entities situated in the transcendence that does

not close over into a totality. In the face-to-face, the I has neither the privileged position of the subject nor the position of a
thing defined by its place in the system; it is apology, discourse
pro dono, but discourse of justification before the Other. (TeI, 269–
70/293)

The creation of the subject is the creation of the sense of the face-to-
face relation. Separation marks the alterity of the face and the ipseity
of the I named by the accusing face. This sense is bestowed otherwise,
donated differently. This *Sinngebung* is a generative function issuing
from the Other who lies outside of subjective life and interrupts the
tranquillity of Desiring and Enjoying. This bestowing of sense creates
or gives birth to the sense of relation, and through this birth the moral
consciousness of the subject, the I, is secured as separated from its
origin. To be sure, Levinas will write that "... enjoyment is the very
production of a being that is born" (TeI, 121/147), but the birth of the
subject in moral consciousness is separated across an absolute interval
from the site of its birth or creation. The subject of enjoyment is nourished by what it lives from. The subject of moral consciousness, on the
other hand, is troubled by the condition of its birth, by what created
its "own" sense of unicity.

The separation opened by the Other in the sensibility of the face
disrupts the subject, not just by the appearance of an enigma, but
further by separating the I from its origin. This is what provokes
Levinas to claim that the experience of the foreignness of the Other
is not mystery or ambiguity, but the "traumatism of astonishment"
(TeI, 46/73). It is also this foreignness of the other human that marks
the uniqueness of the human face, as it is only the human other that
can be absolutely foreign to the Same (TeI, 46/73). The Other as foreign
produces a *traumatism*. This word will gain much cachet in *Otherwise
than Being*. Trauma is produced in the Same precisely because the
Same recognizes the very strangeness of this Other to be not only in-
congruous with the possibilities of representation, but also, perhaps
more profoundly, to be the origin of the sense of the encounter and
therefore the origin of my unicity. Recognition that the I is irreversibly separated from *and* generated by the Other in moral consciousness is traumatic for the subject that returns to itself. Traumatism does
not simply arise from recognition of the insufficiency of epistemic
powers, but rather from the gap or interval opened between the Same

and the origin of its sense in the ethical face. It is a trauma that provokes the immemoriality of original trauma, the original disruption of the plan of the Same, and a trauma of the encounter for which ". . . the subject is left without words."[27] The I is without words because in terms of its origin and sense it has already been spoken for.

In what sense is it legitimate to identify the structural problem of the face-to-face with the problem of the bestowal of sense? We have already seen the extent to which the language of the face-to-face is linked with the language of creation, birth, and origin. The latter terms describe the logic of sense-bestowal, albeit a sense-bestowal turned against idealism. It may be said that the issue in *Totality and Infinity* is transcendence and that this problematic is best kept within the boundaries of the problem of appearance. In this case our discussion of the structure of manifestation as expression and *kath auto* would have been adequate for the exteriority of the face. Indeed, as we have noted, the infinity of the Other is what calls my powers into question (TeI, 170/196). Do not expression and *kath auto* call into question my power to grasp what appears? That questioning is not sufficient. The singularity of the expression of the facing face is not merely an excessive manifestation: it is a moral summons. It is this summons that brings forth a deformalized and concrete (that is, sensualized) sense of Descartes' notion of the Infinite,[28] and the summons that comes from the human Other implicates or catches the I in a one-way relational structure. Hence transcendence, in the ethics of the face-to-face, must be understood as intentional. It must be understood as transcendence in relation. "What is essential in the ethical," Levinas writes, "is in its *transcendent intention*" (TeI, xvii/29). This relation is the production of infinity in relation to the subject, the inscription of the infinite in the finite. The relation of production, i.e., the relation of the bestowal of sense, requires that we push the question of transcendence beyond the problem of appearance and toward the issue of donation. In this regard, Levinas will write that

> [t]he facing position, opposition par excellence, can be only as a moral summons. This movement proceeds from the Other. The idea of infinity, the infinitely more contained in the less, is concretely produced in the form of a relation with the face. And the idea of infinity alone maintains the exteriority of the Other with respect to the same, despite this relation. (TeI, 170/196)

This relation is maintained without the exteriority of the Other losing its infinity in the finitude of the boundaries of the oneself. The oneself in the relation of a moral summons—moral consciousness—does not see the Other. Rather, and this is decisive for our reading, Levinas will say that "[t]ranscendence is not a vision of the Other—but an original donation [*donation originelle*]" (TeI, 149/174). Donation, as we have learned from phenomenology and the problem of sense-genesis, is not a mere modality of appearance. *Donation is the production of sense.* Such a reading of the genesis of moral consciousness confirms Levinas's claim in the "Preface" that unsuspected horizons endow meaning *(prêtent un sens)* (TeI, xvi/28). Concretely, this means that the social relation (the face-to-face) bestows sense *(prête un sens)* (TeI, 24/53) imposing a metaphysically asymmetrical sense upon the I, the Same, thereby lodging infinity firmly within the space of totality.

The familiar turn of phrase "Other who comes to teach me" captures this donation or ethical bestowal of sense in a provocative figure. When Levinas wrote in 1959 that sense-bestowal in the sensible is ethical, he appealed to the respectfulness of the bestowal set out from the alterity of the sensible. In *Totality and Infinity*, that same respectfulness underpins the donation of the transcendence of the face—exteriority as the deformalization and concretion of the Cartesian notion of the infinite that precedes finite thought. Respectfulness is secured by the double after-effect of the imposition of sense from the outside: first, the essential passivity of the subject and, second, the suspension of freedom. Passivity will become an essential theme in the essays that follow *Totality and Infinity*, when Levinas turns to the structure of time for a legitimation of his language of alterity, but the theme will have a kind of secret purchase in the 1961 text. The passivity of *Totality and Infinity*, which is not yet the passivity of the trace, is reflected in the anteriority of the sensible and the transcendental function of the various modalities of sensibility. Levinas's analysis of the body in *Totality and Infinity* contends that the embodied I "lives" the contestation of the priority of consciousness—a contestation that takes the subject to the "living from" structure of elemental life (TeI, 102/129). The suspension of freedom follows from this passivity. Freedom is called into question in the moral summons because it is passive in the constitution of ethical sense.[29] The sense of the ethical is imposed upon, not created or accepted by, the I. This one-way traffic, this *sens unique*, forms the kernel of what Levinas will spend the remainder of his philosophical career trying to articulate. The articulation of *sens unique* as a sense-bestowing has already begun in *Totality and Infinity*. In so doing, *Totality and Infinity* extends the significance of the concluding remarks in the 1959 essay "The Ruin of Representation": The subject is always already subjected to *une Sinngebung éthique*.

The General Economy of Exteriority

In this final section, I want to make some brief remarks on the character of exteriority in general that emerges from our reading of *Totality and Infinity*. These remarks are necessary to round out our consideration of the problem of sense, as well as to begin making the transition to Levinas's work subsequent to *Totality and Infinity*. Before examining the issue of exteriority in general, however, let us pause and consider the consequences of our study of the sense-bestowing structure of alterity.

We have heretofore insisted on reading *Totality and Infinity* as a book about sense. Noteworthy is the absence of this sort of reading in the secondary literature on Levinas. This reflects, I think, a general lack of appreciation of his contributions to a phenomenology of sense. The problem of sense has been our guide for understanding what precisely is entailed in the absurd logic of the anteriority of the posterior. If we take *Totality and Infinity* to be a book about sense, then three basic tendencies in readings of that book are complicated, if not contested. First, our reading of the problem of the ethical under the rubric of the transcendental allows us to excavate the structures that underpin the straightforward empirical descriptions. Levinas is not simply engaged in empirical description. The empirical character of his descriptions cannot be taken in absence of the transcendental problematic. The intertwining of the empirical and the transcendental languages describes exteriority as sense and attaches the genesis of that sense to the alterity of sensibility. Second, the donative aspect of the face-to-face complicates the view that in *Totality and Infinity* the Other appears before a pre-formed subject or I. On many occasions, Levinas's own characterization of the welcome of the Other lends itself to the claim that the subject is already an I that meets the Other. But, our reading of the sense-bestowing function of the face understands the unicity of the I to be a subjectivity whose very sense of itself is bestowed from the outside. The sense of moral consciousness is generated in the summons from the Other. Though we have used the trope "imposed on the I," this turn of phrase ought to be seen as a (perhaps misleading) mere device, as this notion of the I must be understood as created, born. It therefore has its origin prior to its freedom. Third, the troubling and interruptive character of the face distinguishes the exteriority and sensibility of the face from the economy of exteriority in general. Thus, the "ultimate situation" of the face-to-face maintains a one-way structure in sensibility that is decisive precisely where the sensibility of the affective life of Desire and Enjoyment falters. This decisiveness turns on the *mise en question* of freedom and spontaneity introduced by the facing face. It is only the relation set out from the human Other that is capable of marking the relation of separation, and thus it is only the human Other that establishes the relation of passivity.

The question of exteriority, then, is the question of sense. The question of sense is a genetic problematic. The sense question turns on the query "whence sense"? The idealism of Husserl's phenomenology gives us the logic of creation, birth, and origin as the defining characteristics of the transcendental. Levinas's notion of the exterior employs those very characteristics against idealism. The boundaries of creativity, birthing, and origin are, in the facing relation, grounded in the exterior. Thus, the very structural items that make idealism possible are passively bestowed. The subject is created, born, and located at an origin prior to itself. What Levinas has learned from Husserl is that *this* logic of the transcendental constitutes a *genuinely radical philosophy*: phenomenology. The strength of Levinas's overturning of idealism is that it employs the logic of its adversary. The adversary's logic—the logic of idealism—constitutes the most radical boundaries of philosophy as phenomenology. Exteriority is not simply a notion to be juxtaposed to phenomenology, but a critical modality of sense that works according to the logic of idealism and against the powers of the constituting ego. Levinas's phenomenology is not an eidetic science. It is perhaps better understood as a phenomenological nominalism and a transcendental sensualism, notions which oppose idealism while adopting what is most provocative about its logic.

This reversal of the logic of sense-bestowal renders the following general features of exteriority. First and foremost, exteriority is a transcendental problem. Exteriority conditions subjectivity. Though the exterior has its locus in sensibility, it is not reducible to the language of the sensible. We see this in Levinas's "Preface" to *Totality and Infinity.*

We began our exposition of the structure of the exterior with the problem of manifestation: expression and *kath auto*. The self-sufficiency of the signification of exteriority is a necessary condition for the break with idealism, insofar as manifestation must be possible without the predelineating function of the constituting subject. The undoing of form and signification according to itself is constitutive of how the face that refuses constitution manifests.

However, Levinas's concern is not only with the structure of signification. He wants to go further, to understand the intentionality implicated in affective life: Desire, Enjoyment, and the Ethical name modalities of relation. Thus, sensibility figures as the moment where the self-standing signification of alterity performs its transcendental function. This transcendental function consequently reinscribes the question of the exterior within the problem of sense. (We might add, it is this insistence on the primacy of relationality that saves Levinas from reiterating a two-substance metaphysics). The face that issues a moral summons distinguishes itself from the Desired and the Enjoyed by way of calling freedom into question. This questioning pushes the problem of sense genesis to the purity of passivity, as this questioning decisively renders the unicity of the I as created prior to its creativity. Exteriority, then, has a two-fold transcendental appearance: first, the tranquillity of the elemental life and, second, the one-way flow of sense in the face-to-face. Both transcendentals figure constitution otherwise than idealism and both insist on the intentional character of sensibility.

With these issues in place, we can see that there remain unclarified issues—issues that provoke Levinas to rewrite the structure of ethics in his subsequent work. Levinas turns to the genetic logic of sense in order to make sense of exteriority, yet that articulation does not employ the temporal language of phenomenology's account of genesis. Herein lies the soon to be exploded hidden resource of Husserl's thought. This temporal language is already implicit: the subject is created, thus late to itself. The passivity of the genesis of sense implicates an absence at the original ground of presence. The sensibility of the face still struggles to secure the strict singularity of this materiality. The structure of passivity is necessary for the logic of sense-bestowal in *Totality and Infinity*, but the details of that structure are left underdeveloped. It will be the underlying contention of the following two chapters that these problems guide Levinas's turn to Husserl's reflections on the time-structure of consciousness. The structures that emerge from Husserl's work on time open Levinas to the underlying structure of sense-bestowal from the outside. In *Totality and Infinity*, the temporal language that Levinas employs turns primarily on the notions of futurity and the instant. The logic of sense-bestowal, however, demands another time. The structures of materiality, diachronic time, and the trace answer this demand. These new demands indicate a breakdown within the text of *Totality and Infinity*: Although the logic of sense-bestowal from the outside calls for the structure of absence to be found in diachronic time, the resources at Levinas's disposal have still not radically broken with the language of presence. The matters uncovered in 1961, however, make such a break absolutely requisite. It is with this necessity in mind that we proceed.

Four

Sensation, Trace, Enigma

Rethinking Sensibility in the 1960s

It is as though the space between us were time.

—William Faulkner

How is it possible for the subject to be late to itself? What sort of language is capable of describing this lateness? How can we conceive separation if separation is unclosable? In *Totality and Infinity*, the economy of exteriority plays the role of the language of alterity. The genetic prerogative instituted the one-way traffic of sense. Lateness and separation point to the structure of passivity; this is already evident in *Totality and Infinity*. But the analyses in *Totality and Infinity* do not systematically treat passivity in its "lived" temporal dimension.

Between *Totality and Infinity* and *Otherwise than Being*, Levinas takes up just that dimension of passivity. His exposition of the time-structure of passivity again turns to Husserl's phenomenology as the indispensible resource. Sensation, trace, and enigma name the component parts of the intentional structure of passivity; all are components of the diachronic time of relation. From our considerations a notion of experience will emerge that is composed of absolute difference. Levinas will call this *heteronomous* experience, and the concrete structures of time legitimate the structure of this experience. Further, as we shall see when we turn to *Otherwise than Being*, Levinas's rethinking of passivity prepares the ground for his articulation of a sense otherwise than the exteriority described in *Totality and Infinity*. The interim essays between *Totality and Infinity* and *Otherwise than Being*, however, do not directly address the problem of sense. What they do address is the problem of relation, specifically the temporal language necessary for the structure of separation. Out of this temporal configuration of relationality, Levinas is able to pose the question of sense and sense-genesis, as it is only when the temporal structure of the transcendent-intention is made evident that a fully legitimated *Sinngebung* from the outside can be spoken of. Thus, these interim essays and our reading of them represent Levinas's concrete re-working of Husserl's phenomenology. This reworking sets the ground for what we will call *impressional sense* in *Otherwise than Being*, a sense constituted in the appeal to a nonmodified and irretrievable materiality. Without the structures that emerge from his rereading of Husserl in the 1960s, such a sense may seem posited by fiat. But, with these structures concretely worked out, such a posit is both justified and necessary.

Thus, the present chapter will focus on Levinas's essays on Husserl and Husserlian themes immediately postdating *Totality and Infinity* up to the period of publication of *Otherwise than Being, or Beyond Essence*. Three essays serve as high water marks from this period: "Intentionalité et sensation" (1965), "Trace of the Other" (1963), and to a lesser extent "Phenomenon and Enigma" (1965). The task set before us is to anticipate the structural basis for (and consequences of) Levinas's claim in *Otherwise than Being* that "[p]henomenality . . . cannot be separated from time" (AE, 39/31). How does Levinas arrive at this conclusion, and how might such a claim require us to rewrite the story told in *Totality and Infinity?* In following this query, we restrict our considerations to the texts written before 1968. This is the date of publication for the groundbreaking essay "La Substitution" in the *Revue Philosophique de Louvain*. It can be argued that with the publication of "La Substitution" the fundamentals of the ethics of *Otherwise than Being* have been made fully explicit. Thus, the essays contemporary with this publication and those following it are already informed by the ethics of *Otherwise than Being*. The essays that precede "La Substitution," then, retain a more transitional flavor and therefore better serve us as we read Levinas in transition. His transition is from the language of alterity in *Totality and Infinity* to another sort of language underlying the ethical in *Otherwise than Being*. While we will periodically refer to post-1968 texts, the above mentioned three essays will comprise the core of our exposition.

Another Look at Husserl

In his essays on phenomenology following *Totality and Infinity*, Levinas's exposition of the structure of passivity intertwines time and materiality. This intertwining returns us to the question of sensibility. We have already seen how Levinas's turn to sensibility in 1959 takes up the "other" horizon of intentionality—the problem of the exterior and the sensuous, which Husserl himself, perhaps unwittingly,[1] designates as a transcendental item. This turn to the transcendental functioning of sensibility reveals a configuration of intention set out from the sensible. Under this model, the intention does not configure the object(s) at issue, but rather is itself configured by the object: there is a bestowal of sense from the outside. This inversion of the transcendental in Levinas's hands inverts the philosophical eros, an inversion that erupts from within philosophy's own rules of play. In the present considerations, we revisit this theme again, with the problem of time as our accomplice. This accessory to the investigation will reveal another strategy of critique, as well as, for Levinas, a certain *rapprochement* with Husserl. This will be a reconciliation, as will be the case with any ethical work, that entails a gesture of *ingratitude* (cf., TrA, 191/349), an encounter that is altogether "disconcerting" (TrA, 195/353) to the Husserl of the famed "principle of principles" and its intentionality of immanence.

Sensibility, then, provides the point of departure for the following readings. In the course of these readings, three central phenomenological themes come into view and direct our unfolding of the problem of sensibility: modification, recuperability, and phenomenality. The theme of modification will be addressed in Levinas's account of the problem of sensation in the essay "Intentionalité et sensation." This account visits sensation as it appears in Husserl's reflections on the temporalization of intentionality, which trace the genetic movement of materiality through passivity. With Husserl, Levinas will articulate how the temporal distance in an intertwined time and sensation introduces a modification that renders the origin of intentionality strange to the intention that "petrifies" the subject (IS, 162). Such a modification, captured in the structural item of the *Ur-impression*, will prove to be the precise and concrete temporal term that justifies or legitimates the language of the trace. Building on the structure laid out in the "Intentionalité et sensation" essay, the motif of recuperability, we will then pursue Levinas's explicit critique of the privilege of presence in phenomenology, a critique that discovers the trace and its destructive effect on the philosophy of identity. The nonrecuperability of the trace, mapped onto the logic of modification demonstrated by time and sensation, constitutes Levinas's fully justified break with presence. We will shown how such a break makes "heteronomous experience" possible, that peculiar experience in which the famed "beyond being" is put in concrete relationality without conversion into the categories of knowledge. The issue of the manifestation of exteriority—so much a part of our discussion of *Totality and Infinity*—is revisited in Levinas's conception of the enigmatic *entretemps* in "Phenomenon and Enigma." What will emerge from this consideration is the peculiar mode of signification arising from the anterior moment of passivity.

These thematic alterations trace following movements: first, an articulation of the pure structure of time; second, an examination of how and why this structure of time is necessary for the break with identity and presence that underpins the idealist conception of intentionality; third, the overturning of phenomenality, which is nothing other than the conversion of appearance into enigma. "Intentionalité et sensation" establishes, for Levinas, the necessity of Husserl for the rethinking of time and sensibility. "Trace of the Other" argues that the trace, in its immemoriality, structures presence. "Phenomenon and Enigma" tells us precisely how immemoriality structures presence.

Such is our interpretative orientation. Additional preliminary remarks, however, are also in order. What are we to make of the philosophical and ethical status of the essays under consideration? The question of the philosophical status of the essays has two intertwined aspects: the character of Levinas's own findings and the relation those findings have to the Husserlian problematic. This is a methodological question. Now, Levinas himself has said that the issue of philosophical method does not capture the essence of his own thought (e.g., DQVI, 140ff). But, it also must be said—Levinas's hesitations notwithstanding—that the conversion(s) of intentionality in the interim essays from the 1960s constitute a specifically phenomenological method of explicating the structure of the ethical. Philosophically, then, our reading of these essays concerns the modification of the structure of intentionality. This modification will lead us another logic of sense-genesis.

And, insofar as Husserl conceives intentionality as the very method of phenomenology, as well as the fact that the interim essays deal with implicit and explicit readings of Husserl, Levinas's translation of intentionality will bear an irreducible relation to Husserl's own aims and methods. What, then, is the nature of this relation? Levinas's reflections on Husserl in the 1960s form something like a "double reading" of Husserl's texts. The reading is doubled in the following sense: In Levinas's account, Husserl's texts bear witness to both a witting and an unwitting participation of phenomenology in the destruction of the purity of presence. Levinas will, on the one hand, claim that the problem of time rooted in Husserl's own analyses introduces modifications to the structure of intentionality that break with a fundamental presupposition in Husserl's work: the teleological possibility and actuality of immanence and recuperability. Thus, it is fair to say that Husserl exits metaphysics in his very attempt to give metaphysics its final grounding in the presence of constituted time. To this end, Levinas will seize upon Husserl's unwitting admissions. On the other hand, it is also the case that Levinas thinks Husserl and phenomenology itself to be fully conscious in its transgression of metaphysics. It is therefore not simply the case that Husserl's texts are at tension with themselves; this which would be the claim of a double reading. There is a question of intent—not just the intent of the author Husserl, but also, perhaps more significantly, the intent of the phenomenological program. Indeed, Levinas will contend that the program of phenomenology itself, the guiding demand that the matters and methods be purged of metaphysical structures, makes the destructive aspects of the problem of time both possible and necessary. Recall here Levinas's remark in "Lévy-Bruhl et la philosophie contemporaine" that the *Logical Investigations* already prepares the ruin of representation (LB, 55). In this sense, Husserl is at peace with himself in his ". . . radical *Abbau* of Western metaphysics."[2] Husserl, in Levinas's treatment, is both the unwitting destructor of his own foundation grounded in presence and the happy accomplice to this ruination: a passive and active transgressor. This doubled relation to presence blinds Husserl to the full implications of his discoveries. It is Levinas who will recover these "forgotten horizons," explicating their "full implications." But the fact that such horizons are "forgotten" indicates that there is a certain, albeit peculiar, presence of them already in Husserl's work.

The primary concern of the present reflections, then, is with the structure of intentionality found in Husserl's treatment of the problem of time. In this regard, the present reflections are not explicitly concerned with ethics. To the extent that we remain focused on the modification of intentionality, the exposition is primarily on the way to ethics. However, to the extent that the problem of intentionality introduces the structure of the Other in the Same, the diachronic time of sensibility, and the enigmatic signification of alterity, the exposition is already implicitly ethical. The preparatory character of Levinas's essays—preparatory, that is, for *Otherwise than Being*—must be stressed. Yet it must also be confessed that the following reflections are always parasitic on the question of ethics. That is, we must admit that one cannot now read these essays in retrospect except with a view from and toward their terminus: *Otherwise than Being*. One might characterize the interim essays as proto-ethical, which is not to say they are wholly removed or distanced from the ethical. Rather, the following reflections postpone the explicit thematization of ethics proper in favor of an antecedent consideration of the sort of structures necessary for the language of alterity as the relation of passivity. It is the fully justified language of alterity as passivity that exposes the terms of Levinas's ethical thought and the logic of sense-bestowal ethics implicates. In other words, the present considerations are proto-ethical in the sense that we are concerned with the passage to the language of alterity and therefore with the sort of structures that such a language may be said to presuppose. Let us turn to Levinas's proto-ethical reading of Husserl in "Intentionalité et sensation."

Time

It is an all too common a mistake by critics of Husserl to limit the scope of his phenomenological inquiry to the actively constituted boundaries of idealism. This is acutely true in the time-analyses of materiality, where such a limitation conceals the radical horizons indicated and then often set aside in Husserl's own analyses. The structural and constitutive function of the sensual in lived-experience has occasioned numerous critiques of Husserl, from Scheler to Merleau-Ponty to Tranduc-Thao to Derrida. What these criticisms often fail to note is the extent to which the very horizons employed in critique (viz., those of the sensible) are explicitly disclosed *and* suspended by Husserl himself. Take for example the following remark Husserl makes in *Ideas I* regarding the character of the *hyletic* moment of intentional life:

> [W]hen we characterized the stream of lived-experiences as a unity of consciousness, that intentionality, disregarding its enigmatic forms and levels, is also like a universal medium which bears in

itself all lived-experiences, even those which are not themselves characterized as intentive. (Hua III, 171/203)

This is a remarkable comment. Husserl here admits that within the matrix of intentions that constitutes the field of lived-experience there are nonintentional components. On this nonintentive component of lived-experience, he writes further that

> [w]hether everywhere and necessarily such sensuous lived-experiences in the stream of lived-experiences bear some "animating construing" or other (with all the characteristics which this, in turn, makes possible), whether, as we also say, they always have *intentive functions*, is not to be decided here. On the other hand, we likewise leave it undecided at first if the characteristics essentially making up intentionality can have concreteness without having sensuous foundations. (Hua III, 172/204)

Although Husserl's analysis stumbles upon something quite enigmatic—the animating function and nonrelational/relational structure of the sensuous—and groundbreaking—the possibility of a *necessary* sensuous foundation—the articulation of the implications of such discoveries is postponed. And while the implications are postponed, the context of Husserl's remarks make clear the high stakes of reflection on the sensuous moment of lived-experience: It is nothing less than the question of the unity of consciousness as intentional.

Now, it is important to be absolutely clear how and why this indication of a possible nonintentional[3] aspect of *hyle* is inseparable from the problem of the intentionality of consciousness in general. The inseparability of the nonintentional *hyle* from the accomplished structure of consciousness as intentional inheres in the basic structure of relation that intentionality names: consciousness is always a consciousness *of* and *to* the world. Intentionality describes the basic structure of our presence to the world. The "of" structure of relation opens upon the horizons of predelineation explicated in a phenomenological idealism. In the "to" aspect of the relation, this relational presence to the world already of itself implies that our consciousness is also inseparable from its sensual aspect. The structure and character of this sensuality is therefore disclosed by nothing other than Husserl's claim that phenomenology is the matter (Hua III, 167ff/199ff) and the method (Hua IX,

270) of intentionality. Despite Husserl's suspension of an articulation of the full implications of the sensual in lived-experience, phenomenology is always led back to our sensible presence to the world through the very matter of its method.

Husserl chooses to leave the status and interrogation of these nonintentive moments to another occasion. "Intentionalité et sensation" is one of the few attempts to take seriously the positivity of the enigma of materiality disclosed in Husserl's phenomenology.[4] Although Levinas's reflections on Husserl's notion of sensation contend that Husserl's treatment of the problem is profoundly truncated, they also attempt to provide a descriptive analysis of the implications that are borne within the problem of the *Ur-impression* from within the horizons disclosed by Husserl himself. The implications of this problem contest some of the central features of idealism: the primacy of the ego, the coincidence of immanence and transcendence, constituted temporality, the unity of consciousness. Levinas will replace those features with figures of irreducible alterity. The implications of the sensible as nonintentional, however, can only be explicated if we free the *hyletic* from its explicit "subordination to the phenomenology of transcendental consciousness" called for in *Ideas I* (Hua III, 178/210). The question with which Levinas is occupied is quite straightforward: What horizons of relation are implicated in the materiality of the *hyle*, the sensation, or the *Ur-impression* when it is wrested free from the relation of correlation? What this freeing entails is nothing less than the simple yet exceedingly important assertion that the *morphe* and *hyle* correlation does not exhaust the possibilities of conceiving the sensible.

Levinas's interrogation of sensation, *hyle*, and *Ur-impression* (all the modalities of the medium of the sensuous) without figures of correlational predelineation amounts to nothing other than the interrogation of what Husserl calls primal sensibility *(Ursinnlichkeit)* in one of the "Beilagen" to *Ideas II* (Hua IV, 337/348). Nevertheless, the turn to a nonintentional (i.e., nonconstituted) notion of sensible is not without a significant paradox and something of an anticipatory remark regarding this paradox is in order. This paradox lies in the problem of precisely what kind of descriptive language is possible for a phenomenology of primal sensibility or what Levinas will call a "phenomenology of the noumenal." (LC, 43/21). Descriptive language is problematic here because of the peculiar presence a noncorrelational sensibility has in lived-experience. Although, the sensation is something akin to the condition for the possibility of lived-experience, the sensation is not reducible to its appearance within lived-experience. As Husserl himself claims in *Ideas II*, the sensation in its primal functioning affects the Ego as foreign and is thereby fundamentally and originally pregiven. The affect*ing* moment of the sensation preceeds its givenness (Hua IV, 336/348). The givenness of the sensation is not coincident with the primal sensation as such. Rather, the givenness of the primal sensation in lived-experience is merely a *clue* to what has already passed. The possibility of a language for describing this "already passed" lies in the phenomenological reflection on time and genesis and it is to this problem that Levinas's essay returns us.

Levinas's task is to follow the Husserlian problem of materiality as it translates itself into a phenomenology of primal sensibility.[5] The end of these reflections is the development of an account of the paradoxical double character of the sensuous, the one side manifest as the correlational *hyle* and the other side manifest as the nonconstituted item of what has already passed. Levinas will create a term for this double character: the trace. We begin first, however, with Levinas's account of the problem of sensation and primal sensibility as it first emerges within Husserl's texts.

The initial consideration of "Intentionalité et sensation" is a reconstructive characterization of the Husserlian problem of the relation between the two-fold appearance of intentionality: the intentionality that is constitutive of the ideality in perception and the *hyletic* moment of sensuous generation.

It is noteworthy that, in taking up the question of intentionality, Levinas collapses the question of the structural integrity of intentionality with the question of consciousness and its unity or disunity. For, as Levinas notes, ". . . consciousness that is consciousness of the object is consciousness not objectivated to itself . . . [a consciousness that] is *Erlebnis*" (IS, 149). Conceiving consciousness *as Erlebnis itself*, we are forced in principle to understand sensations to be constitutive of consciousness as such. Therefore, as we shall see, the question of the structural function of sensation is not simply the task of fine-tuning the analysis; rather, it is a question of the unicity or rupture of the boundaries of subjectivity. This is to say, if we find that the problem of the function of sensation is structurally recuperable within the phenomenological field, then we can secure the unity of intentionality—and, by extension, the unity of consciousness, the subject. If, on the other hand, sensation threatens the recuperable boundaries of the phenomenological field, then we are taken to the punctured fringes of the field and are given a consciousness that is not—even as a teleological claim—immanent to itself. These are consequences from Husserl's phenomenology itself, evidenced where Husserl writes that "[c]onsciousness is nothing without impression" (Hua X, 100/106).

The first consideration in Levinas's essay takes up the familiar theme of the primacy of theory in Husserl's conception of intentionality. From *Theory of Intuition* through *Totality and Infinity*, Levinas aimed at concretely breaking with the primacy of representation, so it is not entirely unexpected that the problem of theory emerges here as a central point of contention. The strategy in *Totality and Infinity* consisted in the identification of a primary intention (a "transcendent-intention") that is able to sustain the work of the secondary intention(s) and therefore the work of representation and knowledge. In "Intentionalité et sensation," published only four years after *Totality and Infinity*, this same problem is taken up in terms of the contrastive yet constitutive relation between adumbrations (*Abschattungen*) and the ideality that predelineates the unity of sensual differentiation. In his introductory remarks, Levinas notes that intentionality is understood by Husserl as an aiming that correlates mean*ing* or intend*ing* (French: *prétendent*, German: *meinen*) with the multiplicity of appearances of the object *meant* or intend*ed*. Ideality put forth in the intending is a unifying identification across the multiplicity of those appearances (IS, 145f). The adumbrations of which the "external" appearance of the perceived object is composed are, from the standpoint of constituting consciousness, merely aspects or differentiations of the unity predelineated by the ideal correlate of thought (cf., Hua III, §§1–4).

Thus, within the scope of phenomenological idealism, ideality and adumbration are two moments of one and the same intention. Despite the different modes of appearance, the intentionality of idealism is able to sustain both the immanence of ideality and the transcendence of adumbrations. Indeed, as Levinas notes, even this transcendence is an immanent content.

> The *Abschattung* is not an aspect—already objective—of the thing, but an immanent content, lived and nevertheless an abridgment of the objective. Intentionality, the opening of consciousness onto being, hereafter plays the role of an apprehension (*Auffassung*) in

> regard to these contents on which it bestows an objective sense
> *(sens)*, which the intention animates *(beseelt)* or inspires
> *(durchgeistigt)*. (IS, 149)

The aspect or profile is not itself an objective moment standing outside the boundaries of the reflective subject. The profile does not stand over against the ideality that is phenomenally opposed to it. For Husserl, of course, this distinction between ideality and *Abschattungen* is a phenomenal distinction and therefore a distinction regarding the differing modes of appearance.[6] Husserl, under the rubric of the reduction, can only name this difference in terms of phenomenal differentiation. Precisely because Husserl's practice of the reduction moves within this conception of the phenomenal, the particularity characteristic of the appearance of the profile, though opposed to ideality in the phenomenal 'how' of its appearance, does not signify a break with consciousness. When bound by the logic of correlation, particularity does not put ideality into question (i.e., with regard to the legitimacy of ideality's first position), but is only understood *as* particular in terms of its difference from identity. Because with Husserl "idealism is already in intentionality" (IS, 146), the transcendence of the profiled appearance is itself an immanent content. As Levinas notes, for Husserl intentionality *is* the correlation between noesis and noema—a correlation that "expresses . . . the solidarity between the object and its modes of appearance" (IS, 146).

Further, if—by way of his strict identification of the object and its mode of appearance—Husserl's account of the appearance of intentionality renders transcendence an immanent content, then the object does not pose a threat to the unity of consciousness. Levinas writes:

> Across the multiplicity of moments where consciousness is unfolded as a "lapse of time," consciousness becomes identified and is maintained, in its identity, in an aspect of the object; and, across the multiplicity of these aspects, an objective pole, identical and ideal. (IS, 147)

In terms of the sensuous moment of the adumbration, then, consciousness is not threatened in its unity. It is not threatened in its unity precisely because the particularity that might outstrip the idealist intention, the adumbration, is understood by Husserl as an "abridgment" of the objective which, in turn, is animated by the ideality carried in the noetic pole of the intention.

Nevertheless, there remains an aspect of sensation, even within this static mode of analysis, that lies on the "other side" of adumbrations. To this point, Husserl's account of sensations closely follows that of Berkeley, insofar as sensual aspects of experience—as aspects that are on the "objective" side of perception—are still understood as contents of which I am conscious, a consciousness without which the terms fail to make sense. If sensations are merely aspects of the *Erlebnis* of and within which I am conscious, then the items of the intentional complex are wholly recuperable within the intentionality of the phenomenological idealist. This is the case insofar as Husserl, as Derrida has also noted,[7] develops his analysis predominately from within a constituted temporality. But, as Levinas recognizes, sensations are also conceived by Husserl as those elements within *Erlebnis* which are not themselves acts, i.e., do not play an active role in constitution, but rather are nonintentional contents that demand another mode of access: through the passivity of sensibility. Within the scope of static analysis, however, the passivity of sensations remains hidden, insofar as the static analysis always yields—at the very least—a resemblance or analogy between sensations and objective qualities (IS, 149). This analogy holds, for Husserl, despite the tension such an analogy encounters with the claim that *hyletic* contents lie at the basis of intentionality—a claim that implicitly admits a nonintentional foundation of intentionality. This admission, however, does not threaten the structural integrity of intentionality, of consciousness. That is to say, even though Husserl acknowledges the non-intentional status of sensations, the static method of analysis is always inadequate to the task of sustaining this nonintentionality. The nonintentionality of primal sensations demands a genetic account of impressional consciousness and such an account returns us to time as the fundamental or essential element *(Wesensform)* of genesis (cf., Hua XVII, 319/319). The element of time in the analysis of impressional consciousness, in Levinas's rendering of the issue, will allow us to speak of the alterity of the primal sensation in terms of a radical and irreducible absence.

Turning to Husserl's temporal reinterpretation of the problem of sensations, we begin to see the emergence of Levinas's own passage to the language of alterity as absence *within* Husserl's own reflections. And, further, we see that only in this temporal approach to sensations is Husserl able to fulfill the claims made in the static analysis of the problem. Only the temporal analysis of sensations is able to provide sustained analysis of the nonintentional content indicated at the base of accomplished intentionality. It is also of note that in turning to time as the medium of the explication of primal sensibility, Levinas has deepened both his own earlier reflections on the sensible, as well as deepened his own critique of the predominate role of theory in Husserl's phenomenology.

The static exposition of sensations leaves intentionality intact, self-contained and unthreatened. Intentionality remains safe in its modality of being precisely because the problem of sensations is taken up, in the static analysis, in terms of the constitutive relation. That is to say, if Husserl models sensations on the adumbrative character of the appearance of an external object, then sensations are already ideal—abridgments, as Levinas writes—of the objective. On the one hand, then, the constitutive or correlational relation between consciousness and its object—where the object is sensation proper—determines sensation as tangled in ideality and hence emerges as ideality laden, aspects of the subjective, or simply the objective *as* within the subjective. Sensations necessarily show themselves as aspects of the subjective within the constitutive relation. The contrastive relation tells a different story. In the contrastive relation, irreducible difference emerges between ideality and the materiality of the sensible. This irreducibility is established in the very name Husserl gives to original sensations: impression. As Husserl will write in *Ideas II*,

> The word "impression" is appropriate only to original sensations; the word expresses well what is "there" of itself, and indeed originally: namely, what is *pregiven (vorgegeben)* to the Ego, presenting itself to the Ego in the manner of something *affecting it as foreign* . . . This non-derived *(Nicht-abgeleitete)* impression . . . breaks down into primal sensibility and into Ego-actions and Ego-affections. (Hua IV, 336/348; my emphasis)

Husserl here outlines what could be called the "double-character" of the sensuous. On the one hand, primal sensibility stands on the "side" of the foreign as what performs the affect*ing*. On the other hand, the impression stands on the side of the Ego as the affect*ed* strata of lived-experience. When the structural item of sensation passes over into the

Ur-impression, the impression has two distinct moments: the moment in which the impression appears as sensation within constituted boundaries and the moment wherein the *Ur-impression* is, as Levinas calls it, "non-ideality *par excellence*" (IS, 155). The constitutive relation is an identity relation of ideality and sensation, despite the initial phenomenal appearance of difference. The appearance of difference in the constitutive relation is reconciled in terms of a higher level constituted identity. The difference that matters—i.e., a difference that signifies otherwise than the space of coincidence—is only articulated in the contrastive relation, which is the relation set out from the primal, affecting sensation.

This relation set out from the pregiven, foreign sensation is most thoroughly described when Husserl turns to the temporal foundation of the accomplished intention. When the pregiven sensible "content" of intentionality is given its temporal interpretation, there appears, in Levinas's words, "an other sense of intentionality" (IS, 151). This "other" intentionality is an "other" structure of the relation between sensation and the accomplished intention. A peculiar intentionality is necessary to name this relation. The intention or relation that emerges out of the structural moment of *Ursinnlichkeit* is peculiar precisely because its very sense is defined by its break with the conventional conception of relationality as immanence and temporal coincidence. The intentionality proper to *Ursinnlichkeit* and the language necessary to articulate it is to be found at the site of the *break up* of the immanent, coincident, and correlational sense of relationality. This break up of the idealist notion of relationality is articulated in terms of the specifically temporal "space" or gap between the relata in question.

Hence, we must seek the terms of this relation within what emerges from out of the structure of the living-present, the primordial sense of the time and temporality of consciousness as intentional presence *to* the world. As the "source of intentionality" (IS, 152), the living-present becomes that temporal space wherein *hyletic* contents, initially revealed at the basis of intentionality in the static analysis, are given their proper articulation as items of difference. Time, in Levinas's words, is the very "feeling of sensation, which is not the simple coincidence of the feeling and the felt, but an intentionality" (IS, 153). This intentionality, this relation itself, opens up the fundamental difference already indicated in the static analysis, viz., the difference between the "intentionality that aims at identifiable idealities" and "impressional consciousness" (IS, 152). Between this difference, Levinas writes, "exists a bond" (*un lien*) (IS, 152). This "bond" marks as essentially separated *and* related impressional consciousness (i.e., consciousness as the impression, consciousness at its impressional origin, consciousness "to" the impression and thus not consciousness "of" the impression) and the ideality manifest in the accomplished intention. But Levinas's claim is that we must understand this as a relation without immanence or coincidence. It is a relation of what he will call *sens unique*: the one-way traffic of the genesis of consciousness out of the sensation. *Écart* and *lien* describe neither a contradiciton nor a negation (and so are not subsumable under a Hegelian logic), but rather a *diachronic relation*. In the end, this temporal articulation of distance-relation will make it possible for Levinas to articulate an ethical relation of nonimmanence, a relation across the infinite distance of, to use the language of *Totality and Infinity*, the interval. The simultaneity of *Écart* and *lien* underscores the aporetic character of the sensation problematic—its double character—and deformalizes a justified description of the face-to-face as both one across the interval *(écart)* and one of concern *(lien)*.[8]

As constituted by the paradoxical coupling of *lien* of *écart*, and in terms of the one-way traffic of the sensation, impression and ideality must stand in a contrastive relation. This contrastive relation (their irreducible separation, as the bond is not one of immanence) must be articulated as "precisely a temporal distance" (IS, 153). The distance is not merely spatial—an inner separated from an outer—but temporal, as the former is the separation manifest in the static analysis and therefore a separation that is wholly bound within the recuperable intention of the idealist. The temporal explication of the structure of intentionality, an explication that manifests the temporal distance, announces that there is "a diachrony *in* intentionality" (IS, 154; my emphasis). This diachrony names the distance, gap, and bond between consciousness as accomplished in the intention that aims at idealities and the impressional consciousness that is structured *from* the originary sensation. Intentionality does not call for diachrony to be spread over it. Rather, diachrony is announced within the exposition of the temporalization of its structure, viz., at the very origin of the primordial spreading out of the flux.

Although this gap is opened up between two moments of consciousness, this is not to suggest that the diachrony in intentionality designates an absolute separation without structural implications.

Rather, precisely because the diachrony is *in* intentionality, impressional consciousness and the accomplished intention intertwine at the genetic source. This intertwining brings into relief the conditioning relation between impression and ideality. Sensation, which passes over into retentional modification of the original impression in the flux of absolute subjectivity, lies at the generative basis of the living-present and therefore at the basis of intentionality itself (cf., Hua X, 66–70/69–72, 99–101/105–107, 133/136). The *Ur-impression* is the "original creation" *of* consciousness (and not created *by* consciousness) and becomes modified as retention in the flux of absolute subjectivity, yet ". . . the flux is only the modification of the proto-impression that ceases to coincide with itself" (IS, 155). The *Ur-impression* is anterior to retention and indeed makes retention possible, which amounts to the fact that the original sensation is non-modified and therefore precedes its own possibility as appearance, as given. In other words, the *Ur-impression* lies at the very origin of consciousness and this sensual origin, in and after its creative functioning, cannot but fail to maintain its presence within the life of consciousness precisely because its status as original necessitates its noncoincidence with modified givenness. The sensual origin, however, is absent, defined by the very lapse of time between the original sensation and the accomplished intention. This original sensation ". . . is the source of every consciousness and every being" and as such "is original creation, the *passage* from nothing to being" (IS, 155). "Thought remains exiled" without this origin, without the passage into presence from an absolute passivity and absolute absence. Thought as intention, the field within which idealism works, is generated originally from its sensual origin in the *Ur-impression,* an origin that is enigmatic, foreign, and thus "without foundation, without an apriori" (IS, 162). The lapse in the passivity of the separated relation forgets, of necessity and without the possibility of recuperability, its origin. It is and remains an immemorial past—a trace.

To be sure, in the flux of the living-present of subjectivity, this origin undergoes its modification in the translation of sensation into retention. However, Levinas writes, "retention . . . [is] not a constituted content" (IS, 154), in the sense that it is not constituted by the activity of the accomplished intention. The only constitutive item of retention is the condition of the *Ur-impression,* which itself only enters through the absolute passivity of the sensual relation. Further, in Levinas's words

> ... it [the sensation] conditions every constitution and every idealization. The gap is retention and retention is gap: consciousness of time is the time of consciousness

[and therefore]

> ... the flux that is the very feeling of sensation, Husserl names absolute subjectivity, more profound than objectivating intentionality and anterior to language. (IS, 154)

Retention, despite its modified structure, nevertheless bears the mark of the original sensation of the *Ur-impression*. The accomplished intentionality discovered in the living-present of subjectivity recuperates only constituted contents; the temporal interpretation of sensation as *Ur-impression*, even in its modification as retention, stands apart as a nonintentional content, as a nonconstituted item that lies at the very generative source of intentionality. Lying at the generative source of intentionality, the sensation can be said to condition every constitution and ideality. This conditioning relation is precisely the bond across the gap: the aporetic, double-character of the sensuous preserved in the one-way conditioning relation of the *Ur-impression* to constituted time. Thus, the very grasp that would seek to recuperate sensation within the boundaries of constituted ideality (underpinned ultimately by a constituted time) finds itself already conditioned by that which it seeks to recover. It is precisely this state of affairs that leads Levinas to conclude that "... the act is therefore posterior to the materiality of the constituted object" (IS, 155).

Sensation, then, lies at the very origin of intentionality. We can say, in light of the preceding reflections, that the sensation is also already time. That is to say, time is implicated in sensation insofar as the very structural features of sensation (viz., as difference) necessitate a temporal articulation. Time announces and describes the *distance* of the gap and separation that characterizes the sensation as originally pregiven. The difference is temporally, not spatially and not phenomenally, described. But this flows both ways. In addition to time underpinning the very articulation of the character of sensation, sensation can also be said to structure time. Sensation structures time as the space of passage from the nonintentional into the intentional; it is the space of the passage from, and bond of, the outside of being to being. Sensation can be said to give birth to or to create the time of the living-present and the time of absolute subjectivity, but the *Ur-impression* is only articulable as a temporal distance. The impression, we might say, lends itself to the time of the living-present from *out* of time; at its origin, time is radically out of phase with itself.[9] Thus, despite the fact that Levinas employs the distinct terms "sensation" and "time," what lies at the origin of intentionality, according to the analysis itself, is a nonintentional sensation/time. Sensation/time indicates the primordial inseparability of the two terms, insofar as each can be said to condition the other: sensation as a temporal gap and time as a passage from absence into presence through the sensation.

At this point we can see the implications of this consideration of intentionality for Levinas's own extension of Husserl's meditations, as it is precisely the problem of alterity or radical otherness that closes the "Intentionalité et sensation" essay. The implications are merely indicative, as the essay still lacks the fully developed notions of trace and enigma so central to his conception of alterity. Nevertheless, the disclosure of the sensation/time that lies at the originary basis of intentionality—this "other intentionality" (IS, 151)—brings the essential structural items that underpin "trace" and "enigma" into relief.

In the aporetic nonintentional intentionality at the origin of accomplished and constitutive intentionality, Levinas has here discovered what he calls a "mystery." The "mystery" of intentionality lies in its genetically originating from a nonintentional content that, of structural necessity, is always other than the immanence of constituted contents. Insofar as consciousness or subjectivity must be conceived *as* time, this nonintentional content is the generative source of accomplished intentional consciousness. Conceiving subjectivity as time, we cannot simply think of the temporality of consciousness as the consciousness *of* time. Quite the contrary, Levinas writes that "consciousness of time is the time of consciousness" (IS, 154) and thus "consciousness of time is not reflection on time, but temporalization itself: the *too-late* of the solidification of consciousness is the very 'after' of time" (IS, 154). The radical temporalization of the intentionality of consciousness—which is designated as the sensual-temporal stratum of our consciousness "to" (not "of") the world—renders what is given as constituted within time late to its origin. The "time" of the origin (which is outside of the time of the living-present of transcendental consciousness) has already passed at the moment in which the sensation is retentionally modified as a given content of consciousness. To put it another way, accomplished intentional consciousness, understood as the matrix of recuperable intentionalities within the constituted boundaries of the living-present, is late to itself. When consciousness returns to itself, it does not find an original time in coincidence with itself, but rather finds itself as act or activity and thus posterior to the passivity of the materiality that enacted the passage of creation. This is the so-called mystery built into the primordial structures of intentionality: the noncoincidence of the intention with itself and the generation of the intentional from the nonintentional. Levinas captures this noncoincidence with the term *écart*—gap or separation. Levinas writes:

> The mystery of intentionality rests in the separation from . . . [*écart de . . .*] or in the modification of the temporal flux. Consciousness is senescence and investigation of lost time. (IS, 156)

Consciousness is "lost time." It is lost time because it is temporal and time is consciousness. At the most primoridial, impressional level of its "life," consciousness does not have the security of the distance of a "consciousness of" time, as consciousness is *already* temporal at the moment of its solidification and petrification and thus is already structured by its separation from its origin. It is already nonintentional in the very activity of its intentionality, separated from itself and noncoincidental in its very solidification. In its phenomenality, diachronical consciousness or the split temporality of sensual intentionality is *already* sensation/time. Diachronical consciousness is the temporal, material conception of subjectivity that allows Levinas to contest thoroughly the primacy of identity. To a certain extent this has always been Levinas's philosophical aim, but it is only with his reading of Husserl's description of primordial temporality that alterity and identity are decisively shown to be intertwined.

In "Intentionalité et sensation," this interweaving of alterity and identity is first described as the moment of creation. Levinas writes, regarding the creative function of the sensation/time, that it is a " . . . creation which merits the name of absolute activity, *genesis spontanea*, but it is at the same time . . . the passivity, receptivity of an 'other' penetrating in the 'same' " (IS, 156). Levinas gathers this reflection directly from the first "Appendix" to *Husserliana X*, where Husserl writes that

> [t]he primal impression is the absolute beginning of this produc-
> tion, the primal source, that from which everything else is con-
> tinuously produced. But it itself is not produced; it does not arise
> as something produced, but through *genesis spontanea*; it is primal
> generation. It does not spring from anything (it has no seed); it
> is primal creation. (Hua X, 100/106)

Impressional consciousness is wholly passive and the sole activity in
the constitution of this consciousness lies in the generative act on the
"side" of the impression itself. This impression, which is "other" than
accomplished consciousness, is inseparable from the subjectivity of the
living-present; "consciousness is nothing without the impression" (Hua
X, 100/106). This infusion of what Levinas calls "the other in the same,"
alterity in identity, is an activity insofar as it generatively conditions
the accomplished intention, yet—paradoxically—it is an activity enacted
through the relation of radical passivity. This creation is named as
passivity for the very reason that it is neither subject to nor conditioned
by the activity of active or passive *synthesis*. On the contrary, what
Husserl discovers in this peculiar origin of consciousness is

> . . . a first intentional thought which is time itself, a presence to
> self across the first gap [*écart*], an intention in the first lapse of time
> and the first dispersion; he perceives at the heart of sensation a
> corporeity, that is to say, a liberation of the subject with regard to
> the very petrification of the subject, a border, a freedom which
> undoes the structure. (IS, 162)

The structure is undone precisely insofar as the act of accomplished
intentionality is exhibited in its conditionality. The presence to self,
as the analysis of the *Ur-impression* displays, is already possessed by
the unrecuperable absence produced by the lapse in passage across
separation. Self-presence is thus obsessed by the notion that the very
possibility of the presence to self necessitates crossing the temporal
gap between sensation and the ideality of presence. For this reason,
Levinas will describe diachronical subjectivity as "hetero-affective,"
juxtaposed to, of course, the auto-affective subjectivity of transcendental consciousness. The petrification of the subject is already undone,
already liberated from itself and possessed by the non-I. With the
structural item of the impression, Husserl's reflections on time—

despite the explicit privilege given to constituted time—find again the power of surprise.

It is precisely this possession and obsession, this failure of presence to self secretly indicated in the accomplished intention, that makes possible another intentionality and thus another mode of intentional analysis that is able to sustain the anteriority of the relation or bond to alterity. Levinas makes this claim in the following rhetorical questions:

> Is consciousness, essentially impressional, not possessed by the non-I, by the other, by "facticity"? Is sensation not the very negation of the transcendental labor and the evident presence which coincides with the origin?[10] (IS, 162)

The answer, of course, is yes on both accounts. Consciousness, impressional at its origin, is only possible across the gap, across the separation. This passage across carries over the non-I or the other into the very unicity of the subject, but only *as* absence where the trace of the origin serves as the presentational *clue* to an original diachrony.

Therefore, the unicity of the subject is not pure; its accomplished intentions are conditioned by the passivity of the sensation/time. Indeed, the formal structure articulated by the temporalization of intentionality demands the recognition that the traditional priority given over to the accomplished intention—and also the foundational flavor of static analysis—must be overcome by the recognition of the conditionality of such an intention. The sort of teleology that Husserl holds out for, the hope for a coincidence of presence and origin at the conclusion of the task, is disingenuous with regard to the discovery of the diachrony in intentionality, a diachrony evidenced in Husserl's own reflections but subsequently suspended as a field of investigation. This disingenuous or compromising teleological gesture betrays, as Derrida has made clear, the fundamental discontinuity between the principle of evidence in phenomenology and the implications of the description of the structure of time.[11] Fidelity to this diachrony, to the possession/obsession produced by the non-I or other in the subject, disclosed as a necessity by Husserl himself, will finally bear its fruit, for Levinas, in the fully developed ethics of the facing relation in *Otherwise than Being*. And it is Husserl's imposition of the irreducibility of this noncoincidence that makes both possible and necessary the passage over to such an ethics—

a passage, as Levinas puts it in *Totality and Infinity*, of *unnatural movement*, seeking "higher than one's origin, a movement which evinces or describes a created freedom" (TeI, 54/82–83).

With this much in place, we are prepared to explore, with Levinas, the implications of his discovery of original and primary passivity, a passivity that makes it possible for us to "surmount the inevitable naiveté of spontaneity" (IS, 161). To surmount spontaneity is to put in question the scope and legitimacy of the subordination of the *hyletic* to the predelineating structures of transcendental consciousness. Of central importance here is the claim that sensation/time lies at the origin of intentional consciousness. This claim establishes an originary priority to passivity and its content. Sensation/time is not an aspect of intentionality, but the very possibility of intentionality—the nonintentional *Ur-impression*, the origin, without apriori and without foundation. That the very disclosure of this possibility is to be found in the absolute subjectivity of Husserl's temporalization of intentionality—or, better, the recognition of the temporal already within the intention—points to the positivity of Husserl's thought for Levinas. That such a diachrony has its peculiar evidence in Husserl's analysis points to the necessity of Husserl's work for a notarized language of alterity as trace and therefore for the structural passage to the ethics of *Otherwise than Being*. And, as we have shown, Levinas's exploration of this nonintentional origin and the diachronic language necessary for its description fulfills the terms of the promissory notes Husserl leaves us in *Ideas I* regarding a phenomenology of the *hyletic*. Further, we can identify at this preliminary juncture the positivity of Husserl's work for Levinas's own language of alterity, with anticipations of the following two sections on "trace" and "enigma."

The "trace" and the "enigma," as structures that lead to the distinction between the Saying and the Said, become the very language of alterity in *Otherwise than Being*. The possibility of trace and enigma is justified by the passivity of the relation. This passivity is brought into relief in the consideration of the function of sensation in the temporalization of intentionality. If we see the sense in which this passivity—and the gap indicated by temporal distance—bears an evidential moment in the intentional/nonintentional structure of the living-present, then we see how Levinas's consideration of intentionality and sensation justifies the language of trace and enigma. By extension, the same justifies the distinction between the Saying and the Said. To be sure, this evidence is anything but an employment of the "principle of principles." Levinas's consideration of intentionality and sensation is evidential, not in the sense that it brings the trace into presence, but only insofar it shows an irreducible diachrony built into the very notion of intentionality—a nonintention co-implicated in the intention, and, even further, a sensation/time at the origin of intentional consciousness. Hence, there is an originary priority to passivity and its content. Sensation/time is not an aspect of intentionality. It is the very possibility of intentionality—the nonintentional *Ur-impression*, the origin, without apriori and without foundation.

Presence

Our shift from "Intentionalité et sensation" to "Trace of the Other" amounts to a (overlapping) thematic shift from the question of the temporalization of sensibility in the former to the critique of presence in the latter. This shift alters the theme insofar as the explicit concern with presence in "Trace of the Other" initiates a new set of terms and their coextensive horizons. Still, as we shall see throughout the present section, there is an essential overlap insofar as the temporalization of sensibility is already a critique of and departure from (though lodged within) presence. To be sure, in chronological terms "Trace of the Other" (1963) predates "Intentionalité et sensation" (1965). But our concern here is with the alteration of the structure of intentionality through time. Thus, our first step is to make thematic the subjection of intentionality to time and then, from that subjection, explicate the consequences of such analyses. We have begun precisely this task. "Intentionalité et sensation" has already given us the decisively incontrovertible modification of intentionality through Husserl's reflections on genesis and materiality. Therefore, from that essay, we are now able to pose the terms from which to explicate the implications of that modification.

"Trace of the Other" shows us how the terms of the analysis of sensation/time impact the question of presence. Levinas will here insist that presence implicates—within itself, through heteronomous experience—a trace-structure, a trace-genesis. Read under the terms of the "Intentionalité et sensation" essay, this trace-structure finds a mode of legitimation across the "gap"—the "irreversible lapse" (TrA, 199/357)—that underpins sensation/time and thereby can be seen as situated immanently within Husserl's conception of intentionality and time. Further, if we keep the findings of "Intentionalité et sensation" in view, we are better positioned to understand how the provocation of the "ethical movement" *in* consciousness ". . . involves a surplus for which intentionality is inadequate" (TrA, 196/353), but which still must be approached ". . . by situating it with respect to the phenomenology it interrupts" (TrA, 199/356). Intentionality understood as relation to immanence is inadequate and *that* phenomenology is interrupted. But what of this other phenomenology, captured in the intention set out from sensibility? Ethics takes place in the movement of consciousness. But this movement—without return—takes the intentionality understood as relation to immanence to the point of its breaking, its puncture. This displaced and punctured intentionality, already glimpsed in its pure form in "Intentionalité et sensation," will make the structure of another kind of ethics possible. This intentionality, as we shall continue to see in more detail, can only be understood in its being situated in relation to the phenomenology it interrupts.

As with the "Intentionalité et sensation" essay, "Trace of the Other" opens with a discussion of the general problem of identity and, specifically, the identity of the experience of the philosophical subject. By setting out with the problem of identity in view, the issue for Levinas is that of interruption or rupture of identity. This opening move parallels the concern in "Intentionalité et sensation" with the space of critique set up as the unity of consciousness and, in the decisive moment of the analysis, the medium of time. The security of "Being" or knowledge characterizes, according to Levinas, the movement of philosophy in the West. As such, philosophy always "bears in itself the possibility of idealism" (TrA, 188/346). When rendered actual, this is a possibility in which ". . . the Other, in manifesting itself as a being, loses its alterity" (TrA, 188/346). Idealism has always been the privileged route of investigation in Western philosophy and may, perhaps, be named as the "very definition of philosophy" (TrA, 189/347). Idealism ensures the return to self, the return to the "I," and thereby fails to encounter otherness as such. Idealism fails to encounter an Other that might have what Levinas calls the "wild barbarian character of alterity" (TrA, 187/ 345). Instead, as the object of knowledge, that which is other or foreign (*étranger*) is "naturalized" at the moment it has a sense or meaning— at the moment it becomes known (TrA, 187/345). "Every experience," within the prerogative of the philosophy of identity, ". . . is at once converted into a 'constitution of being'" (TrA, 188/346). To appear, we might say, is to be already known, to have been already submitted to the epistemological economy. Any legitimate sense of alterity will give way to the figure of Ulysses, who always returns to his native island; in philosophy, this return is the "recuperation" of every movement in ". . . the light that should guide it" (TrA, 189/347). This is the incontrovertible recuperation of difference in identity guaranteed by something outside the mere appearance of difference. What passes from presence is re-presented in memory and projected into a future, making even the passage of time safe for the *telos* of recuperation and presence. For this project, Levinas writes, "[t]he traces of the irreversible past are taken as signs that ensure the discovery and unity of a world" (TrA, 188/345). Time would seem to pose no threat. That which appears in time appears within the texture of a homogeneous conception of experience. And, this homogeneous conception of experience finds its ultimate grounding in the supremely recuperable horizon of constituted time.

To this movement—a movement that ensures recuperation of difference in identity, the conversion of transcendence into immanence—Levinas opposes the "movement without return." Figuratively, Levinas opposes the figure of Abraham, who meets with no possibility of a future return to his land of origin (TrA, 191/348), to that of Ulysses, who ". . . through all his peregrinations is only on his way to his native island" (TrA, 188/346). The root of the opposition that Levinas seeks to provoke is displayed by the double sense of transcendence, a double sense that rehearses at the formal level the discussion of the two-sided conception of *Abschattung* in "Intentionalité et sensation." On the side of the philosophy of identity, transcendence always returns to immanence, just as the adumbration always returns to unity. Within this idealist prerogative, the appearance of transcendence is recuperated at the moment one returns to the identity of transcendence in the consciousness of that which transcends. All is recuperable if what transcends is only "consciousness of" the movement of transcendence. Such is the case according to the philosophical eros.

Still, against this privilege of identity and on the other side of thought and being, philosophy also bears the clandestine mark of the "enigmatic message of the beyond being" (TrA, 189/347). The "beyond being" articulates a transcendence outside the "paralytic" (TrA, 194/

351–352) economy of manifestation. This transcendence outside being is ". . . other absolutely and not with respect to some relative term," unrevealed and buried, not because knowledge is insufficient to the task of explicating its sense, but precisely because it is ". . . wholly other than being" (TrA, 190/347). The absolutely other lies outside of being, beyond knowing, and is therefore irretrievable within the boundaries of the philosophy of identity. The philosophy of identity explicates the being-sense only of that which appears. The genuine sense of alterity testified to in the various appearances of the beyond being in philosophy's history does not appear under an epistemic category. Although the beyond being refuses epistemic categories, this is not because knowledge is insufficient to the task of its explication. Rather, knowledge presupposes both a univocal sense of being and the fully illuminated presence of what appears to the knowing subject. Therefore, according to Levinas, the beyond being, by its very structure, is foreign to the boundaries of knowledge. The beyond being, as named by the One of Plato's *Parmenides*, is ". . . foreign to definition and limit, place and time, identity with oneself and difference in relation to oneself, resemblance and dissemblance, foreign to being and knowledge" (TrA, 189/347).

However, if this genuine sense of alterity is beyond being and fails to appear within the boundaries of knowledge, then an obvious question arises: "In what sense does the absolutely other concern me?" (TrA, 190/347). The question of concern is decisive. If the beyond being is irreducible to the I, then it might at first appear to be an item incapable of entering into a relation with the subject. Indeed, to enter the boundaries of the concerned subject would seem to convert what is putatively beyond being into an appearance. If the beyond being is translated into an appearance, it is then an object convertible into an identity across its difference. How can this beyond being concern me without losing its sense of beyond? Without a sense of relation, the beyond being would seem an insignificant construction. Literally, it would not signify and so would not weigh on the subject. If this is the case, we must ask further how and why it is unnecessary to renounce philosophy at the moment of contact with the transcendence of alterity. Can transcendence be captured in the movement of the Same, where the movement does not convert the transcendence of the Other into the immanence of the Same? If the movement of the Same cannot sustain a relation to this alterity, then it would seem necessary to abandon philosophy in favor of a non-philosophical empiricism, as Derrida had already noted in his review of *Totality and Infinity*.[12]

Such a complete abandonment is, in fact, not at all necessary. The concern that the beyond being imposes on the I is possible in what Levinas calls "heteronomous experience." This peculiar conception of experience evokes the alterity of the beyond being within the experience of the Same without the submission of what signifies in heterological experience to the logic of identity. Conceiving experience as heterological, Levinas is able to sustain a relation to philosophy and the movement of the subject (intentionality), while simultaneously puncturing the boundaries of the synchronic logic of identity that defines philosophy. Heteronomous experience punctures the very logic that would seal ignorance of radical transcendence.

Heteronomy, as the logic of experience that meets with alterity, opposes itself to homogeneity. Opposed to the homogeneous experience of the Same, heteronomy presents the interruption of identity in the concretely experienced emergence of alterity *both* within *and* outside the boundaries of the Same. Interruption can be said to begin (or have begun) within the boundaries of the Same insofar as heteronomy is concretely produced in the movement of the Same and in the relation of the Same to the wholly other. As the effect of the imposition of the wholly other, interruption can also be said to emerge outside the boundaries of the Same. In this doubled movement, heteronomous experience signifies the following four, closely intertwined features (see, TrA, 190/348). First, this peculiar conception of experience is the experience of the foreignness of the absolutely exterior which, according to the logic of identity, is contradictory. Thus, the task of the exposition of heteronomous experience is to elaborate the structure of this experience without renouncing the contradiction introduced by the exterior. Contradiction is the very life of the interrupted subject. Second, in its break with the immanence of the logic of identity, heteronomous experience "disengages" *(dégage)* the movement of transcendence. This disengagement unbinds transcendence from its essentialization in the consciousness of transcendence—that reflexive position which renders the transcendent an immanent structure. Third, heteronomous experience designates an "attitude" wholly incontrovertible into a category. It is incontrovertible in the sense specified above: not due to an underdetermined knowledge, but because the movement toward what is beyond being leaves the boundaries of epistemic possibility, even knowledge in its telic form. This incontrovertibility loosens the analysis from the boundaries of philosophical anthropology and the phenomenology of the mundane.[13] Fourth, the movement of heteronomous experience, in its departing the Same toward the Other, is not recuperated in the identification of the consciousness of the movement. Heteronomous experience does not return to its point of departure. Capturing this gesture—this Abrahamic wander—constitutes a decisive interruption of the philosophy of identity by another kind of experience.

With these structural features in view, we can say that heteronomous experience warrants the description "movement without return." Precisely because it is a movement without return, experience as heterological is experience in a wholly different sense. Indeed, as Levinas points out in a later essay, it is customary to understand that "[t]he notion of experience is inseparable from the unity of presence, or simultaneity" (DP, 101n3/187n3). Heteronomous experience, however, derives its sense from nothing other than the break with presence, and so with the implicit recognition of, as we have already seen, the diachrony already in time. Experience, as heterological, is to be understood with an oppositional regard to the simultaneity and presence it interrupts.

Nevertheless, heteronomy remains an experience to the extent that it names the Same in relation, viz., in relation to the face. The problem of articulating this heterological structure of experience as an experience leads Levinas to the face of the Other as the paradigmatic, fundamental mode of heterological relationality. The phenomenality or mode of signification of the face consists primarily in the undoing or unraveling (*défaire*) of the form which would seek to contain it, already dissimulated in its exposure to the intention (TrA, 194/351). This formulation in many ways repeats that of *Totality and Infinity* (e.g., TeI, 37/66). To this effect/affect of unraveling, Levinas attaches a number of terms that express the enigma of this interruption: *Ingratitude* provokes the sense in which the movement toward the Other cannot be converted into a relation with reciprocity, which, positively, is a relation with to the Other ". . . who is reached without showing himself touched" (TrA, 191/349).[14] *Patience* designates the possibility of maintaining the heterological relationality of "*l'action à sens unique.*" Patience is a one-way sense, a unidirectional flow of sense, and surplus manifest in the Other as singular existent. Patience is that peculiar action which accomplishes its act ". . . without entering the promised land" (TrA, 191/349).

Liturgy, in the original sense of "a putting out funds at a loss" (TrA, 192/350), is invoked by Levinas as the patient action of ethics in relation to the face. *Desire*, as in *Totality and Infinity*, is contrasted to "need" with the aim of specifying the movement of desire with a proper conception of the Other (TrA, 193/351).

With these four terms, Levinas outlines the descriptive task that explicates the sense of movement without return. Ingratitude, patience, liturgy, and desire capture moments of heteronomous experience and the initial conditions of its maintenance; all four terms describe the subject as this experience. Heteronomous experience, so far only provisionally conceived, accomplishes the task announced at the outset of "Trace of the Other": the break with the philosophy of identity. This break with identity breaks up the primacy of consciousness and the intention that issues from it. "Consciousness," Levinas writes, "loses its first place" (TrA, 195/352). In "Signification et sens," a 1972 revision of "Trace of the Other, Levinas will say that the first position of consciousness is "called into question" precisely because "[t]he absolutely other is not reflected in consciousness" and thus must issue from an absolutely exterior (SS, 53/97). Recalling the idea of infinity, which was used to characterize the exterior in *Totality and Infinity*, Levinas again situates the analysis of "Trace of the Other" in relation to the intentionality of representation (also, SS, 52/96). The verdict, of course, is that the "marvel of the infinite *in* the finite," of the Other in the Same, provokes an "upsetting" or "overturning" *(bouleversement)*[15] of intentionality (TrA, 196/354) at the moment of its inadequacy to the alterity of the Other. Alterity enters heteronomous experience ". . . precisely out of an absoluteness" that is ". . . the name for fundamental strangeness" (TrA, 194/352). The Other signifies out of an absoluteness, an absolutely unencompassable (TrA, 199/356) that guarantees the foreignness of both the signification and the signified.

We have arrived at the decisive question: How can we articulate this absoluteness, a foreign signification that nevertheless signifies? To be sure, the conception of heteronomous experience herein outlined has done much to articulate the absoluteness of the relation to this Other. However, a question still remains unresolved: "How is the face not simply a true *representation* in which the Other renounces his alterity?" or, put more bluntly, "[H]ow is such a production [of signification] possible?" (TrA, 195/352). The alterity necessary for the relation to be heterological must maintain the character of strangeness. If we negotiate an articulation of the absoluteness out of which the Other may be said to signify, then, according to Levinas's account, we have found a kind of justification of this "name for fundamental strangeness." To conceive absoluteness properly, Levinas writes, ". . . we will have to study the exceptional signifyingness of a trace" (TrA, 195/352). Study of the trace-structure establishes both that alterity signifies outside the boundaries of representation and how such a signification is possible. As Levinas puts it in one of his additions to "Trace of the Other" in "Signification and Sense," the study of the trace-structure will allow us to ". . . fix with precision the conditions for such an orientation" (SS, 43/91).[16]

The trace-structure produces the extra-ordinary signification of alterity. The trace is fundamentally a temporal structure. Heterology and the experience that moves without return will thus turn to time for its final justification. Such a turn is implicated already in the first four sections of "Trace of the Other," but the articulation of both the context and its stakes was first necessary. The context, of course, is the problem of justification and the securing of conditions of orientation in heteronomous experience, which already implicates the stakes involved in the exposition of the trace. The stakes are quite straightforward: the concrete justification of heteronomous experience, and so the justification of the relation to the absolutely other. The account of this legitimation is accomplished in two steps. First, the function of the trace within the boundaries of experience. Second, the structure of the trace as a temporal item.

First, then, the function of the trace. The primary function of the trace is to articulate the possibility and actuality of a concrete break with the philosophy of presence. The break with presence does not simply juxtapose absence to presence. It does not simply posit a "world behind our world" (TrA, 198/355).[17] Rather, this break requires the interruption of presence by the absolutely absent and, further, the founding of the living-presence of the face in the very item that disturbs the order of the present and its "life." The trace is therefore defined both as the descriptive term for the absolutely absent and, more concretely, as that from which the other proceeds without "indicating" or "revealing" the absence. (TrA, 198/355). The trace seals absence as absence. The trace is not a modification of presence; absence, as the trace, is not a faded "previously present moment."

The signification of the trace is thus neither an indication nor a revealing, neither a revelation nor a dissimulation. It is, rather, a "third way excluded by these contradictories" (TrA, 198/355). What the trace signifies in the relation of the Same to the face is not the transcendent itself. Such a signification would render that which transcends immanent to the consciousness of the transcending. For Levinas, we must consider the signifying of the trace as radical absence. The relation of the trace to the face must be understood as

> . . . the unique openness in which the signifyingness of the transcendent does not nullify the transcendence and make it enter into an immanent *order*; here on the contrary transcendence refuses immanence precisely as the ever bygone transcendence of the transcendent. In a trace the relationship between the signified and the signification is not a correlation, but *unrightness* itself. (TrA, 198/355)

Again, the issue returns Levinas to the question of how one can articulate *radical* transcendence, original transcendence outside the boundary and economy of being. This is what prompts Levinas to write that ". . . a trace signifies beyond being" (TrA, 198/356). The beyond being is signified in the trace according to the heteronomous logic of "beyondness" itself, insofar as its signification is that of the transcending of transcendence. Or perhaps more precisely, trace signification is that of the already having transcended of the transcendently quasi-present face.

This peculiar signification of the trace brings us to the structural moment of Levinas's break with presence. In turning to the trace, Levinas negotiates a passage through presence to the absolute absent. This is possible only on the basis of, in Levinas's words, ". . . this third direction of radical *unrightness* which escapes the bipolar play of immanence and transcendence proper to being, where immanence always wins against transcendence" (TrA, 199/356). However, the unrightness of this third direction is made possible in what appears as present. It is for this reason that Levinas writes that "[t]he supreme presence of a face is inseparable from this supreme and irreversible absence which founds the eminence of visitation" (TrA, 199/356). In the presence of the face, the pretension of order is complicated in the signification of the absolutely absent. Thus, we can talk of heteronomous experience as a sustaining of contradictories—the present and the absolutely absent—without having to abandon the language of experience. To make this contradiction work (to make it produce a sense), we must conceive the trace and its signification as a structuring of presence by the irreversible absent. If we found visitation—the living presence of the face—on the trace, then heterology may properly claim itself as the *disturbance* of presence and identity. The relation of the trace to presence, when conceived in terms of the structural work of the trace on what appears, seals an irreversible lapse between both what is disclosed and what structures disclosure (TrA, 200/357).

This brings us to the temporal structure of the trace. We have already seen the temporal language of absence implicated. To be sure, the absence signified in the trace is not the spatial absence rendered in the problem of perspectivity. As we saw above, such a conception of the absent—the absence characteristic of *Abschattungen*—is already within the economy of immanence. The trace and the absence it signifies calls for a temporal language. The temporal feature of the trace, and the position it assumes, has its locus in the problem of memory. Memory is a conservation of the past which allows the present to extend itself, ecstatically, across history and past-passed time. But, the trace defines itself precisely in terms of its break with the boundaries of memory. The break of the trace with the boundaries of memory positions the trace as unrecuperable in recollection. This is why Levinas will characterize the trace as an *immemorial* past. Immemoriality renders the trace outside of recollection and it powers of re-presentation. Re-presentation is the power of recollection to make what has passed present again. The signification of the trace, however, is not faithfully rendered in any variant of presentation. Thus the trace cannot point to a complex of memories or to a modified sense of past, present, or future. Levinas writes that

> A trace qua trace does not simply lead to the past, but is the very *passing* toward a past more remote than any past and any future which still are set in my time—the past of the other, in which eternity takes form, an absolute past which unites all times. (TrA, 201/358)

The signification of the trace signifies as a trace only to the extent that it refuses to indicate a modification of the past. The trace is absolute in its unencompassability and is therefore not to be understood on the model of modification, transformation, or alteration. In other words, the remoteness of the trace cannot be understood in terms of the remoteness of a memory that transforms or alters its content. Nor can the trace be understood in terms of the modification of what has passed. The trace is, in a word, an "immemorial" past. Memory and the recuperability of the past both presuppose a constituted time, a time based in the ecstatic intertwining of presence and absence. It might be said that the trace as "an absolutely bygone" past (TrA, 200/357) is an absence more absent than absence. This language is legitimate to the extent that absence is understood, within the time of memory, as a modification of presence. Further, Levinas, underlining the transcendental dimension of the trace, will say that the trace structures presence without entering the recuperable horizon of memorial time. The trace maintains an irreducible relation to what appears, but does not belong to the appearing. This is the paradox that conditions moral consciousness. Immemoriality, on this account, is the condition for the possibility and impossibility of memoriality. That is, immemorality is the condition for the possibility of the play of constituted time *and* the impossibility of the memorialization of what makes memorialization possible. Thus, Levinas will add that a trace ". . . is a presence of that which properly speaking has never been there, of what is always past"; the trace is an item that does not remain in the world (TrA, 201/358).

Relation

In the preceding two sections, the relation of materiality and trace to accomplished subjectivity and its play within presence has become clear. In his account of both sensation and trace, Levinas describes an alterity as related across time. This description brings the "gap" or "irreversible lapse" that marks the relation of the Same to the Other into relief. Sensation and trace name not only alterity as such, but the way in which alterity already structures the boundaries of the Same. Thus, again, Levinas insists on the transcendental status of alterity—the way in which the alterity approached plays an irreducible constitutive role of the boundaries of the Same.

Still, there is a piece of the puzzle missing. Levinas remarks in "Trace of the Other" that the articulation of the beyond being must not only answer the question of the legitimacy of the phrase "beyond being," but also the question "in what sense does the absolutely other concern me?" (TrA, 190/347). Levinas's insistence on the constitutive function of the trace has answered much of what that question demands, but there remains an ambiguity at the heart of this question. His accounts of sensation and trace open a gap or lapse between the Same and Other. As a result, the sense in which this gap/lapse may be conceived as a relation is left unclear. The insistence in "Intentionalité et sensation" on the nonintentional character of sensation and the insistence on the absolute absence of the trace in "Trace of the Other," coupled with the central role of "gap" and "lapse," only exacerbates the difficulty of articulating the sense of relation. If there is no relation and therefore a straightforward separation, then it is difficult to fully justify the claim that the absolutely other *must* concern me. It becomes, then, a question of how to conceive the structure of the relation between trace and presence. How is this structuring possible? How can the establishment of this heterological relation be articulated? How are we to understand the movement of passage across the irreversible lapse at the moment that its irreversibility is sealed? What is this *interval*?

To establish a legitimate sense of relationality across this gap or lapse, we turn to the problem of passivity as it is taken up in "Phenomenon and Enigma." Levinas puts the problem of relation in this way:

> Something takes place between the dusk in which the most ecstatic intentionality, which, however, never aims far enough, is lost (or is recollected) and the dawn in which consciousness returns to itself, but already too late for the event which is moving away. (EP, 211/68)

This something that takes place is something akin to the temporal transition from the absolutely absent to the presence, where presence understands itself as too late to its origin. This something is located between dusk and dawn. Dusk and dawn, of course, figure two distinct temporal moments: Dusk, the movement toward the origin of itself (absence) and dawn, the presence to self already in exile (presence). The relation lies between these moments. So, Levinas terms this "something" the *entretemps*, a betweenness of and in time in which is found the modality of relation across the gap or lapse in diachronic time. A figure like *entretemps* is indispensable for understanding the structure of diachrony as diachrony, inscribing in the splitting of time a passage that leaves at least a "trace" of relation in its passing out of time. The *entretemps* makes a third way of articulating the splitting of time in diachrony possible. This third way is an articulation that neither renders a "simple parallelism of two orders" nor "reestablish[es] the simultaneity of one single order" underlying and conditioning diachrony (EP, 210/67). The relationality described by the *entretemps* makes it possible to link diachrony to disturbance. *Entretemps* is the way in which diachrony is expressed in a singular instant: disturbance. Disturbance happens between the radically absent and the faltering present, on the basis of the immemorial and in the hypostasis of the subject. And so disturbance is between the splitting of time, between—the relation of—diachrony. Disturbance is nothing other than the presence of enigma in heteronomous experience. Disturbance, enigma, *entretemps*—each is the intertwining and incompatibility of the trace with presence. With the *entretemps* established as the locus of the trace's passage into and out of presence, Levinas can sufficiently demonstrate the relation across the gap or lapse. When deformalized, this structure answers the question of how the absolutely other can and must concern the subject. The structural burden borne by the *entretemps* is therefore quite heavy.

The sense of this betweenness of time, this passage, brings us back to the notion of passivity. "Phenomenon and Enigma" implicates passivity in the conception of the *entretemps*. The essay "Language and Proximity" details that implication in its exposition of passivity. "Language and Proximity" argues that Husserl's notion of passivity has a two-fold sense, one conservative and one radical: passive synthesis and the relation of absolute passivity. The first sense of passivity is the passivity Husserl wants in order to seal the borders of constituted time. Passive synthesis seals constituted time because it fails, of necessity, to open upon what has already passed. Constituted time only recovers simultaneity. It is a passivity without trace. Passive synthesis, though it works as a pre-reflective structure, is still a spontaneity and activity and so an event preserved in memory. Indeed, the passivity in passive synthesis is characterized by Husserl as the "passively active" constituting labor of the subject in pre-reflective life. It is thus the work of passivity in constituted time. The exemplary instance of this modality of passivity is to be found in retention. Retentional passivity, Husserl writes, "is an intentional modification in the realm of pure passivity; it takes place according to an absolutely fixed law without any participation of the activity radiating from the ego-center" (EU, 122/110) and this lawfulness in passivity "concerns *all* phenomenological data" (EU, 122/111). The key words here are modification and lawfulness. The term modification signifies that what is construed by Husserl as passive is not absolute, but an alteration of activity. The term lawfulness secures the activity of passivity in the eidetic stratum, which effectively neutralizes what initially appears to be enigmatic. The coupling of modification and lawfulness warrants joining the two terms "passive" and "synthesis." This joining might seem a contradiction in terms, as synthesis is virtually synonymous with activity. But, it is not a contradiction on this account, insofar as the lawful work in passivity of acts of modification makes the pre-conscious labor synthetic. Passivity, for Husserl, has its laws. Because it has its laws, passivity is always synthetic. On this rendering of passivity, then, Husserl fails to question the primacy of activity. Activity remains the source of passivity and the work of the passive remains caught under eidetic lawfulness.

But there is another sense of passivity. This passivity, more passive than passivity as passive synthesis, is manifest in the notion of creation. We have already glimpsed this notion above in the problem of origin and sensation. Levinas revisits creation in an attempt to articulate absolute passivity as such, without conceiving the work of the passive in terms of pre-reflective synthetic activity of the subject. To this end, Levinas reminds us that at the moment of creation and the work of the trace, we arrive at a pre-egoic stratum of genesis. Thus, Husserl's conception of passivity as the clandestine work of the subject on sensations or retained impressions is preempted by the very terms with which Levinas approaches the problem. The time of creation is the very presupposition of the boundaries within which retention may be said to play. The passivity that labors in constituted time is artificially juxtaposed to activity, inevitably parasitic on precisely what would be opposed in the juxtaposition. The time of creation, however, is an absolute passivity that is pure. It is not a modification of activity. Levinas writes that

> . . . there is a consciousness which is a passive work of time, with a passivity more passive still than any passivity that is simply antithetical to activity, a passivity without reserve, the passivity of a creature at the time of creation when there is no subject to assume the creative act, to, so to speak, hear the creative word.

> Consciousness as the passive work of time which no one activates
> cannot be described by the categories proper to a consciousness
> that aims at an object. (LeP, 223/114)

Levinas's insistence here on passivity without reserve speaks to the problem of modification indicated above. Consciousness does not work in passivity. Consciousness itself is the work of (and worked upon by) time through the passive. The passivity to which Levinas turns in attempting to articulate the *entretemps* cannot be understood on the model of synthesis. This latter model serves only to smuggle back in to the analysis the very item being put in question: active consciousness. Nonmodified passivity is found in the time of creation, the time that Husserl identified as the first impression of impressional consciousness. In impressional consciousness, with its hinge located in the *entretemps,* lies the secret radicality of phenomenology's confrontation with time and genesis. And, in this development of passivity, Levinas names, not another structural item, but the very relation between consciousness and its origin: the Same and the trace, with the meeting point of the *entretemps.*

This relation, then, is the enigma of the alterity that bears the trace. The term *enigma,* which signifies in proximity, comes to stand for the signification of not only the trace, but also the passage through which the trace structures presence. The signification in proximity expressed in the enigmatic calls forth the terms of the exposition of sensation/time. Proximity is the very contact of the sensation in and across time—the absolute production of diachrony. Levinas's identification of the trace through the enigma seals the immemoriality of what appears as the face and, through passivity, establishes a relation that does not render itself phenomenal. Yet it signifies. The enigma therefore binds the analyses of sensation and trace above. The enigma also secures the relation between that which conditions presence and that which arrives late to itself in the living-present. The enigma is dusk and dawn at once, the relation of the Same to the beyond being. It is only through this passage—the anteriority of what enters through the relation of passivity—that Levinas is able to demonstrate the immemoriality of the "object" of heterological experience and the necessity of its concernful relation to the subject. Its transcendental or constitutive status, is secured through the relation of passivity. What, then, of ethics?

The interim essays, as we have read them, show how at its origin in time consciousness is already outside of synchronic time and the constituted boundaries of simultaneity. There is a diachrony already within time and the consciousness of time. Heterology, and the way in which it indicates a structuring of its presence by the trace, allows us to retain a notion of "experience" despite the fact that the beyond being to which the subject is related in heterological experience is defined by its incommensurability with presence. This relation of passivity—this punctured intentionality—is already at the threshold of ethics. How does the face exemplify this relation? How does the face impose obligation in passivity? How does such an alteration of our understanding of the relation of separation, already at issue in *Totality and Infinity*, alter the language of the ethical? It is up to the text of *Otherwise than Being* to demonstrate how this disturbance and its constitutive function on the living-present is already the ethical relation.

Five

Impressions of Sense

Materiality in *Otherwise than Being*

> Materiality describes responsibility.
>
> —Levinas

> The original source of all affection lies in the *Ur-impression*.
>
> —Husserl

We concluded the preceding chapter with a three-fold structure: sensation, trace, and enigma, held in relation through passivity. These three elements intertwine the problem of materiality with the problem of time and relation. The explicit link between materiality and sense has been at issue for Levinas since the 1940s, moving from the general constituting function of sensibility to the general economy of exteriority. The insertion of the problem of time advances Levinas's discussion of alterity, as it yields a new language with which to speak of the enigma of the material. Time and materiality make it possible to account for the singular as such. The problematic left standing after *Totality and Infinity* indicates the necessity of this conjoining of time and the sensible. This necessity issues from the fact that it remains unclear how convincingly Levinas argues for the strict singularity of alterity on the basis of the findings of that text. The exteriority of the face, according to the account in 1961, signifies *kath auto* and not *tode ti*. This liberates manifestation from the synthetic work of the universal. The logic of sense-bestowal from the outside furthers this endeavor to radically articulate singularity, yet a gap remains in the analysis. This gap is the decisive logic of the singular that could secure the singular as enigma, and so not as an instant of a general economy of transcendental sensualism. The problem of time guarantees the enigma and decisively determines the singular as singular. The prepatory work for this is done via materiality and the trace.

To exhibit how the time structure at work in *Otherwise than Being* justifies the determination of singularity as singular, we will again turn to the problem of the production of sense. The production of sense in *Otherwise than Being*, as we shall see in detail shortly, does not produce an excessive sense, but an impoverished sense. Consider the following passage from "Beyond Intentionality," which indicates the functioning of a sense determined prior to the possession of sense by thought. Levinas asks:

> [D]oes not sense, in senseful thought, possess—perhaps prior to presence or to re-presentable presence, and to a greater extent than these—a meaning which is already determined and through which the very notion of sense comes to the mind before it is specified in terms of the formal structure of reference as it refers to a world unveiled, to a system, to an aim? (BI, 100)

To possess sense, to have it "come to mind," prior to an aim is to have sense whose origin lies outside the intentions of the ego. Levinas puts it directly when he asks in "La conscience non-intentionelle":

> [I]s intentionality the only mode of the "giving of sense" *(dona-tion de sens)*? Is the sensed *(le sensé)* always correlative with a thematization and representation?. . . Is the given seized upon only in its ideal identity? (CNI, 136)

In our reading of *Otherwise than Being*[1] we will seek the logic of this sense that comes to mind before the synthetic and synchronic work of the subject. Our exposition of this logic will concretely answer Levinas's first question from "Beyond Intentionality" in the affirmative and thus the second set of queries in the negative. We will find that the intentionality set out from the subject, that of aiming at or opening upon, is not the only mode of sense-bestowal and that sense breaks with thematization, representation, and ideality only when the privilege of presence is put in question. This putting into question of presence reveals the surprising character of this "other" sense issuing from the hither side of the Said (AE, 44/35).

The questioning of Husserl's privileging of presence and its re-presentation (cf., CNI, 134ff) requires that we think time and sense together. But for the priority of presence to be radically put in question, this questioning necessitates thinking sense-genesis in terms of what is structurally prior to presencing-presentation *(Gegenwärtigung)* and re-presencing-re-presentation *(Vergegenwärtigung)*. Sense and time, thought together in genetic analysis, produces what Levinas calls a "diachrony of truth" (DMT, 241). Thinking sense in terms of the diachronic structure of time significantly alters the prevailing conception of sense-bestowal in *Totality and Infinity*. Sense in *Otherwise than Being* is produced out of another language of absolute difference. This other absolute difference initially follows the same general logic of sense uncovered in our reading of *Totality and Infinity*. However, with the introduction of temporal language there is produced, not excessive exteriority, but what we will here call "impressional sense." The term "impressional sense" is derived from the genetic function of Husserl's *Ur-impression* exploited in Levinas's rethinking of the language of alterity.

In order to manifest the structure of this impressional sense, our exposition will have the following component parts. First, we will consider how the methodological problematic in *Otherwise than Being* insists on the primacy of relation and how the method departs from the reduction. From that insistence on relationality, we will consider what Levinas demands as both the terms of that relation *and* the status of the exposition that establishes the relation. This demand brings the genetic problematic into contact with the necessity of thinking the I and the Other as absolute singularities. The problem emerging from this contact is how one is to articulate the relational structure of that genesis while maintaining the absolute difference of the related terms. Time is the element of this relation. The relation of absolute difference is possible only through the anterior movement of passivity. How is this passivity possible? The exposed body and the impressional materiality of the face give us the tools to answer to this question. The logic of this bestowal of sense, impressional sense, will finally be situated within the logic of ethical subjectivity, the for-the-Other of the oneself.

Description and Approach

The attention given to method in *Otherwise than Being* is present only in fragments. Levinas's work works according to a definitive logic, but the particular items of that logic are left, for the most part, to the reader's appropriation of scattered and enigmatic remarks. This is not to say that *Otherwise than Being* is not a methodological work. It is to say, though, that the question of method requires considerable effort on the part of the reader. The following preliminary considerations reflect such an effort. We will contend throughout that in *Otherwise than Being* Husserl's phenomenology provides the decisive clue to the issue of both matter and method. The matter and method of the text lies in Levinas's rethinking of intentionality and sensibility in terms of time, and so the temporal element of sense produced out of absolute difference.

The methodological problem in *Otherwise than Being* commences with a familiar phenomenal beginning: the face approaches. This is a constant point of descriptive departure for Levinas's work, though the alteration of logic introduced here by time produces another language of alterity. In this familiar context, Levinas will claim that phenomenology has the right to a legitimate descriptive and structural claim, despite the fact that he will also insist that the face that approaches stands "... in contrast with a phenomenon" (AE, 155/120). The phenomenality to which the face is opposed and contrasted is that of thematization. In *Otherwise than Being*, what is problematic about thematization is that it is underpinned by the privilege of presence. The principle of evidence, the *telos* of the project of phenomenology as a self-grounding science, the re-presentational status of what is recollected, the foundational status of positionality, the *nunc stans*, and the neutrality thesis—these features of Husserl's project (and after Derrida's work this remark is almost cliché) situate the *logos* of the phenomenal squarely within the boundaries of the play of presence.

Yet there remains another side to Husserlian phenomenology: the forgotten horizons of possibility. These forgotten possibilities do not revert to possibility as such, but rather question the idealist prerogative at its source. Perhaps paradoxically, phenomenology is more than a science of the phenomenal, more than a philosophy of presence. Levinas writes that

> [p]henomenology can follow out the reversal of thematization into anarchy in the description of the approach. Then ethical language succeeds in expressing the paradox in which phenomenology finds itself abruptly thrown ... Starting with the approach, the description finds the neighbor bearing the trace of a withdrawal that orders it as a face. (AE, 155/121)

Phenomenology is this paradoxical situation. In the presencing or coming forth of the face, it finds the very structural items that already question the boundaries of presence. In the order of the face, phenomenology finds the items that already indicate the failure of presence (AE, 115/90). The *telos* of presence, as expressed in the principle of evidence, is put in question in the *experience of phenomenology*. The experience of phenomenology experiences *concretely* the demands placed on description by the approach of the Other. The letter of phenomenology is not exceeded by way of an appeal to an extra-phenomenological event. The rupture of the juridical constraints of Husserl's *practiced* method is enacted within what phenomenology itself manifests. The experience of phenomenology puts in question the *logos* of the phenomenological method, a questioning that is first initiated concretely by the anarchical "order" of the manifestation of the face. Therefore, the approach itself commands the reversal of thematization. Or, perhaps, the approach commands the recognition of the reversal that has always already made thematization possible (cf., NS, 253).

How is phenomenology possible in and after this reversal? How is it possible to think phenomenologically in the face of the paradox of anarchical manifestation? Recall here that Husserl refers to intentionality as both the *primary theme* (Hua III, 167f/199f) and the *method* of phenomenology (Hua IX, 270). Intentionality is both what phenomenology takes as its matter of investigation *and* the manner of proceeding in that programme. Thus, while maintaining the paradoxical presence of phenomenology in that which betrays the very juridical boundaries that define it as a system, Levinas will still insist on the intentional character of the analyses of *Otherwise than Being*. *Otherwise than Being* is a book about relation. It is therefore a book about the intentionality constitutive of the ethical approach of the Other. In concluding the text, Levinas gives us perhaps his clearest formal statement of its methodological underpinnings, while at the same time situating the work within the general problem of relationality:

> Our analyses claim to be in the spirit of Husserlian philosophy, whose letter has been the recall in our epoch of the permanent phenomenology, restored to its rank of being a method for all philosophy. Our presentation of notions proceeds neither by their logical decomposition, nor by their dialectical description. It remains faithful to intentional analysis, insofar as it signifies the locating of notions in the horizon of their appearing, a horizon

> unrecognized, forgotten, or displaced in the exhibition of an
> object. . . . (AE, 230–231/183)

Precisely what this horizon is—the forgotten, unrecognized, and displaced horizon—comprises the descriptive content of *Otherwise than
Being*. Rendering that content phenomenologically comprises the task
of our present reflections.

Now, it is notable that this passage distinguishes the notion of
appearance within the forgotten horizon(s) from the horizon of appearance proper to the exhibition of an object. What exactly constitutes the
mode of appearance proper to this forgotten horizon, however, is not
clear. The passage therefore states the method of the text primarily in
terms of the negative: it is neither a method of logical decomposition
nor a method of dialectics. What this passage does make clear, though,
is that the horizon in which Levinas's presentation unfolds falls within
the scope of intentional analysis. Retaining the name phenomenology
and the method of intentionality makes both possible and necessary the
fundamental relationality that orients Levinas's method. In the end, we
will find that only in the exposition of time and sensibility as the element of this relation is the forgotten horizon of relation and "appearing" fully reactivated. But at this juncture, some further remarks
concerning relationality are in order.

Relationality here, it must be said, is relation ". . . without rejoinder" (NS, 250). That is, the intentionality uncovered as the structure of
ethical subjectivity does not rejoin with its origin. It is thus not a relation of coincidence and reciprocity. It is, rather, a relation maintained
across the interval of absolute difference, an interval that separates the
ethical I from the Other who accuses concretely (AE, 212/167). Levinas
takes us to the fundamental paradox of ethical subjectivity: the question of a nonintentional intentionality. Thematization is inadequate; this
much is clear. Yet, we cannot say that the reversal of thematization in
anarchical manifestation—what is proper to the "appearing" of
alterity—simply erases the relational character of Levinas's descriptions.
Levinas writes that

> [t]he trace in which a face is ordered is not reducible to a sign:
> a sign and its relationship with the signified are synchronic in a
> theme. The approach is not the thematization of any relationship,
> but is this very relationship, which resists thematization as anar-

chic. To thematize this relation is already to lose it, to leave the absolute passivity of the self. (AE, 155/121)

The anarchical logic of the approach is the relation itself. The absolute passivity of the self is that structural moment to which we are directed for the exposition of this relation. The absolute passivity of the self, therefore, forms the core of Levinas's reflections on relationality. The main problematic Levinas faces in the absolute passivity of the self is this basic question: How do we make sense of the sense produced in this relation? Such an account must proceed without neutralizing the weight of the interval across which the relation is maintained. Levinas puts it this way: the issue is that of articulating ". . . the improbable field where the Infinite is in relationship with the finite without contradicting itself by this relationship" (DP, 123/184). This relation is the intentionality of the ethical subject. It is not simply the case that thematization is overflown by the relation of the I to alterity, but rather that the *arche* of thematization is late to the anarchy of the relation. The economy of the thematic alters and neutralizes the uneven sense of relationality produced in the ethical relation. The infinite institutes relation with the finite without losing its infinity. How is this possible? A phenomenology of excess provides the answer to this possibility.

As he has made clear in his varied reflections on its possibility, phenomenology, for Levinas, always exceeds itself. Indeed, it is perhaps the very imperative of phenomenology that this exceeding take place. This exceeding manifests in the extension of the legitimacy of phenomenology's structural claims beyond the economy of appearance. So, phenomenology is a term that Levinas will only use with caution. He must be cautious, for the term will always bring with it the specter of the *logos*. The *logos*, in turn, will always bring with it the possibility of rendering *Erlebnis* memorable, namable, identifiable, appearing, and re-presentable (AE, 54–55/42). Yet, and this is decisive, the life of lived-experience, the *Leben* of *Erlebnis*, will also entail the irreducible possibility of exceeding and rupturing, in the pre-reflective life of the subject, the synchronic immanence of the Same. Memory, identification, appearance, re-presentation—for Levinas, these depend upon the integrity of egoically constituted meaning and time. The radicality of pre-reflective life lies in the relationality initiated and instituted by *hyle* before *Abschattung*. To interrogate *hyle* prior to its preservation in memorial time is to "encounter" the "explosive and surprising character" of the *Ur-impression* as it functions prior to retention (PE, 94/212). To borrow a turn of phrase from *Totality and Infinity*, the pre-re-flexive life of the subject is the locus of the *origin prior to origin*. In the language of *Otherwise than Being*, the locus of this "life" lies in the pre-original. Phenomenology's turn to pre-reflective life entails the employ-ment of items that radically contest the *logos*. This contestation is radical precisely because the items that call the primacy of the *logos* into question contest it at its genetic root. Thus, when Levinas writes that ethical subjectivity, ". . . does not enter into that play of exposings and dissimulations which we call a phenomenon (or phenomenology, for the appearing of a phenomenon is already a discourse)" (AE, 132/104), this does not pronounce the end of thinking in and through Husserl's phenomenology. Rather, Levinas is only noting the limits of any logocratic construal of the phenomenal. Only in the exposition of the structure of the Oneself, even as this exposition breaks with the first position of auto-affection, will Levinas's work calls forth the most radical, fringe aspects of Husserl's work. This fringe operates, for Levinas, as the moment of legitimation for his language of alterity.

Can this legitimation be authorized by Husserlian phenomenol-ogy? Can exceeding phenomenology's juridical constraints on evidence be anything other than an offense to the Husserlian prerogative? In a peculiar rethinking of the phenomenological method, Levinas's re-sponse to this offense is that the phenomenological reduction itself authorizes what exceeds evidence. The teaching of the reduction, Levinas writes, is the teaching of a "permanent revolution," a revolu-tion that will "reanimate or reactivate the life that is forgotten or weakened in knowledge" (PE, 92/211). Relations of knowing, and the evidential principles entailed in that disposition, limit our descriptive tools. But to reanimate this life weakened by the epistemic prerogative is to open upon another set of tools. The reduction, we might say, concretizes intentionality. And, insofar as the concrete exceeds what is known, the reduction brings another language of description out of pre-reflective life. From this reduction that reactivates life forgotten by knowledge (and Levinas notes that this is the very "style of Husserlian phenomenology"),

> [d]ormant intentions brought back to life will open lost horizons, ever new, disturbing the theme in its identity as a result, reawakening the subjectivity of identity where it rests in its ex-perience. The subject as intuitive reason in accord, in the World,

with being, reason in the adequation of knowledge, thus finds itself brought into question. (PE, 92/211)

The path outlined by the reduction, which initially, in Husserl's hands, seems to lead toward a Cartesian ideal of certainty, also reverses the relation constitutive of sense generated by idealism. A reduction that reactivates these lost horizons ". . . would be a teaching of a sense *despite* the failure to achieve knowledge and identification, a failure affecting the norms that the identity of the Same commands" (PE, 93/211). To be sure, Husserl will produce safeguards against this failure—viz., a teleologically oriented intentionality of unfulfillment/fulfillment, which betrays, according to Levinas, a secret voluntarism. The obscurity of the pre-reflective, in Husserl's hands, bears within it elements of clarity as potentialities, and the reflective turn renders this potentiality actual.

Yet, there remains an uncontained moment revealed by the reduction. This uncontained, anarchical moment provides Levinas the decisive clue to navigating a passage outside the boundaries of Husserl's *interpretation* of the reduction. Husserl's interpretation of the reduction as the movement into and out of the pre-reflective, the movement from obscurity to clarity, initiates a forgetting of the hither-side of pre-reflective life. Levinas's movement outside or to the hither-side of the pre-reflective is commanded by the reduction itself. This movement is commanded to the extent that the reduction establishes both the limit and methodological opening of the phenomenological "system." This opening is seen in recalling the lost horizons shown, yet weakened, in Husserl's own reduction. Husserl's reduction thus works, not just to bring obscurity into clarity, but also to bring relations that relate otherwise into relief. The reduction, which signifies the Cartesian path for Husserl, is *at the same time* the movement to the hither-side of comprehension, the said, presence, the *logos*, and ontological difference (AE, 55/43). The reduction leads us to the relation without rejoinder, which is constitutive of the production of sense from out of absolute difference. The reduction, then, becomes in Levinas's hands the path *from* the Said (presence, clarity), or the intermingling of the Saying and the Said (presence/absence, clarity/obscurity), *to* the unraveling of the Said through explicating how the Said is late to itself and conditioned across another time.[2]

To construe the reduction in this manner is no longer to end with Husserl (PE, 97/214). It is to begin with Husserl in order to exceed the letter of his work. The movement of the reduction is for Levinas always the reactivation of lost horizons. What is recollected in this reactivation? What history is told? The movement in the reduction recalled by Levinas "remembers," not the passage from this initial moment of pre-reflective unclarity to understanding (as this is the movement of Husserl's idealism—see PE, 97/214), but the passage from pre-reflective life to what constitutes that life from outside, beyond accomplished egoic life. The reduction is thus a movement to the hither-side of the living-present. It is the movement to absolute passivity and diachronic time, which opposes itself to the absolute activity and synchronic time of idealism from out of the very matter that motivates idealism—the pre-reflective life of the subject. The reduction is not reducible to the bracketing of a being; this sort of bracketing would be a clear offense to the Levinasian problematic. Instead, the reduction is the methodological point of access to the originary—or, on Levinas's rendering, the *pre-original*. Thus, Levinas will write that "[t]he movement back to the Saying is the phenomenological reduction in which the indescribable is described" (AE, 69/53).[3] Precisely how this movement in the reduction may claim to hold a first position—i.e., may disclaim its affiliation with activity and freedom—is explained by another kind of sense-genesis, whose logic is captured in the temporal analysis of impressional sense. But that gets us ahead of ourselves. Let us first consider the "terms" of the relation we have begun to articulate(the component parts of the Oneself as for-the-other. Once the terms of this relation are made clear, the final purchase of this other sense-genesis will be clear.

Singularity and Subjectivity

Our reading of the relation constitutive of ethical subjectivity as for-the-other in *Otherwise than Being* must first contextualize the set of concerns guiding Levinas's analyses. This contextualization helps us to gain some clarity regarding what is at stake in Levinas's reworking of the Husserlian notion of the living-present. To this end, let us first consider some issues left standing in *Totality and Infinity*.

At the conclusion of our reading of *Totality and Infinity* above, we indicated some shortcomings in the analysis of the logic of sense-bestowal from the outside inherent in that text. This set of shortcomings provides a context for both the differences between and strands of continuity in *Totality and Infinity* and *Otherwise than Being*. We will revisit the importance of these differences and continuities at the conclusion of the present chapter, with the findings of our reading of *Otherwise than Being* in view. First, though, a brief review of the problem of singularity handed down from the logic explicated in *Totality and Infinity*, as well as an initial indication of how that same problem is taken up in *Otherwise than Being*.

Our insistence on reading *Totality and Infinity* as a book about sense allowed us to recover the transcendental, generative function of the anteriority of the posterior. Exteriority precedes the spontaneity of consciousness. The materiality of the exterior therefore signifies otherwise than the materiality derived from the labor of thematization. Signification is reconceived by Levinas on the model of manifestation *kath auto*, and not *tode ti*. Now, Levinas will make clear in *Otherwise than Being* how manifestation, as opposed to thematization, does not submit to the constituted time of the Same. In *Totality and Infinity*, however, Levinas's conception of time is still dominated by notions of the instant and futurity passed down from his work in *Existence and Existents* and *Time and the Other*. The very logic of sense-bestowal from the outside renders the ego late to itself, as it finds itself already constituted through the relation of passivity. The time of the ego is inadequate to the time of the constitutional work of materiality. This much is evident in the logic of *Totality and Infinity* in the figure of the transcendental function of sensibility, but the exposition remains limited by the temporal language within which this passivity labors. The analysis is left wanting.

The question following *Totality and Infinity*, and we have seen this in the previous chapter, becomes how to articulate this lateness, this genesis from the outside, and therefore this transitional movement in and through passivity. Phenomenology, in Husserl's hands, has always insisted on describing passivity in terms of the primordial structure of time. Levinas adopts this insistence. The legitimacy of Husserl's demand that passivity be temporally described issues not simply from the authority of Husserl's pen, but from the very demands of the language of origin and creation. Origin and creation, as affects producing the ego from the outside, require, in order to be rendered appropriately, a diachronic language of time and alterity. The lateness of the subject to itself infuses an irreducible absence at the origin of self-presence. The demand put to descriptive language is quite direct: the language of presence must be put out of order. To be sure, the order of presence is disrupted by the very logic of sense-bestowal from the outside in

Totality and Infinity. This much is clear from the language of excess that dominates that text. Nevertheless, it is unclear how successful instant and futurity can be in fully disrupting presence, as it is unclear how adequately excess displaces the language of experience and/or empiricism. The language of singularity and the logic of a reversed sense-bestowal can only be maintained in this full disruption, so a more decisive language must be developed to contest even Levinas's notion of a radical empiricism.

Thus, the gap in the analyses of *Totality and Infinity* obtains in the failure on Levinas's part to conceive the logic of a reversed sense-bestowal temporally. The genesis of sense originates in the materiality of the sensible. This tells us about the character of Levinas's transcendental sensualism. But how can this sensualism relate across the interval of separation? And, perhaps even more decisively, how can this interval rest assured of its integrity? How does it not collapse under the weight of a project of teleological recuperation? What protects separation against the specter of the teleological aim? The time structure of *Otherwise than Being* secures this separation and seals its interval as a refusal of closure.

Ethics is wholly a matter of the relation of singularities across an interval. When understood on the relational model of intentionality structured from the outside, the question of the singular, already at issue in *Totality and Infinity*, presents the structural item in which the mutation of the intentional subject into the ethical subject of the for-the-other—of the Other into the Same or of alterity into identity—"happens." The aim of *Otherwise than Being* is nothing other than the exposition of the structure of the for-the-Other (AE, 152/119). Ethical subjectivity requires a two-fold sense of singularity: the irreplaceable singularity that "lies in me" (AE, 195/153) or the ipseity of the I and the singularity of the Other who concerns me or *illeity* (AE, 15/12). Levinas's analyses develop the language within which one can legitimately speak of both the ipseity of the I without *arche* (AE, 145/114) and the recurrence to oneself that does not betray the subject's identity as already put in question (AE, 146/145). The analysis also seeks a language within which the alterity of the Other can both concern me and signal itself as a singularity more "extreme" than designation as *tode ti* (AE, 109/86). Despite the radicality of both senses of singularity (i.e., their refusal of universality and sublation), they nevertheless hold in a relation without rejoinder. This relation without rejoinder, as it is called in "Notes sur le sens," must be conceived as a one-way relation.

Levinas makes this link clear in "Language and Proximity" when he writes that the ethical relation marks a *reversal* of subjectivity. This reversal is literally the inversion of the ecstatic logic of relation that understands intentionality in terms of an "aiming at" or "opening upon." As Levinas will write in a note to *Otherwise than Being*, ". . . the ego obsessed by all others, supporting all others, is an inversion of intentional ecstasy" (AE, 110n24/192n24). The mutation of the relations of opening and aiming into the relations of proximity and obsession is ultimately the movement from the knowing subject to the responsible subject. The reversal of subjectivity in its ethical relation with alterity is the transformation of the knowing subject

> into a subjectivity that enters *into contact* with a singularity, excluding identification in the ideal, excluding thematization and representation—an absolute singularity, as such unrepresentable . . . The precise point at which this mutation of the intentional into the ethical occurs, and occurs continually, at which the approach *breaks through* consciousness, is the human skin and face. Contact is tenderness and responsibility. (LeP, 225/116)

The invocation of contact again requires our return to the now familiar problem of how sensibility decisively alters intentionality and sense. Sensibility, which was such an important part of *Totality and Infinity*, is described in *Otherwise than Being* as the site of the relation of singular to singular; it is that site where "[o]ne can show the latent birth of justice in signification" (AE, 89/71).

Thus, in addition to the necessity of the purity of both the singularity for whom I am concerned and the singularity of who I am in this concern, there is also the correlative problem of indicating ". . . the element in which this *concerning* occurs" (AE, 15/13). The problem of the element in which concerning occurs is nothing other than the problem of intentionality. The structure of relationality as the element of (ethical) concern cannot manifest a conjoining relation of sublation or subsumption. The issue, rather, is necessarily how one may articulate a relation that is one of absolute separation, and therefore a relation composed of absolute difference. For Levinas, it is a question of what kind of language is able to maintain, without resolution by a third thing, something that appears to reflection as a contradiction. The genetic problematic answers to this demand. Only under the rubric of the genetic can we say that the beyond being signifies *before* the event of contradiction in reflection (AE, 198–199/156), for only this rubric can provide the language of the *before*. That is to say, the genetic problematic, when put under the Levinasian, intersubjective reduction, rests ultimately on the diachronic time of the interval—the contradiction of two times in proximity. This time-structure becomes the very element of the relation without rejoinder, and so it is able both to sustain a contradiction and articulate the sense of beforeness that defines the signification of the beyond being. Materiality produces this diachrony, this contradiction. What is produced in this diachronic relation is what we would like to call *impressional sense*. In Levinas's rendering, the genetic character of this impressional sense delivers the creation and legitimation of an ethical subjectivity that is "an orphan by birth" (AE, 133/105). The orphaned creature called the ethical subject literally embodies the contradiction of the necessity of both absolute difference *and* relationality. Separated by the interval of infinity from the source of its birth, ethical subjectivity is orphaned as the very condition of its being. Absence of the "parent" is separation from the impressional origin of self-presence in the ethical relation. The sense, this *impressional* sense, of the orphaned subject is the sense of the subject's self-presence in moral consciousness.

Our reading of *Totality and Infinity* has, of course, already discovered the genetic aspect of the problem of sense in the language of creation and origin. The singularity of the Other in *Otherwise than Being* and related essays has this same productive function. Indeed, Levinas will speak, with Husserl, of the figure of a creation "without seed" to characterize the productive activity of the *Ur-impression*. This productive work is described by Levinas's through a reconstruction or restaging of the passage from the sleeping ego to wakefulness: the awakening of the Same by the Other. Levinas's essays "De la conscience à la veille" (1974), "Philosophie et éveil" (1977), and the concluding remarks of "La pensée de l'être et la question de l'autre" (1975), all explicate the terms of awakening, namely, the transition from sleep to wakefulness, underscoring their significance for articulating the otherwise than being. Awakening, which ultimately leads us to the question of time, announces, beneath Husserl's understanding of its logic, what Levinas calls the denucleation of the subject. The denucleation of the subject brings us to the logic of movement of the awakening of the subject, as for-the-Other, by the neighbor.[4] Awakening is already ethical, insofar as, when fully articulated in terms of the intertwining of materiality and time, it inscribes the Other in the Same. As we shall see later, this inscription makes possible the logic of substitution.

Awakening, which puts into question the Same by the Other, grounds the subject "beyond knowledge, the condition of philosophy" and Husserl's thought, despite its idealist pretensions, attests to this rupturing affect/effect (PE, 98/215). In the *Phenomenological Psychology* lectures, Husserl writes that awakening happens before the play of the *hylé-morphe* correlation, that is, before life manifests the world to the I. The I can be ". . . awake for these or those objects and in various ways," and thereby assume its positionality and constituting modality of relation. But, Husserl writes,

> . . . it can also be a dull, sleeping I. That is, nothing stands out either immanently or transcendently, everything has flown together indistinguishably. Then neither is the I itself in its way a prominent subject pole . . . The sleeping I in its peculiarity is of course revealed only from the perspective of the awake I by a reflection of a peculiar sort which reaches back and seizes it. More closely considered, sleep has sense only in relation to waking and implies a potentiality for awakening. (Hua IX, 209/160)

The dull and sleeping I, then, is the potential ego of the yet-to-be-I of pre-reflective life. This will become extremely important in our consideration of the function of the *Ur-impression* in the flow of time. However, it is at this point significant that Husserl here stumbles on something quite radical—the enigma of the constitution of the I from out of pre-reflective life—but nevertheless reinstitutes a conservative gesture in his final remarks on the implication of a potentiality in sleeping life.[5] The constitution of the I from out of sleeping life renders awakening as the passage or bridge from nonegoic to egoic life. This is a passage that, on a more radical reading of the issue, implicates a non-I at the generative source of the I. What prompts the I to awakening? Something other than the I startles it to wakefulness. Further, if the transitional moment of passage conditions the wakeful life of the subject, then must not active and accomplished egoic life be inseparable from traces of the passive, sleeping ego lying at its origin?

This transition or passage imparts an irreducible impurity to wakeful life. Such impurity is inherent in the very question of genesis, where, if we question the status of potentiality in sleeping life, we also question the purity of self-presence and any putatively secure self-identity. With precisely this passage from *Phenomenological Psychology* in mind, Levinas writes that the passage of awakening entails a "scission of identity" that is "otherwise than being." This scission inscribes an irreducible difference ". . . into the heart of the Same, which pierces the structure of being while inspiring and animating it" (DCV, 50). Awakening is not a twisting free from pre-reflective life. Rather, the hitherside of this pre-reflective life, marked by absolute difference, animates and inspires accomplished subjectivity and its sense of unicity.

Thus, in reading Husserl's account of awakening, Levinas is concerned with the dilemma awakening poses for the problem of self-presence. For, as he makes evident in *Otherwise than Being*, the question of intentionality as an aiming that begins with the ego is inextricably bound up with auto-affection. "[S]ubjectivity taken as intentionality," Levinas writes, "is founded on auto-affection as an auto-revelation, the source of an impersonal discourse" (AE, 142/111). To this auto-affection and impersonality, Levinas wants to oppose *hetero-affection* (AE, 155/121), the concrete and "personal" relation with the Other that ". . . precedes the auto-affection of certainty" (AE, 152/119). Hetero-affection is a relation that begins in absolute difference and, in the final analysis, maintains this difference on the basis of the diachronic time of ethical subjectivity. The exposition of the structure of the one-self as ethical demands the relation of hetero-affection because, as Levinas writes, "the oneself cannot form itself; it is already formed with absolute passivity" (AE, 132-33/104).

Hetero-affection, this affection from the outside, is traumatic in its awakening of the sleepful ego. This hetero-affective awakening takes place in what Levinas calls a passivity more passive than passivity. From out of this radical passivity comes the truth of the reduction: the reversal of the constitution of the subject. Levinas writes:

> But isn't the Self that emerges and in which the identification of the *hyle* with itself is broken in its turn an identification of the Same? We think that Reduction reveals its true sense and the sense of the subjective that it allows to be signified in its final phase of intersubjective reduction. The subjectivity of the subject shows up

there in the traumatism of awakening, despite the gnoseological interpretation that, for Husserl, ultimately characterizes the element of spirit. (PE, 95/213)

The trauma of this awakening awakens the ego, not just from its sleeping state of passivity, but even further from the dogmatic slumber induced by the privileged position attributed to the transcendental ego. It is an intersubjective reduction that yields the structure of

> [a]n awakening that begins with the Other—who is Other—who, incessantly, puts into question the priority of the Same . . . An awakening and sobering by the Other that does not let the Same alone and through which the Same from the outset resembles the living and, while it sleeps, is exceeded. It is not an *experience* of inequality posited in the theme of an understanding, it is the very event of *transcendence* as life. (PE, 96/214)

This distinction introduced by Levinas, between the experience of inequality or noncoincidence as a theme and the event of transcendence as life, is crucial. It brings us to the crux of the genetic problematic. Under the genetic problematic, transcendence is conceived as ". . . palpably prior to any *position* of the subject and to any perceived or assimilated content," a transcendence in or awakening of the life of a subject who is ". . . already unsettled by the Infinite" (PE, 98/215). Egoic life is exceeded in its sleeping state, but not in a wakeful moment where insufficient powers of intuition are confronted with an excessive theme. If Levinas's contention was simply that egoic life is exceeded in its theme, then one could say the analysis would be operating at the levels of *Abschattungen* and unfulfilled intentions. Under the rubric of the genetic, however, the accomplished life of the wakeful ego has already been exceeded at the very moment of its identification in and out of pre-reflective life. Identity is generated in this awakening, but not by way of a dormant sameness. It is generated from absolute difference.

The methodological function of the intersubjective reduction is significant, as it reminds us of Levinas's reworking of Husserl's genetic program in the *V. Cartesian Meditation*. In the reduction to the *Eigensphäre* (which initiates the account of intersubjectivity for Husserl), Husserl begins with a nonegoic sense of life from out of which the I-ness of the I and the Otherness of the Other in relation to the I—the intentionality of this relation—is constituted. At the primal level in which the analysis begins, the ego, for Husserl, is only an ego in a metaphorical sense.[6] The I only becomes a unique I on the basis of the appearance of the body of another ego. Thus, the intersubjective site of the reduction brings us to the genesis of the I from out of a pre-egoic sphere, a transcendence in life that precedes the life of the theme. Levinas identifies this as the task of the reduction in the *Cartesian Meditations* when he writes that the

> [i]ntersubjective reduction is not simply directed against the "so-lipsism" of the "primordial sphere" and the relativism of truth that would result from it . . . The explication of the sense that a self other than my self has for me—for my primordial self—describes the way in which the Other tears me from my hypostasy, from the here, at the heart of being or at the center of the world where, privileged and in this sense primordial, I posit myself. (PE, 95/213)

If understood under the genetic problematic, and thus as a tracing back to an originary tearing, this tearing of the I from its hypostasy is neither destructive nor degenerate. Rather, Levinas will write, ". . . in this tearing, the ultimate sense of my 'me-ness' is revealed" (PE, 95/213). This revelatory moment exhibits the original, primal sense of subjectivity, as well as the genuine sense of the reduction as an intersubjective reduction—what Levinas calls the "final (i.e., most primordial) phase" of the phenomenological method (PE, 95/213). This "sense of subjectivity" is a theme that will occupy us throughout the present chapter, but it is important here to underline the genetic movement of both Levinas's reactivation of the reduction and the structure of the awakening it reveals.

Levinas's turn to the structure of awakening thus constitutes a turn to the pre-reflective genesis of subjectivity. This genesis ultimately identifies the origin of the identity of the I as a nonintentional, generative source that endows sense through the anterior relation of passivity (CNI, 138ff). The genetic character of this nonintentional origin of the subject is emphasized by Levinas in the distinction of pure passivity from the description of consciousness as caught or seized by passivity. The seizing upon of consciousness by passivity, the infection of the ego, presupposes an I already formed that is compromised by the upsurge of passivity. Infection is mixture, and the infection of an already formed I by passivity is thus a mixture of the active with the passive. Pure passivity, on the other hand, is a one-way giving of sense wholly unmediated by activity. The giving of sense from a nonintentional "item" does not eliminate the issue of relationality, but rather reverses the relational direction of its flow of sense. Absolute passivity is anchored in one source: the resistance of materiality as transcendence to identity, a resistance more ancient than being (NS, 255). The resistance of what moves across absolute passivity is not the resistance of the world characteristic of descriptions in existential-phenomenology, e.g., Scheler and Merleau-Ponty. The difference Levinas is after is captured by the genetic account of the intertwining of alterity and unicity. Further, this identification of passivity as the anterior item in the awakening of the subject makes it necessary, in Levinas's words, ". . . to put in question experience as the source of every sense" (DMT, 241). Experience is the play of activity and passivity. Sense, however, is not reducible to the economy of exhibition (DMT, 241). This is decisive. Sense may be generated otherwise. The structure of awakening already indicates how the logic of this *Sinngebung* works without the economy of exhibition. How is this movement outside experience, and thus to the pre-original origin of this passage named awakening, to be articulated? To answer this, we turn to how Levinas appropriates the most radical elements of the phenomenological conception of the living-present.

Awakening to the Other

The logic of awakening in many ways mimics the logic of sense-bestowal in *Totality and Infinity*. But, the logic of sense-bestowal in *Totality and Infinity*, as we have seen, remains underdeveloped. The structure of the passage from the Other to the Same in that text, a passage of constitution and donation, does not yet have the temporal language necessary to maintain the gap or interval that qualifies the relation as asymmetrical and as a reversed intention. Also, it remains unclear how successfully Levinas has broken free of the language of presence. So too, then, it remains to be seen how awakening can be twisted free of the language of presence and thus how awakening can name the unmediated inscription of the Other in the Same. To alter this logic of sense-bestowal and awakening—i.e., to render the terms necessary for a legitimated language of alterity that fully questions the privilege of presence—Levinas turns to Husserl's account of time. Levinas's reading of Husserl's account in *Otherwise than Being* must be read under the rubric of genesis. Such a reading allows the logic emergent from that reading to impact the general problem of sense-bestowal directly. In his reading of Husserl's *temporal* account of genesis, Levinas will exhibit the necessary mutation of the reduction to Absolute Subjectivity into the reduction to Responsible Subjectivity. This mutation, as we shall see, is a self-mutation on the part of phenomenology. The movement from an Absolute to a Responsible subject is nothing other than the movement from an impersonal temporal flux to a facing materiality lending itself to time from outside the living-present. This "lending" is the interruption of the flow of time that first figures or describes my awakening to obligation.

For Husserl, the primordial form of consciousness is the original flux of time. This primordial consciousness—absolute subjectivity—is composed of the originary items of the living-present. It is in the living-present, as Levinas notes, that "Husserl finds the genesis of every being and of every sense" (DMT, 124; also NS, 237). In Husserl's phenomenology, this turn to time has a double-effect. First, it secures the ground up from which sense is constituted. Second, and more controversial, the turn to time appears to institute an irreducible absence into the heart of presence, a trace of a fundamental sleep into the wakeful life of the subject. The living-present is simultaneously the site of both the closure and opening of the system of idealism. The closure of the system, indicated in the representational structure of the sense of absolute consciousness, putatively secures ideality across difference. The opening of the system, indicated in the nonmodified structure of the sense of impressional consciousness, discovers an alterity at the very heart of the Same. In its awakening transition from sleeping consciousness—the consciousness immersed in pre-reflective life—to wakeful life—the active life of the constituting ego—Husserl's phenomenology already points beyond itself toward the outside of its origin.

This moment of awakening that initiates a temporal articulation ultimately interests Levinas. The genetic problem of this temporal articulation of awakening situates us in the primordial flux of time. This is most decidedly not the time of accomplished subjectivity. To be sure, Levinas writes in *Otherwise than Being* that "phenomenality . . . cannot be separated from time" (AE, 39/31), but the phenomenality subjected to time provides only the *clue* to the deeper structure occupying Levinas's reading of Husserl. The alterity that time comes to articulate is not the time statically constitutive of an object of perception. It therefore cannot be understood on the basis of the temporality of a phenomenal object. Rather, primordial time, in both Husserl's and Levinas's hands, addresses the more general question of identity, as well as the specific question of the genesis of the subject across time. This is already implicit in the account of the intersubjective reduction above, wherein Levinas maintains that the awakening revealed in that reduction is an awakening induced by and from the Other. The awakening revealed in the intersubjective reduction bestows the very I-ness of the I, set out from the Other and given to the Same. Thus, the temporality of fulfilled/unfulfilled intentions appropriate to the logic of the phenomenal is inappropriate to the genetic matter at issue. The issue of genesis demands that the absolute structure of time be called to the fore. Hence we cannot call forth that conception of time applicable to perceptual experience. The language of alterity in *Otherwise than Being* will bear empirical marks (sensation, materiality, skin), but the affect/effect of that empiricality is wholly transcendental. Intertwining empirical language with the transcendental prerogative produces both the necessity and authority of the genetic problematic.

This brings us to a fundamental distinction already found in Husserl's reflections on time. The time, the living-present, from which phenomenality cannot be separated, is split by a decisive distinction, noted by John Brough.[7] This is the distinction between the temporality of immanent temporal objects and the absolute flow of consciousness (see Hua X, §§34-38). The problem of the temporality of objects may tempt the reader of Levinas, insofar as the presentation of the body of the Other, according to the *V. Cartesian Meditation*, entails an irreducible analogizing apprehension in which the Other is never fully given. The temporality of the perceptual object *could* yield the ground of the heretofore unfulfilled intention appropriate to the encounter with the Other person. However, this is clearly not the central task of *Otherwise than Being*, even in its confrontation with Husserl. Rather, Levinas wants to interrogate what in *Dieu, la mort et le temps* he calls the "pre-history of the I" (cf., DMT, 153, 202). The pre-history of the I, as he remarks in a footnote to *Dieu, la mort, et le temps*, is already indicated in *Totality and Infinity*, but Levinas explicitly entrusts writing this pre-history to

Otherwise than Being (DMT, 202n2). To write this pre-history is to write a history that cannot assume a narrative form. The very "pre-ness" of a pre-history demands that such a writing break with reminiscence and memory (DMT, 153). Levinas iterates this same point in *Otherwise than Being*, by demanding that the text not speak in a narrative or epic voice (AE, 16/13). For, as he has made clear elsewhere, the narrative structure of sense gathers the diachrony of time into presence and representation (DR, 171/105), which, in turn, renders diachrony nothing but a mere privation of synchrony (NS, 238). This history demands a language of transcendence as the manner of writing pre-history, a language capable of animating presence or the Said with absence or the Saying. This language would therefore not be the narrative account of experience, which would only neutralize the terms at issue (PE, 98/215). It is on this basis, then, that Levinas insists we put in question the notion that experience and its immanent contents yield the source of every sense. Questioning experience as presence thus leads us to the pre-history of an I irreducibly absent from the self-presence and history of experience. To interrogate this pre-history, Levinas's analysis takes up the structure of the living-present. Levinas finds, however, not a seamless flow, but an already fractured scene of transition into the wakeful play of retention and protention from out of the material moment of passive genesis. The language of the pre-history of the I is the language of materiality, absence, and diachrony—that is, the ethical language that describes responsibility.[8]

We can say, then, that Levinas's turn to the problem of passivity and materiality aims at negotiating a passage out of the synchronic living-present toward the rupturing that produces diachrony. This turn to time brings into focus what Husserl considers the originary forms constitutive of the problem of the genesis of sense. Husserl makes this explicit in *Formal and Transcendental Logic*, where he writes that

> [t]he all-embracing essential form *(Wesensform)* of intentional genesis, to which all other forms relate back, is that of the constitution of immanent temporality, which governs each concrete life of consciousness . . . [A] life of consciousness is inconceivable apart from life given originally in an essentially necessary form of facticity, in the form of the universal temporality wherein each lived-experience of consciousness *(Bewußtseinserlebnis)* has its identical temporal locus, which it receives throughout the stream-

ing changes in its typically modified manners of givenness within a living-present. . . . (Hua XVII, 318/318)

The very *leben* of *Erlebnis* is initiated through time. This time is the space of the genesis of life, a genesis that springs from a necessary form of facticity. Thus, the life of consciousness that comes to bear the power and freedom of constitution is generated from a form of facticity given through and across time. Indeed, Husserl goes on to say later, in the text just quoted, that every item given in time in the mode of consti-tuted modification ". . . refers us back . . . to its absolute primitive mode—to a consciousness that, to be sure, becomes modified forthwith but is not itself a modification" (Hua XVII, 318/318–319).

This originary form of the element of genesis is Absolute Subjec-tivity. Absolute Subjectivity is conceived as the pure flux of time, the flux of time that is structurally prior to the positionality of the idealist ego and out of which the terms of intentional relations of constitution are generated. Absolute subjectivity is the "universal peculiarity of all lived-experience" (Hua III, 161/192). It is an "enigma *(Rätsel)*" not taken up explicitly in *Ideas I*, but altogether presupposed.[9] In a now famous passage from his time-consciousness lectures, Husserl writes:

> This flow is something we speak of in conformity with what is constituted, but it is not "something in objective time." It is *absolute subjectivity* and has the absolute properties of something to be designated *metaphorically* as "flow"; of something that originates in a point of actuality, in a primal source point, "the now," and so on. In the actuality-experience, we have the primal source-point and a continuity of moments of reverberation. For all of this, we lack names. (Hua X, 75/79)

Absolute subjectivity is the flow of time. This flow is not in objective time, which is to say it is not the time manifest in a particular object of perception, and thus is neither subject to, nor an instantiation of, a higher-level structure of time. We lack names for this flow precisely because it is that originary, pre-reflective flow out of which the very structures that render naming possible must emerge. In this flow, there is not yet a positional I from which to divide time and estab-lish identities. Absolute subjectivity is not a perceptual act. It is, rather, pre-actional.

There is in Husserl's account a significant ambiguity regarding the status of the ego in the reduction to absolute subjectivity. On the one hand, the absolute flow of absolute subjectivity is designated as impersonal and therefore pre-egoic. On the other hand, the absolute flow is characterized as something constantly watched over by absolute consciousness.[10] There is much at stake in this ambiguity: the pre-egoic appearance of the absolute flow already decenters or displaces the ego-pole at its source, yet Husserl will still seek to smuggle in some form of consciousness not subject to time. The time-consciousness lectures term this originary, pre-egoic flow the "flow of flows" and the "subjectivity" designated by this term renders the idealistic work of constitution or act(s) of giving sense secondary. This work, Husserl writes, is "not consciousness in the original sense" (Hua X, 292/303). This aspect of absolute subjectivity is supported by Gadamer's account of Husserl's C21 manuscript on time, where Gadamer writes that ". . . the special feature of the primal level [is] that in no sense can one speak any longer of an activity through which its ontic sense comes about as a valid unity."[11] Absolute subjectivity, then, is ". . . the transcendental stream of consciousness itself" out of which the I is passively constituted.[12] Regarding the temporalization of the monad, the concrete I/ego (cf., Hua I, 102ff/67ff), in the "primal modality of the present *(Gegenwart)*" (Hua XV, 666), Husserl writes the following:

> The Absolute is nothing other than absolute temporalization *(absolute Zeitigung)* and its explication *(Auslegung)* as Absolute that I discover directly as my standing-streaming primordiality is *already a temporalization,* a temporalization of this into something primally existing. And so the absolute sum of monads, that is, the primordiality of all monads, *only is by virtue of temporalization.*[13]

In the flow of flows, I encounter my position, my standing in the stream of time, as having already been temporalized. On Husserl's own account of the ego's reflection on the flow of time, the I finds itself late to this temporalization at the very moment in which I come to see my position as a monad in reflection. The enigma of this pre-egoic flow should not fail to remind us of Hyppolite's comments at the conference in Royaumont regarding a "subjectless transcendental field," a conference where Levinas was both a speaker and participant.[14] The *absoluteness* of this absolute temporalization marks it as an uncontaminated, pre-egological flow. Primordial time is radically, unmediatedly anonymous.

This is not, of course, the only way Husserl will conceive the primordial flow of time. In his remarks on the structure of the pre-personal flux, Husserl will cast the primordial flow of time in the role of the constitutional origin of egoic life. In playing this role, the primordial flow does not threaten the first position of the I. On Husserl's other account, and this betrays a conservative gesture, this origin of egoic life—the pre-egological flow—is already constituted as a flow by a wakeful and watchful absolute consciousness. If this flow is watched over by an absolute consciousness, portrayed by Husserl as atemporal, then the ground of the ego is already secured above the time flow of the temporal subject, above the subject subjected to time.[15] In this regard, Husserl will write that "[s]ubjective time becomes constituted in the absolute timeless consciousness which is not an object" (Hua X, 112/117). Or, with regard to this constitution, Husserl will also claim that all contents—that is, all that emerges from out of the flow—are ". . . contents of the primal consciousness that constitutes temporal objects and that in this sense is not itself content or object in phenomenological time" (Hua X, 84/89). Thus, the absolute subjectivity conceived by Husserl has a double structure. It is at once a pre-egoic subjection to the flow and a constitution of the flow from a nontemporal position. The flow both subjects the subject and is subjected by the subject. This double structure leads Husserl to write in the *Cartesian Meditations* that the ego is both ". . . the active and affective subject of consciousness" (Hua I, 100/66). The ego is both radically active and radically passive, which is to say, simultaneously determined as unmodified activity and unmodified passivity. This produces a provocative tension in the Husserlian account of the status of the ego. Adjudicating this tension will prove decisive for Levinas. Levinas's adjudication begins inside the component parts of Husserl's account of time, so we need first pause to outline the items constitutive of primordial time.

Although we lack all names for this absolute and impersonal flow, we do not lack a grasp of its essential constitutive items: impression, retention, and protention. These three essential items comprise the lived phenomenological Now and so produce the absolute element within which the Now wells up. It is, of course, well known that this phenomenological Now is not the atomic Now of linear, measurable clock time. Rather, when thought within the boundaries of primordial time, the

Now is essentially and inextricably extended into past and future. Borrowing a term from William James, Husserl characterizes his conception of the Now as one with irreducible "fringes" (cf., Hua X, 151/155). In this sense, the Now "is not," insofar as the Now cannot make sense without an appeal to the component parts "pastness" and "futurity." As Husserl writes in one of the *Beilagen* to the *Lectures*:

> [W]e have as the essential modes of time-consciousness: "sensation" as presentation (making originally present), and the retention and protention that are combined with it essentially but that also attain to self-sufficiency . . . [and] the positing re-presentation *(die setzende Vergegenwärtigung)* (memory), the co-re-presentation *(Mitgegenwärtigung)*, and renewed re-presentation *(Wiedergegenwärtigung)* (protention). (Hua X, 107/112)

Husserl's introduction of the *positing* function of re-presentation becomes significant when Levinas purges Husserl's phenomenology of certain limiting presuppositions. But, for now, this much at least can be said of the structure of the living-present: the living-present is composed of the complex of modifications produced in the three-fold function of re-presentation—origin, Now, and future. What is called the "Now" in the phenomenological present of lived-experience points to the past as that from which it has arisen and the future as that toward which it aims. The Now ". . . is precisely only an ideal limit, something abstract, which can be nothing by itself" (Hua X, 40/42).

The function of protention is quite straightforward. Protention designates the intentionality, subjected to time, proper to the anticipatory mode of relation. Protention takes up what is held in memory and throws it toward the future in act(s) of anticipation. The welling up of the Now, as it emerges within the intentional life of lived-experience, is constituted in part by this orientation toward the future. Futurity, in turn, is itself rooted in a definitive interrelation with what has passed and is retained (sedimented) in memory. Protentive intentions are built upon retention. Taking up of what has passed, what is retained, in acts of anticipation gives the flowing Now a temporal thickness.

The relation between retention or pastness, and the impressional sensation, however, is considerably more complicated. Retention is produced by the impression and thus what is retained is itself only a modification of what is impressed. On this, Husserl is precise:

> [W]e teach the *a priori* necessity that a corresponding perception,
> or a corresponding primal impression, precede the retention . . .
> [E]very retention intrinsically refers back to an impression. (Hua
> X, 33–34/35–36; see also 311–319/323–330)

The primal impression is that source from which any durationally
present and thematized object arises. It is the source of that retentional
complex which, along with the protentive taking up of what is retained, composes the phenomenologically temporal present. Husserl
writes that

> [t]he "source-point" with which the "production" of the endur-
> ing object begins is a primal impression. This consciousness is in
> a state of constant change . . . [W]hen the consciousness of this
> [e.g.] tone-now, the primal impression, passes over into retention,
> this retention itself is a now in turn, something actually existing.
> (Hua X, 29/30–31)

This originary "source-point" hands over the content to lived-experience, as both a primary sensory impressional presence and, further,
subsequent to its constitutional modification, a retentive and recollective
pole in the temporal nexus of the living-present. "[E]ach later retention,"
Husserl remarks, "is not only continual modification that has arisen
from primal impression; each is also continual modification of all earlier
continuous modifications of that same initial point" (Hua X, 30/31). The
structure of the flow of time is nothing other than the mixture of retention and protention in the phenomenological Now. This Now, to the
extent that it emerges out of the retentional/protentional nexus, is
possible only on the basis of the productive work of the primal impression. Hence, the primal impression is the originary source-point and
the generative condition for the possibility of lived-experience itself
(Hua X, 66–70/69–72, 99–101/105–107, 133/136).

Now, what interests Levinas here is the dual function of this *Ur-
impression* in Husserl's understanding of the living-present. To set the
stage for Levinas's work on the *Ur-impression*, we should pause to note
three aspects of this account of the structure of the flow. First, Husserl
will characterize the movement from impressional consciousness to
retentional consciousness as a "passing over." Second, Husserl says that
the modificational activity of retention "has arisen" from the impression.

And, third, Husserl considers the impression productive of the retentional complex to be a singular, "same initial point," which secures the purity of the impression as itself unique and uncontaminated by the retentive work of memory. To anticipate what is to come, Levinas's reading of Husserl's account of absolute subjectivity will show

1. that this "passing over" already indicates a diachronic structure of time;

2. that the having "arisen" from the impression names the material and temporal movement of awakening;

3. that the "same initial point" that the impression manifests signals the absolute singularity and non-iterability of the alterity that produces the Same.

When this reading is completed, the mutation of absolute subjectivity into responsible subjectivity is accomplished. To initiate this mutation, however, Levinas must first purge Husserl's reflections of the prejudicial impurities that compromise the radicality of Husserl's account of genesis.

In Husserl's account of absolute subjectivity, we have seen the tension between the flow that constitutes and the flow that is constituted. Though this tension is, on the face of it, undecidable, Husserl's phenomenology always decides for the constituted flow. Despite the fact that this source point, on Husserl's own account, lies outside of the nexus of retentions and protentions (and the succession of modified Now points), it nevertheless remains, within the Husserlian prerogative, *recuperable* through a series of reflective unfoldings of the retentional complex. This is to say, despite the fact that it itself is essentially non-modified, "... the primal impression is nonetheless not impressed without a consciousness" (AE, 41/33; also, Hua X, 29/30). In Husserl's view, if the primal impression is only impressed in the presence of a consciousness, then we can be guaranteed in principle that the primal impression is always nascently "present" in the retentional moment of the temporal whole. The nascent presence of the impression makes the impression accessible to phenomenological reflection. The folding over of the impression into retention is, on Husserl's account, done without loss. The passage from impression to retention leaves nothing behind.

On Levinas's estimation, it is precisely this gesture, the simple positing of the recuperability of the primal impression, that compromises the methodology of phenomenology vis-à-vis the possibility of speaking of or admitting a radical sense of alterity. Levinas writes in *Otherwise than Being* that

> [i]n Husserl, the time structure of sensibility is *the time of the recuperable*. That the *non-intentionality* of the proto-impression is *not* a loss of consciousness, that nothing can be clandestinely produced, that nothing can break the thread of consciousness, excludes from time the *irreducible diachrony* whose sense the present study aims to bring to light, *behind* the *exhibiting* of a being. (AE, 43/34; my emphasis)

The passing over of the *Ur-impression* into retention is, for Husserl, a pure and coincident passage. Nothing is lost in the transaction. That is, the singularity of the impression is understood, by Husserl, as wholly identical with what it retained. If this passage is made without an interval or a gap, then the production source-point of the impression is already embedded in the retentional complex, without alteration of it in modification. If the impression remains unaltered in retentional modification, then taking up what is retained in protention, and thus the constitution of the phenomenological Now, establishes time as irreducibly constituted. A constituted time is a recuperable time. Representation is literally a re-presentation of what was once present. As Husserl sees quite clearly, this fact of a constituted time requires a structural item from which the constituting is dispensed. Hence, the logic for developing an atemporal notion of absolute consciousness. With this constituting function of absolute consciousness, one might say that the language of presence is given its most provocative justification.

To recover the radicality at work in the productive function of the *Ur-impression*, Levinas targets two aspects (perhaps what Fink called "operative concepts") of Husserl's phenomenology: the voluntary and the teleological. Levinas writes:

> Despite the extension which phenomenology gives the word *intention*, intentionality bears the trace of the voluntary and the teleological. Signification is signifying out of a lack, a certain

negativity, an aspiration which aims emptily, like a hunger, but in a determinate way, at the presence which is to satisfy it. Whether it be an expectation for a representation or a listening for a message, the intuitive fulfillment is the accomplishing of a teleological intention. (AE, 122/96)

Even in the movement of neutral time, the pre-egological flow, Husserl will affirm a sleeping will (AE, 142/111) that, even in its pre-reflective life, teleologically strives toward fulfillment and satisfaction.[16] The fact that Levinas's thinking through Husserl in *Otherwise than Being* begins by questioning these two aspects of subjectivity ought to be considered an advance vis-à-vis the analyses in *Totality and Infinity*. The questioning in *Otherwise than Being* marks an advance in the sense that Levinas's purification of Husserl's phenomenology allows him to employ what is radical about Husserl without standing, ambiguously, as both friend and foe. The phenomenological language employed in *Otherwise than Being* must be understood on the basis of what emerges after this purification. And, the fact that phenomenology bears a *trace* of the voluntary and the teleological (and so not an explicit adoption) indicates the presuppositional character of what Levinas wants to remove from phenomenology. Unwarranted metaphysical speculations must be jettisoned. The removal of such speculative aspects has always been the imperative of a rigorously self-critical phenomenology.[17] Viewed under this approach to phenomenology, Levinas's treatment of Husserl functions, not as a critique and dismissal, but as an extension of the general project.

Levinas's purification of Husserl removes the voluntaristic and teleological underpinnings of Husserl's *interpretation* (and not exhaustion) of the method of intentionality. What Levinas wants to exhibit in this purification is precisely how very differently the structure of absolute subjectivity shows up within his "liberated" method of intentional analysis. Hence, we must here think of Levinas's appropriation of the living-present not so much as a critique of Husserl, as much as a purging of the operative concepts of will and *telos* from the method itself. Perhaps on account of Derrida's introduction of the problem of contamination into readings of Husserlian phenomenology, we have no doubt come to identify impurity as the path to complicating phenomenology. However, there is an important difference between Levinas and Derrida on this question. It is both a difference in language and in intent.

Levinas's reading of Husserl does not simply attempt to complicate presence. It seeks to wholly and completely reverse the order of constitution in the notion of sense-bestowal from the outside. This reversal demands the purity of alterity as singularity. For Derrida, at least in *La voix et le phénomène*, mixture is differance, contamination ceases the progress of phenomenology. Contamination for Levinas is not the critique, but the problem to be overcome. Even in Levinas's account of the Saying and the Said, which displays the contamination of the Said by the Saying, the point will always be to signal, within the presence of the Said, an absolute and pure pre-original. In other words, contamination, for Levinas, is only a point of transition toward what is ultimately a one-way traffic.

Let us first consider the problem of the teleological. The teleological aspect of Husserl's use of intentionality obtains most clearly in the delimitation and closure of the boundaries of constituted time. The boundaries of the living-present are not necessarily rendered present and recuperated in a single intuition. Indeed, what is intuited as the essence of the living-present is the undetermined horizonal fringes that surround the instant seized upon in reflection. Still, the intention that cannot gather the living-present into one vision is not sealed as a failure. It is, rather, only empty. The constituted intentional structure of time insures this. The emptiness of the intention—i.e., its failure to close the retentional complex in memory—is not marked as irreducible. The intention, rather, lacks a fulfillment that, de jure if not de facto, admits of closure as a *telos*. The unfulfilled intention already, of its very structure *as* unfulfilled, hungry, and aiming, points to closure as its end and task. Levinas writes:

> Intentionality remains an aspiration to be filled and fulfilled, the centripetal movement of a consciousness that coincides with itself, recovers, and rediscovers itself without aging, rests in self-certainty, confirms itself, doubles itself up, consolidates itself, thickens into a substance. (AE, 62/48)

The character of time as constitut*ed* secures this possibility, insofar as a constituted time is coextensive with the notion of a closed system. As a juridical matter, the system is not open. Husserl makes this plain in *Experience and Judgment*, where he says that an act that is affected, even through *fiat*, tends of its very nature toward realization (EU, 236/

201). For Husserl, even though an ego may be affected through passivity, the intentional subject awakened from that passivity "wishes to know" (EU, 209/179). The awakened subject, in its wakeful action, seeks identity and determination "once and for all" (EU, 232/198), even where this finality is merely an empty aiming toward or striving toward an end.

How is it possible to ground this constitution of the flow? Does not the constituting function of the primordial flow render closure insecure? This is significant, for certainly if the flow were to shed its being structured as closed, the issue of the legitimacy of an inscription of teleology in intentionality would be put in question. The flow is only secured as constituted when what enters time—as a production of activity or affectivity—is understood as seized upon and held by the will, ". . . an obedience in the midst of the will . . . , a kerygma underlying a *fiat*" (AE, 46/36). This obedience obtains and constitutes, according to the Husserl of *Experience and Judgment,* unity even in subconsciousness (*Unterbewußtsein*) (cf., EU, 210/179). The operative concept of the voluntary shows itself in two fundamental ways: the inscription of possibility in the pre-reflective life of absolute flow and the conception of meaning and intention as *Meinung*.

It is not insignificant that the two occasions we have discussed, in which Husserl announces what would seem a moment of the prehistory of the I, he reinstitutes the notion of possibility or potentiality. In his analysis of awakening, it should be recalled that Husserl at once stumbles on what precedes the auto-affectivity of the I and compromises that which lies "beyond" with the claim that "[m]ore closely considered, sleep has sense only in relation to waking and implies a potentiality for awakening" (Hua IX, 209/160). This same gesture is repeated in his reduction to the impersonal, pre-egoic, absolute flow. As Landgrebe points out, in accounting for the structure of this flow Husserl will posit as equiprimordial with the flux both a *Treibintentionalität* and *Urstreben*.[18] In a response to the problematic relation between absolute flow and constitution, Husserl asks the following question:

> May or must we not, presuppose a universal instinctive intentionality which unitarily constitutes every primal present as standing temporalization and which presses on from present to present in such a way that all content is content of the fulfillment of these

drives and is intended *(intendiert ist)* prior to its achievement? (Hua XV, 595)

The answer is, of course, affirmative. Prior to the wakeful life of consciousness, or even its awakening, a pre-reflective intending constitutes the content yielded to consciousness in awakening and wakeful, reflective life. In order to both safeguard and supplement this dangerous pre-reflective life, Husserl also adds the notion of a primal striving, which, as Landgrebe says, names the most elemental form of activity.[19] It is an activity of the subject that, paradoxically, precedes the possibility of subjective activity. Husserl proposes this instinctive intentionality in order to secure, even in the egoless flow of time, a unitary constitution. As Levinas puts it, the thread of consciousness is not broken (AE, 43/34). Indeed, Husserl must posit this primal activity and this pre-reflective intending, lest the security of a constituted time be lost. The primal striving embedded in pre-reflective life, and the intentionality it manifests, interposes an active will intrinsic to the work of passivity. The genesis of the ego from out of this pre-egological flow is a passive genesis, but the interposition of intentive striving and activity in this flow renders what is produced in passive genesis a recollected and recollectable activity. The primal source of the intentional ego is itself intentional. The pre-history of the I can, for Husserl, be told in narrative form, insofar as the very unity necessary for a narrative is already achieved in the pre-reflective, pre-egoic work of *Urstreben* and *Treibintentionalität*.

The operative concept of the voluntary also shows up in the term *meinen* and its cognate *Meinung*. In pausing to examine the implications of this term, Levinas is led to commend Derrida's translation of *meinen* as *vouloir-dire* in *Voice and Phenomenon* (AE, 46n23/36n23). As it turns out, Derrida in fact translates *bedeuten* as *vouloir dire*. Levinas gets the facts of Derrida's translation wrong, but this is beside the philosophical point.[20] The philosophical point Levinas wants to make here is simply that the much of the phenomenological notion of meaning is caught up with a peculiar sort of pre-reflective will. This will shows itself in phenomenology's genuinely voluntaristic language of meaningfulness. The *vouloir* of the *vouloir-dire* expresses the will as a wanting, a desiring, one that directs and determines the movement of thematization. As early as 1929, for example, Levinas will translate *meinen* as *pensent* (SLI, 83). So, from the outset of his itinerary, it is clear how closely he understands the Husserlian notion of meaning to be tied to thought and the will. It is important, though, to see that Levinas is not simply equating the will with an aiming. Rather, he sees the will as an intending that animates and wants in the act of thematization. In *Otherwise than Being* he will write that

> [t]he mediaeval term intentionality, taken up by Brentano and Husserl, does indeed have in scholasticism and in phenomenology a neutralized meaning with respect to the will. It is the teleological movement animating the thematization that justifies the recourse, however neutralized it may be, to voluntarist language. The *Meinen* in its identifying statement is canceled when it is translated by *visée*. (AE, 47n24/37n24)

The translation of meaning as an aiming misses the neutralized sense of the will that the phenomenological reduction accomplishes. But, this neutralization is overturned in the directionality of animation or constitution, wherein the will is reinstated, albeit in cloaked form. The "meaning to say" that translates the German *Meinung* captures and brings out of hiding the clandestine form of the voluntary and thereby exposes the hidden function of egoic activity. As we have seen in our remarks on the *Treibintentionalität* and *Urstreben*, this hidden activity is crucial to maintaining the teleological, constituted structure of the living-present.

What troubles Levinas in this account of the living-present is quite straightforward and has two basic features. First, the clandestine work of egoic activity represents nothing other than an attempt to ground the primacy of the Same in the pre-reflective life of the subject. Second, and perhaps more significant for our purposes, Levinas insists that the structural item of the *Ur-impression* and its productive functioning tells us quite the opposite story. That is, the necessity of the *Ur-impression* for the retentional complex and the work of modification is a unidirectional necessity. Retention needs the *Ur-impression,* insofar as retention is nothing but the modification of the affected impressional consciousness. The *Ur-impression* precedes this modification and is the condition of the possibility of retention. This is of course an unfortunate and unanticipated absurdity discovered by the idealist prerogative, which contends that the retentional complex conditions the possibility of what appears. By virtue of its temporal place, the *Ur-impression* does not appear, but conditions appearance. It is precisely this state of affairs that prompts Levinas to write that the *Ur-impression* is ". . . non-modified, self-identical, without retention—[it] precede[s] every protention, and thus precede[s] its own possibility" (AE, 41/33). Without the will and a *telos* of wanting, the primal impression recovers its pure status as outside of, yet necessary for, the living-present. How does absolute subjectivity show up under this purified rubric?

This purified "element" mutates absolute subjectivity into responsible subjectivity. Responsible subjectivity is subjectivity understood in terms of the separated relation between singularities. The sense of this relation as interval or separation requires, for its articulation, a diachronic structure of time. The singularity of what stands in a separated relation requires, for *its* articulation, the productive function of the primal impression.

For the Husserl purged of the teleological and the voluntary—the Husserl who interests Levinas—the originary sensation or primal impression (*Ur-impression*), as one of the three fundamental moments of the living-present, signifies the absolute starting point and phenomenal limit of the living-present and therefore of lived-experience. It is this feature of the primal impression that Levinas exploits for the legitimation of his language of alterity in *Otherwise than Being*. The primal impression, for both Husserl and Levinas, is primordial, essential, and definitive. However, they decisively part ways with regard, not to the structural place of the primal impression, but to its *phenomenal-non-phenomenal status*. Whereas the primal impression lies within the horizon of recuperability for Husserl, the primal impression for Levinas necessarily lies outside the living-present as a structural moment. By virtue of its place, the impression is itself *wholly* irretrievable. There can be no real access to the primal impression. Rather, because the primal impression is itself anterior to retention and thereby makes retention itself possible, it is essentially "non-modified" and therefore precedes its own possibility (AE, 41/33). The primal impression precedes its own possibility in the sense that, of its very essence, it is prior and exterior to the modifications enacted by the retentional and protentional nexus. It is, in a word, *pre-phenomenal*. Despite the fact that the primal impression is essential to the very possibility of phenomenal appearance, the impression itself remains an absent yet productive moment of the living-present. Thus, in Levinas's view, it is a productive item that lends itself as an essential temporal moment through the absolute passivity of the anterior relation. The relation or passivity is prior to and constitutive of the phenomenal relation, a relation that is itself structured by the trace and a relation that structures and makes possible the initial presentational clue (*Leitfaden*). The nonintentionality of the *Ur-impression* is "fitted back in the normal order, not leading to the hither side of the Same or of the origin" by Husserl (AE, 42/33). But under the nonvoluntaristic, nonteleological purified structure of time brought into relief by Levinas's reduction, the *Ur-impression* emerges as a non-intentional, productive materiality ". . . before every wanting" (CNI, 138).

The primal impression, then, as an essential, irreducible, and constitutive moment of the living-present, necessarily lies on the hither-side of the living present. The affective effect is therefore "[t]he *signaling* of the pre-original past *in* the present" (AE, 11/9; my emphasis). This signaling, the peculiar nonphenomenal indication of what becomes the trace, is in the living-present as a structural moment, but, because it itself does not appear, it lies outside relations of knowing and being. *The impression "is" Otherwise than Being.* The phenomenal absence of the primal impression, the impossibility of its appearance and the necessity of its productive work, provides Levinas with the sought passage out of experience as the source of all sense. This passage also furnishes the structural justification of his language of alterity, the language of the trace as lapse and radical, absolute passivity. This language marks the most significant break with *Totality and Infinity*. The hither-side of the living-present indicated by the structural moment of the primal impression discloses a wholly other form of alterity(alterity as trace, lapse, absence. Levinas writes that "[t]he hither side, the preliminary, which the pre-originary saying animates, refuses the present and manifestation, or lends itself to them *out of time*" (AE, 57/44). Structurally, this moment of passage "out of time" has its basis in the absent effect of the primal impression. Its effect enters "from the outside" into the living-present, and so is an effect "out of time," yet essential to the structure of the living-present. The impression is the origin prior to origin. In its lending, the impression becomes the locus of the genesis of sense.

It is clear, then, that the impression produces the time of living-present, the time of re-presentation and presence, without itself entering the flow of constituted time. The primal impression is unmodified. Hence, if modification is constitutive of being and presence, then the materiality of the impression can legitimately be called "more ancient than being." Its resistance to presence is a resistance of absolute passivity from outside of presence, thus not the resistance of or within being (NS, 255). What is at play in constituted time is modified as re-presentation, but the primal impression lends itself to presence from out of the time of the living-present. In what sense may it be said that the impression shows up in presence? What is the character of this "lending"? How can we articulate this affect/effect of the impression in presence without reducing the impression to a constituted content? What form does the presencing of what lies outside of presence and time take?

This is a crucial issue, insofar as much of the first sections of *Otherwise than Being* are devoted to the distinction and relation between the Saying and the Said. The Saying-Said issue is homological with, if not synonymous with, the problem of the relation between a radical absence and a manifest presence. In the analysis of the Saying and the Said, Levinas will contend that the traditional primacy of the Said, as present, is undone by the recovery of the generative function of the Saying. That is to say, in its pronouncement and coming to presence, the Said is already constituted by the Saying. This is borne out in Levinas's description of the ethical approach of the face and the peculiar relation of absence and presence that approach implies. The structure of this relation between presence and radical absence, and the animation of the former on the basis of the latter, is captured by the term "trace." The trace is what is given as coextensive with presence, but is structured by the sensation or primal impression that is already outside of time and that enters the living-present through the relation of passivity. Presence, the Said, is already structured by unmodified absence, the Saying. The trace becomes "present" in manifestation, but only in its withdrawal into a pre-original past. The trace, Levinas will say, is the presence of an instant "out of phase with itself," which is a transition or passage tantamount to the dephasing of identity (cf., AE, 11/9, 86/68, 90/72, 207/162). This dephasing is effective and affective already in the living-present in the figure of the trace. The trace, as embedded in the first clue of manifestation, gives itself over to the language of the pre-original. What is present, the time of the living-present, already signals or points to the pre-original past from which presence has come and from which it was produced. This signaling or signification is manifest in the trace, and the signal structured by the trace renders a presence. But this presence that signals the trace is already withdrawn into the pre-original site of its genesis.

The trace, then, is the present or instant out of phase with itself. The trace renders presence *radically* out of phase with itself. The rupture of time cannot be construed as the dispersion of modifications that refer to a primal, re-presentable present. This purified notion of the *Ur-impression* alters the very terms that would save presence from what lies on the hither-side of time. As Levinas notes, if the trace interrupts presence with a radical absence, then ". . . there must be signaled a lapse of time that does not return, a diachrony refractory to all synchronization, a transcending diachrony" (AE, 11/9). Diachrony is constituted in this meeting of the trace with presence. The split time is generated by the production of presence by the *Ur-impression* lying outside of time. The splitting of time in the irretrievable lapse between what produces sense and the presence in which sense is rendered—this is diachrony. This split is important. The lapse between the affective moment of the *Ur-impression* and the re-presentable time of presence legitimates the language of the pre-original. That is, the pre-original maintains its status as prior—as "pre"—when the unrecuperability of the source-point is made secure. The splitting of time constitutive of diachrony is this securing. Diachrony renders the hither-side of time and the consciousness of constituted irreversibly separated, and thus renders consciousness irreversibly dispossessed of itself. The subject is outside itself, separated in its identity by time. Such separation is only possible on the basis of Levinas's purging of absolute consciousness from the structure of time, for, as he notes in "Notes sur le sens," positionality and presence are coextensive (NS, 237). On the basis of this positionality and logic of presence, diachrony would have to be rendered as a privation of synchrony (NS, 238). Levinas's account, however, reverses the terms: synchrony is a perversion and privation of an original diachrony. Indeed, diachrony renders the very terms of synchrony—viz., identity and activity—derivative. Levinas writes that

> This diachrony prevents the one from joining up with itself and
> identifying itself as a substance, contemporary with itself, like
> a transcendental ego . . . The diachrony by which the uniqueness
> of the one has been designated, is the fact that the one is required,
> on the hither-side of essence, by responsibility, and is always
> wanting with respect to itself, always insufficiently divested, in

deficit, like a painful point. This diachrony of the subject is not a metaphor. The subject said as properly as possible is not in time, but is diachrony itself. In the identification of the ego, there is the aging of him that one will never "catch up with there again." It is the diachrony of an election without identification. . . . (AE, 73/57)

The subject cannot recuperate the origin of itself from across time. Rather, the awakening of the subject is provoked from outside presence, outside the life of the subject, and thus the subject is awakened and elected without identification. The subject is constituted out of time in this awakening. The oneself of subjectivity cannot form itself, but rather "is already formed with absolute passivity" (AE, 132–133/104); this passivity signifies subjectivity within and across diachronic time. The diachronic time of the subject is thus "not an insufficiency of an intuition," but rather is both ". . . the anarchy of what has never been present" (AE, 124/97) and the condition of the possibility of intuition, intentionality, and aiming (NS, 253). Synchrony has been dispossessed of its authority.

To be sure, this much was already clandestinely at work in Husserl's reflections on the absolute flow. But, the productive function of the *Ur-impression* and the effect that function has on the notion of the living-present was covered over by the traces of the voluntary and the teleological. Under the intersubjective reduction and with the purging of the voluntary and teleological in place, Levinas is able to show how the logic of the primal impression already interrupts the living-present. This interruption is the very genesis of the ego from outside of time. That is to say, outside the time of presence. The hither-side of the present is the site of what Levinas calls the pre-history of the I. This pre-history cannot be adequately rendered in the narrative structure of the Said. Instead, this pre-history is the very unraveling of the Said in the Saying, the very questioning of presence at the genetic source of what animates presence: the materiality of the impression. The impression, as we saw in detail in our reading of essays from the 1960s, enters through the relation of passivity. Passivity is the point of passage across the interval opened up by the splitting of time, the lapse between the pre-original impression and its retention, and so the absent origin of presence and re-presentation that Levinas calls diachrony. On this account, the very terms of absolute subjectivity mutate into the fundamental structure of responsible subjectivity. Diachrony, passivity, trace, impression, materiality—these are already the fundamental terms of the logic of ethical subjectivity.

Responsible Subjectivity

The function of the impression in producing a diachronic time-structure brings us to the structure of responsible subjectivity. As we have just seen, this responsible subjectivity is a mutation brought about through a recovery of the radicality nascently at work in Husserl's exposition of absolute subjectivity. This radicality is covered over by the metaphysical hangovers of voluntarism and teleology, and is recovered in Levinas's purging of phenomenology's account of time. At this point, what is in place is the sense of a separated relation (diachrony), the site of the nonnarrative structure of the pre-history of the I (the *Ur-impression*), and the genetic project at work in the material constitution of ethical time and the awakening of the I.

What is missing is the exact impact this analysis has on the language of singularity. The stakes are high. It is a question of securing the purity of singularity in order to generate a legitimated language of the subject as for-the-Other. The sense of relationality has its expression in the constitutive function of the *Ur-impression*, which is a relation Levinas names "animation" (AE, 89/71). Animation captures how the life of the Same cannot escape its possession by and obsession with the Other. The I is hostage. That is, the unicity of the I is already animated by alterity. The animation of the I by an alterity produces the obsession that is "unassumable" (AE, 110/87) precisely because it is not a relation set out from auto-affection, which would be the condition of the possibility of assumption. Indeed, Levinas will define obsession as produced when "the subject is affected without the source of the affection becoming a theme of representation" (AE, 127/101). Animation, the relation produced in radical affective life, is therefore a relation set out from the disturbance of memorable time in the hetero-affection manifest concretely in my material proximity to the neighbor (AE, 113/89).

How is it possible for this animation to impose itself on the subject? Or, to be more precise, in what condition do we find the subject such that it may assume the unassumable work of passivity? How can the I be exposed to the Other ". . . antecedent to his appearing, [in] my delay behind him, my undergoing," and thus how can this animation in proximity "undo the core of what is identity in me" (AE, 113/89)? To establish this condition, Levinas turns to the issue of embodiment, described in *Otherwise than Being* in terms of the body's passivity. The essence of the ethical body, for Levinas, lies in the materiality of its proximity to the other. The materiality of the body in proximity to the face of the Other is described as the exposure of the body. Exposure as the condition of the ethical subject makes a reversal of the constitution of the subject's identity possible. This reversal of identity is concretely accomplished in the sense-bestowing function of the pre-original, manifest in the concrete accusation of the facing face. The exposed body is constituted as a unicity through the relation of absolute passivity. Incarnated and passive makes the ethical subject susceptible to trauma, pain, and persecution prior to the will. The vulnerable skin of the subject bears the trace of the hither-side (AE, 156n26/121n26). The exposed body is marked concretely, in its vulnerability, by the pre-history of the I.

Such a conception of the body stands opposed to the body of Husserl's *V. Cartesian Meditation*, as well as to the lived-body of Merleau-Ponty's *Phenomenology of Perception*. Neither Husserl nor Merleau-Ponty give unmediated priority to absolute passivity, though both will appeal to a modified form of the passive in their explorations of embodied life. For both, some form of primordial activity always obtains. Yet it must be said that Levinas's opposition is not complete. That is, he will want to hold on to the genetic account in Husserl's meditation on our pre-reflective embodied life, as well as what he calls the "fundamental historicity of the body" in Merleau-Ponty's work. In this double gesture of opposition and appropriation, the issue of the logic of animation is decisive. Animation is neither the inhabitation of the body by the mind nor the positing of a psycho-physical unity (AE, 139n12/109n12). Both inhabitation and psycho-physical unity are conceptions inherent in the idealist prerogative of Husserl's Fifth Meditation (cf., Hua I, 130ff/99ff). Animation is also not, for Levinas, the coincidence of the sensing and the sensed, the between of activity and passivity, as we find in Merleau-Ponty's notion of our embodied being in the world, as well as his analysis (borrowed from Husserl) of the relationality of the touching-touched.[21] Both Husserl's and Merleau-Ponty's conceptions of the body entail genetic projects that either give a privilege to activity—the former—or intermingle activity and passivity—the latter.

For Levinas, the exposed body of ethical subjectivity is animated as a for-the-Other. It is animated to the point of obsession by the Other through the relation of passivity. There is not a psyche that inhabits the body prior to awakening by the Other. Nor is there a reciprocal or reversible character to our embodied presence to the Other. The body exposed to the Other is animated and awakened otherwise. "The recurrence in awakening," Levinas writes "is something one can describe as a shudder of incarnation through which giving takes on sense, as the primordial dative of the *for another,* in which a subject becomes a heart, a sensibility, and hands which give" (DP, 120/182). The subject is rendered unique—it recurs—as for-the-Other in the interruptive awakening of the body from outside. Levinas writes that in the election of the I by the Other

> . . . I am summoned as someone irreplaceable. I exist through the other and for the other, but without this being alienation: I am inspired. This inspiration is the psyche. The psyche can signify this alterity in the Same without alienation in the form of incarnation, as being-in-one's-skin, having-the-other-in-one's-skin. (AE, 146/ 114–115)

The embodied I is animated and inspired from the outside. It is exposed to what accuses and commands. This is the diachronic truth of the psyche. Exposure is not alienation, which is to say, the notion of the exposure of the body is not opposed to the notion of the I. Rather, exposure generates or creates the I through the relation of animation and inspiration. Incarnation is the locus of the identity of the I, but only where the genesis of the I occurs in the relation of passivity. The identity of this body, the exposed body, is animated without a common time or place—inspiration is diachronic. The diachronic time of animation and inspiration allows us to see the movement of the genesis of a relationship between uneven or unparallel terms. Animation signifies the nonindifference of the body and the noncontemporaneous time of the relation established through the passivity of exposure (AE, 89/70–71).

Animation from the outside is traumatic (AE, 141/111). The trauma of genesis, of awakening and fundamental historicity, is lost in the analyses of Merleau-Ponty and Husserl precisely because they miss the original, pure passivity constitutive of the unicity of the embodied

I. What Levinas takes from Merleau-Ponty is the notion that the body has a history. However, this is not a history for which the subject has words. The history of the ethical body cannot assume a narrative form. It is, rather, a history in that sense in which we spoke of the pre-history of the I. The exposed body has a pre-history that demands the ethical language of diachrony and awakening, insofar as the interruption of the I by the Other leaves the ego speechless (cf., AE, 128/101). This history can, however, begin to be told through an evocative abuse of language (AE, 149n19/117n19). Levinas's famed examples, of course, are Celan's "Ich bin du, wenn ich ich bin" and Rimbaud's "Je est un autre." Merleau-Ponty opens the question of the body's history. Levinas writes it otherwise than narrativity. From Husserl, Levinas will want to retain the sense of the material exposure and subjection of the body to both time and alterity in the pre-reflective, pre-predicative life of the ego. But, for Levinas there is not a concealed identity in this exposure. There is no primal striving of an instinctive intentionality that guarantees, even in passivity, a recuperable and synchronic time coincident in acts of reflection. Quite the contrary, on Levinas's account the exposure of the body is the exposure to and awaiting of assignation. Only out of this assignation is there a unicity to the I. That is, the body exposed to assignation is ". . . unique in the unexceptional requisition of responsibility" (AE, 69/53). "In responsibility," Levinas writes, "as one assigned or elected from the outside, assigned as irreplaceable, the subject is accused in its skin" (AE, 134/106). The exposure of the body accused in its skin is what allows the I to say *me voici* without violence, to say "here I am" in an "exasperated contracting" (AE, 145/114), a saying "with inspiration" (AE, 181/142, 184/144–145) and without a situation or dwelling place (AE, 186/146), saying without the possibility of evasion (AE, 191/150), and to declare the unicity of the oneself as "here I am for the others" (AE, 233/185). The embodied and exposed I is this incarnate, extreme passivity (AE, 139n12/109n12).

The body as exposure and assignative awakening establishes the condition of the subject as passive, as well as securing the singularity of the subject under obligation. What, then, of that Other who is constitutive of ethical subjectivity?

First, it is important to understand the function of the Other as the constituting item of the ethical relation. We have contended throughout that alterity is best understood under the rubric of the genetic. The rubric of the genetic authenticates the sense in which the I is displaced at its origin, as well as how the interval across which the relation is maintained articulates absolute difference. In a certain sense, we could say that such reading demands thinking of Levinas's work as a transcendental project. But, in *Otherwise than Being* Levinas will claim that

> the way the Infinite passes the finite and passes itself has an ethical sense *(sens éthique)* [that] is not something that results from a project to construct the "transcendental foundation" of "ethical experience." The ethical is the field outlined by the paradox of an Infinite in relationship with the finite without being belied in this relationship. Ethics is the break up of the originary unity of transcendental apperception, that is, it is the beyond of experience. (AE, 189/148)

Thus, it seems that the project Levinas sets out is not a foundational problematic. Yet, he will also say that "[t]he foundation of consciousness is justice" (AE, 204/160). There is, then, something of a tension in Levinas's own self-understanding. On the one hand, Levinas's work does not seek to found experience. On the other hand, justice—which Levinas explicitly links with the diachronic structure of sensibility and proximity (cf., AE, 90/71)—founds consciousness. What sense are we to make of this tension between competing characterizations of the transcendental prerogative?

The structure of what we here call "impressional sense" adjudicates this apparent tension. The relation at issue produces a *sens éthique*, but this sense is not something that refers its construction to the transcendental ego. It is not a relation set out from the subject. The sense set out from the transcendental ego is set out from something already determined by the possibility of presence (AE, 208/164) and therefore presupposes the work of auto-affection. The foundation established in this understanding of genesis is firm and unshakable, even if only in a teleological sense, i.e., as the end or purpose of phenomenological research. In this regard, then, Levinas's project cannot be construed as foundational. There is no ground in which the origin, the singularity of alterity, can take root. Levinas writes:

> The for-the-Other of responsibility for the other does not proceed from any free commitment, any present, in which its origin would germinate, or in which an identity identifying itself would catch its breath. (AE, 195/153)

The origin that forms basis of the for-the-Other is thus not a ground in the sense of an identity that could allow the ethical I to "catch its breath," to succeed in its giving, or ultimately to complete its expiation without inspiration.

Impressional sense does not follow this logic. If there were a further ground in which the singularity of alterity could take root, then the anarchy of the Other would be only a privation of the *arche* of this original ground. But Levinas will continually insist on the anarchic character of alterity. The same must therefore be said of the structure of impressional sense. Instead of tracing back what appears to be its genesis in an ego that seeks only identity, impressional sense names that modality of genesis in which we find an absolute, radical, and unmodified singularity. Thus, Levinas will again oppose the radical singularity he seeks to the compromised singularity of the *tode ti* (AE, 109/86, 134/106). The status of this singularity is captured when Levinas, in the passage just quoted, describes it as an origin in which germination cannot take place. The alterity that generates the unicity of the I is not itself a ground, nor does it presuppose one. This invocation of the figure of "germination" harks back to Levinas's reading of the first Appendix to Husserl's time-consciousness lectures. In that reading, Levinas seized upon Husserl's remark that the *Ur-impression* is not generated, does not have a seed, does not grow up, and thus is born through spontaneous generation. The impression itself, according to both Levinas and Husserl, is primal creation.[22] Impressional sense creates without germination. That is, impressional sense is generated through the anteriority of the relation of passivity without the presupposition of a prior ground. There is no nether world from which this alterity descends or ascends to meet the positional I (PE, 98/215). Rather, the impression is the origin of the relationality constitutive of what may be called "world" or context, and therefore must be understood as genetically preceding the position of the subject (PE, 98/215). The transcendental character of Levinas's work in *Otherwise than Being* must be understood on this model, a model structured from the outside without the presupposition of a ground from which the singularity might have arisen or within which it is germinated.

In this sense, impressional sense names the radical singularity of materiality, concretely signified as the singularity of the face. If impressional sense establishes the singularity of the Other and is understood as the singular site of the genesis of subjectivity, then the foundation of subjectivity becomes, quite plainly, the imposition of the

Other on the Same. But, this can only be the case when this imposition is given its constitutive force. It is an imposition of the beyond being that produces being. Impressional sense is not about ontic play, and so is not a question of one being imposing itself on another being. The analysis is transcendental, concerned with genesis, and therefore not merely empirical. This is clearly not a conception of the transcendental that derives its sense from the transcendental ego. Levinas is explicit: Diachrony "breaks the unity of transcendental apperception" (AE, 194/ 152). This diachrony does not originate from a neutral ground nor does it grow up from a soil in which it may germinate. Rather, diachronic time originates in the absolute singularity of the primal impression, the enigmatic singularity of the material that distinguishes itself as absolute difference. This materiality is deformalized as the face that assigns, obsesses, and persecutes. Its status as a singularity is legitimated by the logic of the sense-bestowing function of the *Ur-impression*, which is a bestowal of sense that initiates the two-time contradiction of diachrony in proximity and fates presence to failure. Heteronomy and hetero-affection name the relation structured from the outside. Levinas writes:

> The subject is inseparable from this appeal or this election, which cannot be declined. It is in the form of the *being* of this entity, the diachronic temporality of aging, that there is produced despite myself the response to an appeal, direct and like a traumatizing blow. Such a response cannot be converted into an "inward need" or a natural tendency. This response answers, but with no eroticism, to an absolutely heteronomous call. (AE, 68/53)

This call is heteronomous. The genetic logic of heteronomy demands both that the call come from outside and that it issue from a radical singularity. Thus, the face that manifests itself as a trace of a trace, in a time before the beginning, as the locus of the awakening and constitution of the ipseity of the I without *arche*, is a radical singularity. This singularity is radical in that, across the productive work of the originary sensation, it precedes the possibility of identity and thus the possibility of possibility. The face is a singularity that interrupts the anonymous flow of primordial time and contests, in its enigmatic passage through the anterior relation of passivity, the positionality of absolute consciousness. This is the ethical Other of the relation of unicity to unicity. The complete reversal of this relation establishes the subject in substitution, which is nothing other than the unity of inspiration, animation, and expiation (AE, 151/118).[23]

The structure of the for-the-Other manifests the sense of ethical subjectivity. To be an ethical subject is to be already for-the-Other, a modality of relation that, as we have seen, is prior to the question of the will and without a *telos*. As such, the sense produced in this relation is pre-voluntary and prior to the very boundaries that would make a teleological project possible. This is the fundamental character of impressional sense. By way of this impressional sense, the ethical subject discovers the alterity already in the I and this alterity in the Same names the effect of the one-way genesis of the unicity of the subject. The sense of this "already" is justified through the anterior relation of passivity explicated as a sense-bestowal from the outside. The subject is for-the-Other because difference precedes, genetically, the identity of the petrified I, the ego closed upon itself. The unparallel terms Same and Other, described according to the logic of absolute difference and singularity, make diachrony and assignation possible. The relation of for-the-Other is concretely manifest as the subject accused of something (cf., AE, 142–143/112). This accusation, this incarnate approach, brings together the logic of the intertwined structures of relationality, awakening, time, materiality, and genesis herein discussed. We find in the approach, where the approach is put under the reduction, the unsaying of the Said, the failure of presence, and the lateness of the subject to itself. The phenomenology of this approach, then, yields the clue (the face structured by the trace, the exposure of the body) and the path (diachronic time) to the break-up of pre-reflective life in the bestowal of impressional sense from the outside.

The ethical subject itself is composed of the exposed and vulnerable body and the singular materiality of the face of the Other. This is a relation set out from the nonintentionality of alterity (set out as a one-way relation), constituted in the movement of awakening as the genesis of the unicity of the I from the outside or hither-side of the flow of time, and therefore is a relation whose sense is produced or bestowed by the figure of the *Ur-impression*. To be so constructed is to be the ethical subject of the for-the-Other. To "be" for-the-other is to have felt, at the origin of the unique and irreplaceable I, the "force of an alterity in me" (AE, 146/114). The "adventure" of this subject is decidedly not the "adventure" of cognition. Given this structure of an alterity in me, what sort of notion of subjectivity is required for the signification of the beyond being, the alterity that genetically precedes boundaries of ontological possibility? Levinas writes that it is a

> notion of subjectivity independent of the adventure of cognition, and in which the corporeality of the subject is not separable from its subjectivity, is required if signification signifies otherwise than by the synchrony of being, if intelligibility and being are distinguishable, if essence itself signifies only on the basis of an allocation of sense *(prestation de sens)* that rises again *(remontant)* from the-one-for-the-other, the signifyingness of signification. (AE, 98–99/78)

For our purposes, it is noteworthy here that Levinas turns to the allocation or assignment of sense, as it emphasizes our insistence on the problem of sense-genesis. The sense is that of the for-the-Other, the relation of diachrony where the recurrence of the I finds itself thrown out of the present and toward the hither-side. Levinas writes:

> The recurrence to the oneself refers to the hither-side of the present in which every identity identified in the Said is constituted. It is already constituted when the act of constitution first originates. (AE, 133/105)

This double movement of recurrence and ipseity, and the reference to the hither-side, names the diachronic relationality of the for-the-Other. This lateness of the subject to itself, the recognition of the sense-genesis from out of an absolute difference that precedes identity, and the diachronic time that such lateness implies, is precisely the impressional sense marking the irreducibility of the Other in the Same. The relation is the double movement this lateness describes, where the recurrence is already displaced, but displaced without alienation.

The sense that impressional sense ascribes to the ethical subject, in the concrete accusation of the face, is the sense that names the Oneself, the unique I, as for-the-Other. The body is exposed to this ascription of sense. The face of the Other approaches from out of a pre-original time and in the signifyingness of this pre-original materiality, the Other gives a sense to the I (AE, 99/78). Sense is given even in its withdrawal through the trace, its reference to a pre-ontological past, and thus the lapse in me opened up by the diachronic time of the ethical relation. To be an ethical subject is to be on the basis of the trauma of affectivity—to be, as Levinas puts it, a subject "affected in spite of itself" (AE, 130/102). To be an ethical subject is to be a body awakened from this pre-original past and to find oneself unable to account for the history of the very sense constitutive of my unicity. This pre-history is necessary in order that the absolute outside-of-me may concern me: "But in the 'pre-history' of the ego posited for itself speaks a responsibility. The self is through and through a hostage, older than the ego, prior to principles" (AE, 150/117). To be an ethical subject is to find oneself already referred to an irretrievable origin. "I am a self in the identifying recurrence," Levinas writes, "in which I find myself cast back to the hither-side of my point of departure" (AE, 147/115). The simultaneity of the recurrent ipseity of the I and the casting back to the hither-side is both the contraction and exposure of the embodied subject. To be an ethical subject is to be this double movement. The double movement of ethical subjectivity produces the paradoxical affect of assignation: making the oneself other without alienation, to be dispossessed in obligation, and, ultimately, to be "caught up in the impossibility of evading" (AE, 139/109).

As a way of concluding the present reflections, I want to make a few remarks regarding the difference between the languages of alterity and sense in *Totality and Infinity* and *Otherwise than Being*. First, we should note an important homology: both texts attempt to produce a logic of sense-bestowal that originates from and maintains absolute difference. The relational character of this sense, in both texts, contests the primacy of the intentionality of "opening upon" or "aiming at" by insisting instead on the first position of a reversed intention. A radical affectivity attests to this reversal. Through affectivity, which is the articulation of the structure of the site of reversal, a complete and radical overturning of the logic of sense-bestowal is instituted. Sense-bestowal from the outside, the transcendental function of sensibility, the passivity of the subject, relation across the interval—these figures are what underpin both *Totality and Infinity* and *Otherwise than Being*. What, then, marks the decisive difference?

In *Totality and Infinity*, Levinas's central concern is with the attempt to trace the sense of totality back to the situation in which the putatively secured intentional structure of that totality, the noesis-noema correlation, "breaks up" (TeI, xiii/24). The various intentional analyses of *Totality and Infinity* bring the representational mode of intentionality back to the nonrepresentational source(s) from which all theory and practice are originally nourished, back to that from which all intentional life "lives" (TeI, 102/129). Therein lies the core of the sense-bestowal problematic. This movement from and through affectivity finds its most radical articulation in the face-to-face relation. Levinas terms the face-to-face the ". . . ultimate situation" (TeI, 53/81). Levinas bases both his language of alterity and the logic of a reversed sense-bestowal in the transcendental matters of sensibility affected in the face-to-face relation. The face-to-face relation is thus characterized as an experience ". . . in the fullest sense of the word" (TeI, ix/25). This fullest sense of experience lies in the origin prior to origin: the sensibility of the face. Exteriority produces the very sense of this experience from what is genetically beyond, prior to, and outside the I. Exteriority *par excellence* is the face of the Other and the presentation of the face of the Other manifests a sensible—and senseful—excess. An insurmountable surplus of sense, to which no objectivating mode of intentionality is adequate, is bestowed. In the context of *Totality and Infinity*, then, alterity is excessive exteriority and this exteriority produces an excessive sense. Sense will thereafter take on the figurative character of abundancy and overflowing. Exteriority overflows and explodes the boundaries of simple presence.

In *Otherwise than Being*, quite a different character of alterity and sense shows up. Whereas the presentation of the face indicates the excessiveness of exteriority in *Totality and Infinity*, the face in *Otherwise than Being* serves as a clue to a structure wholly other than excessiveness. The face as a sensibility in *Totality and Infinity* is an excessive sensible that outstrips the grasping of intentionality, but in *Otherwise than Being* Levinas alternatively, and with decisive consequences, characterizes the face as ". . . already a *failing* of all presence, *less* than a phenomenon" (AE, 113/90; my emphasis). The face, Levinas writes, ". . . does not signify an indeterminate phenomenon," but rather is manifest as ". . . a trace of itself, a trace in the trace of an abandon, where the equivocation is never dissipated" (AE, 119/94). In other words, the presence of the face of the Other serves, not as the event of transcendence and its excessive sense, but rather as the impoverished and desolate presence of a radical absence. As we have shown, this absence enters through the passivity of the anterior relation and offers no promise of recuperability. Indeed, the structuring of the nonphenomenal face by way of the trace precludes such a *telos* and thereby denies outright the possibility of closure. *Otherwise than Being* is therefore a book about absence. In terms of that analysis alterity *is* trace, it *is* lapse. Alterity is *pre*original and therefore does not manifest its origin in the presence of an appearance, but in the poverty and unrecuperability of its absence. The face comes from an empty, desert, and desolate space (AE, 116/91). Its origin is the failing of presence—the trace, in a word—the Saying that precedes the Said and escapes the Said while always, in its own absence, making it possible (AE, 58–59/46).

Thus, *Totality and Infinity* may be characterized as a Levinasian phenomenology of alterity *as* excessive presence, the exceeding and overflowing of what could be contained by a conservative logic of presence—i.e., a presence within a recuperable horizon. *Otherwise than Being*, in distinction from this excessive exterior, is a book about absence and how that absence has already passed before the present becomes present. In *Otherwise than Being*, alterity does not overflow the phenomenal. It withdraws behind and before the economy of appearance takes hold. Between the two texts there are two distinct senses of the failure of the phenomenal: 1) the failure of appearance to contain the exterior and 2) the failure of the phenomenal to speak of its poverty. To be sure, on both accounts, the language of alterity always already signifies a *debt*, a debt that opens us to the peculiar sense of the ethical. In both texts the subject is put in question with regard to its putative self-certain subjectivity.

However, the notable shift in Levinas's language alters the terms of this debt and therefore the very terms of the ethical. In *Totality and Infinity*, the excessive exteriority of the Other ruptures the constitutional confines of my own subjective life and the representational modality of my being-in-the-world that the idealist's notion of subjectivity presupposes and assumes. The Other questions my powers. In *Otherwise than Being*, the radical absence of the original manifestation of the Other, and the centrality of that trace in the notion of identity, does not simply call my subjective life into question. Rather, this absence calls the very notions of subjectivity and self-identity themselves into question. And this pushes the problematic of alterity further. I do not meet the Other as an already formed I who is subsequently called into question in *Otherwise than Being*. Rather, the I who meets the Other is one who has already failed in responsibility. That failure itself is irredeemable, a fate sealed in the lapse of passage from the time of the Other to the time of the vigilant I. With the conceptual tools in place in 1961, it is unclear how radically Levinas is able to question the structure of identity. In 1974, however, he is able to contest identity through the temporal structure of genesis. This shift in Levinas's language of alterity thus does not simply signify a shift in emphasis, but alters the very sense and content of the ethical. The *mise en question* effect of the ethical face is no doubt invariant. The effect always produces an *infinite* responsibility. But, the enigma of alterity secured in the notion of sense-bestowal from the outside produces two distinct senses: excessive and impoverished.

What of the difference between the two texts? Perhaps this difference is merely a difference in language and emphasis. Perhaps this difference emerges as a response to certain critics—viz., Derrida—who question the traces of ontological language in *Totality and Infinity*. Or, perhaps the difference is already made necessary by the logic at work in *Totality and Infinity*, even as the text itself was incapable of making good on that necessity. If the latter is the case, and I believe it is the most persuasive account, then we can ultimately appeal to Levinas's remark that, although the pre-history of the I was at work in *Totality and Infinity*, it is only the text of *Otherwise than Being* that is capable of writing that history (DMT, 202n2). That history is a history of an impoverished, not excessive, sense.

But ultimately the question of sense answers more familiar questions, as old and as new as philosophy itself: Who am I? What does it mean to say "I am"? What is my place in the world? These questions are never the same after Levinas's work. For all the talk of contingency in the twentieth century, too much work has anchored itself in some remnant of the will. Levinas, in the name "of the millions on millions of all confessions and all nations, victims of the same hatred of the other human," changes everything. The ubiquity of obligation, irredeemable and irrecusable, must disrupt philosophy's pretensions. And it must disrupt who I am when I say "I am." Am I here for the others, before I am here for myself? If the Other and Others accuse before I answer, what of my place in the sun? How can I be without usurping the Other's place? Perhaps this is impossible. Perhaps this is why, as Pascal says in his *Pensées*, the I is hateful. But, if Levinas's work leads us to this world out of joint with itself, this u-topian space, then we can, with him, begin to encounter and respond to the infinite in us. Paul Celan has, I think, captured something of this effect:

> I find something which consoles me a bit for having walked this impossible road in your presence, this road of the impossible.
>
> I find the connective which, like the poem, leads to encounters.[24]

The impossible. This is the condition of subjectivity in the ethical relation. And it does lead to encounters, encounters that have impossible conditions: excessive and impoverished. The enigma of the connective— is this not the divine comedy in which the intrigue of the ethical is implicated for contemporary thought?

Notes

Introduction

1. There are two partial exceptions to this. First, there is Maria Schafstedde's *Der Selbe und der Andere* (Kassel: IAG, 1993), which is better characterized as a long essay than as a book-length study (it is under sixty pages). Second, there is Nathalie Depraz's *Transcendance et incarnation* (Paris: Vrin, 1995), which Rudolf Bernet rightly calls a Levinasian reading of Husserl (see his "Preface" to Depraz's book, p. 20). Depraz's book, however, does not systematically read Levinas's work on Husserl; it is better understood as "inspired" by the Levinasian problematic. (Indeed, this is how Bernet describes the character of her work.) An important collection of essays, edited by Jean Luc-Marion, on Levinas (*Positivité et transcendance*. Paris: PUF, 2000) appeared too late for consideration here.

2. Here, our reading opposes Robert Manning's *Interpreting Otherwise than Heidegger* (Pittsburgh: Duquesne University Press, 1993), which starts with the claim that "Levinas sees the primary value of Husserl's transcendental phenomenology in the fact that it lays the foundation for Heidegger's phenomenological ontology" (16). Far from being what Manning calls "an obvious polemic" (19), *Theory of Intuition* in fact claims that "Husserl's phenomenology goes further than the goals and problems of a theory of knowledge" (TIPH, 187/130) and that the very issues raised against Husserl may be overcome "with the affirmation of the intentional character of practical and axiological life" (TIPH, 223/158).

3. In this vein, we could also add, among others, Robert Gibbs's *Correlations in Rosenzweig and Levinas* (Princeton: Princeton University Press, 1992). Perhaps we could also add, substituting (somewhat scandalously) Heidegger for Rosenzweig, Manning's *Interpreting Otherwise than Heidegger*. It seems unclear if, for Manning, Levinas is first a Heideggerian or first a phenomenologist "inspired beyond Husserl" by Heidegger. The difference, of course, is immensely important.

4. Richard Cohen, *Elevations*. (Chicago: University of Chicago Press, 1995), 227.

5. Ibid., 230.

6. Ibid., 237.

7. Jan de Greef, "Levinas et la phénoménologie," *Revue de Métaphysique et de Morale* 76, no. 4 (Octobre–Décembre 1971): 465.

8. Ibid., 463. William Large makes a similar argument in his "On the Meaning of the Word Other in Levinas," *Journal of the British Society for Phenomenology* 27, no. 1 (January 1996): 36–52.

9. Stephan Strasser, "Antiphénoménologie et phénoménologie dans la philosophie d'Emmanuel Levinas," *Revue Philosophique de Louvain* 75 (Février 1977): 124.

10. Jacques Collette, "Lévinas et la phénoménologie husserlienne," in *Emmanuel Levinas: Les Cahiers de La nuit surveillée, No. 3*, ed. J. Rolland. Lagrasse: Verdier, 1984, 33n23.

11. "Ethics of the Infinite," interview with Richard Kearney, in *States of Mind*, ed. Richard Kearney (New York: New York University Press, 1995), 180. I should thank Professor Kearney for informing me in personal discussion that Levinas uses the French term *sens* in this passage. Kearney translates *sens* as "meaning," but we here choose the more phenomenologically precise term "sense." The significance of the notion of *sens* is accounted for in chapter 1, below.

12. On the notion of the things themselves, see the remarks in Salomon Malka, *Lire Levinas* (Paris: Cerf), 1984, 18.

13. This, I think, has been a common misunderstanding of Levinas's relation to Husserl. See, for example, Brian Schroeder's remark that "Levinas is united with Husserl's later thinking . . . in the conviction that the meaning of subjectivity is intersubjectivity" (*Altared Ground.* [New Jersey: Routledge, 1996], 172n1). Levinas's exposition of affective life works as a counter to the discussion of the sphere of ownness in the *V. Cartesian Meditation*, though Levinas will not name that text as the "foil." Rather, Levinas will juxtapose affective life to representational gaze of the subject.

14. Emmanuel Levinas, "Entretien," in *Répondre d'autrui: Emmanuel Levinas*, ed. Jean-Christophe Aeschlimann (Boudry-Neuchâtel: Editions de la Baconniere, 1989), 10.

15. On the notion of testimonial language and its status, consider Levinas's claim that the witness is "borne" (AE, 188/147).

16. See, for example, Marbach's observation that the identity of the ego only became an issue for Husserl when the problem of intersubjectivity came to the fore. Eduard Marbach, *Das Problem des Ich in der Phänomenologie Husserls* (The Hague: Martinus Nijhoff, 1974), 108n44.

Chapter One: Unsuspected Horizons

1. This approach will entail crucial changes in how we understand basic phenomenological language. The aim of the present chapter is to lay out some of the basic terms of phenomenology, though throughout the study we will have to note Levinas's alteration of the sense of those terms.

2. For the standard story about the limits of the methodological question, see Charles Reed's remarks in "Levinas's Question," in *Face-to-Face with Levinas*, ed. Richard Cohen (Albany: State University of New York Press, 1986) regarding the failure of intentionality to the idea of infinity and the juxtaposition of "style" to method (73–76). We will contend throughout the present study that intentionality as the problem of relationality as such is the site of Levinas's reflections on alterity.

3. On the enigmatic structure of psychism as the relation with the unrepresentable (what is here called the concrete), see VDVT, 55/101–102, as well as throughout *Otherwise than Being*.

4. *Pace* Jan de Greef's claims in his "Levinas et la phénoménologie," *Revue de Métaphysique et de Morale* 76, no. 4 (Octobre–Décembre 1971): 448–465, especially 461ff.

5. On this, see Ludwig Landgrebe's "World as a Phenomenological Problem," in his *The Phenomenology of Edmund Husserl*, ed. and trans. Donn Welton (Ithaca: Cornell University Press, 1980), 122ff.

6. Cf., J. N. Mohanty, *Transcendental Phenomenology* (Philadelphia: Temple University Press, 1989), 109.

7. Edmond Husserl, *Méditations cartésiennes*, trad. Gabrielle Peiffer and Emmanuel Levinas (Paris: Vrin, 1980), 59. See also *Hua I*, 104/70; Dorion Cairns translates the same as "empirical significance."

8. We might add here that Cairns reserves "meaning" for *Meinung*, no doubt because of the ambiguity of any distinction between the verbal and substantial aspects of the English term—i.e., the substantial is also the gerund.

9. Emmanuel Levinas, "Entretien: Violence du visage," in *Altérité et transcendance* (Montpellier: Fata Morgana, 1995), 175.

10. On this critique of the modern problematic in Husserl's work, see Burt Hopkins, *Intentionality in Husserl and Heidegger* (Dordrecht: Kluwer Academic Publishers, 1991), chapter 1.

11. For some debate on this notion of creativity and constitution, see Eugen Fink's "Die phänomenologische Philosophie Edmund Husserls in der Gegenwärtigen Kritik," in *Studien zur Phänomenologie 1930–1939* (The Hague: Martinus Nijhoff, 1966), 143ff; "The Phenomenological Philosophy of Edmund Husserl and Contemporary Criticism," trans. R. O. Elveton, in *The Phenomenology of Husserl*, ed. R. O. Elveton (Chicago: Quadrangle, 1970), 133ff; Roman

Ingarden's *On the Motives Which Led Husserl to Transcendental Idealism*, trans., Arnór Hannibalsson. (The Hague: Martinus Nijhoff, 1975), 20ff; and Alfred Schutz, "The Problem of Transcendental Intersubjectivity in Husserl," in *Collected Papers II*, ed. I. Schutz (The Hague: Martinus Nijhoff, 1966), 82ff. All three interpret constitution in terms of the creative work of the ego. This creativity has central importance for Levinas's identification of idealism with freedom in "L'oeuvre d'Edmond Husserl."

12. In "La ruine de la représentation" (1959), Levinas will again note how Husserl "wavered between the disengagement of transcendental idealism and the engagement in the world"; in 1959, this wavering is the strength, not the weakness, of Husserl's phenomenology (RR, 33).

13. This same question has been revived recently in France, especially in the work of Jean-Luc Marion, Michel Henry, and Rudolf Bernet. Levinas's work holds an important position in such a debate, since he, like Marion, Henry, and Bernet, understands the problem of the reduction to be tantamount to the problem of the primordial structure of subjectivity. This problem deserves independent treatment and cannot be adequately discussed in this context. But, briefly it can be said that, in the end, the reduction will take Levinas to the hetero-affective genesis of subjectivity, a genesis negotiated through the structures of pre-predicative life. Levinas's conception of the reduction, then, must be subtly distinguished from Henry's notion of a primitive auto-affection (cf., "Quatre principes de la phénoménologie," *Revue de Métaphysique et de Morale* 96, no. 1 [1991]: 16 and *Phénoménologie matérielle* [Paris: PUF, 1991], especially chapter 1) and Bernet's notion of the double-life of the subject (cf., *La vie du sujet* [Paris: PUF, 1994], especially the Introduction), while approaching something close to the logic of what Marion calls the "third reduction" in his *Réduction et donation* (Paris: PUF, 1989), 289–305.

14. Fink, "Die phänomenologische," 110/105.

15. Ibid., 119/112.

16. Ibid., 119/113.

17. Ibid., 118ff/112ff.

18. This is the word Fink uses to describe Husserl's practice. See Fink, "Die phänomenologische," 110/105.

19. On the question of the relation between philosophy and nonphilosophy in Levinas's work, see Robert Bernasconi's "Levinas: Philosophy and Beyond." In *Philosophy and Non-Philosophy since Merleau-Ponty*, ed. Hugh Silverman (New York: Routledge, 1988), 232–258, especially 240ff.

20. It should be noted that Levinas will return to the problem of a reduction without theoretical motivation in the 1970s. See chapter 5, for our treatment of this return.

Chapter Two: The Subject outside Itself

1. See §53 of *The Crisis of European Sciences and Transcendental Phenomenology*.

2. See Hua V, 75/64.

3. For example, see Heidegger's remarks in *History of the Concept of Time*, trans. Ted Kisiel (Bloomington: Indiana University Press, 1985) on the necessity of thinking intentionality otherwise than the theoretical model in the face of a radical (i.e., non-Greek) conception of being (139f) and on the inauthentic mode of Husserlian intentionality as opposed to the authentic mode of being-ahead-of-itself-in-already-being-involved-in (303f).

4. Burt Hopkins has recently argued for this homology. See his "On the Paradoxical Inception and Motivation of Transcendental Philosophy in Plato and Husserl," *Man and World* 24 (1991): 27–47. Also, see Gadamer's characterization of phenomenology as a sort of Platonism in *Philosophical Hermeneutics*, trans. 2nd ed. David Linge (Berkeley: University of California Press, 1976), 147.

5. Cf., Husserl's remark: "This evidential character will . . . give us a descriptive mark, free from presuppositions regarding metaphysical realities, which will enable us to sort out various classes of perception [i.e., inner and outer]" (Hua XIX\2, 755/854–855). Levinas notes this with regard to Husserl's critique of traditional empiricism (ŒH, 32n1).

6. On the problem of Husserlian sense in "L'œuvre d'Edmond Husserl," see also Adrianne Orianne's "Translators Introduction" to the *Theory of Intuition*, xiii–xxiv.

7. The mention of positionality should also direct us to Levinas's remarks on the *Ichstrahl* (see, ŒH, 40).

8. Levinas will of course attribute a hidden voluntarism to Husserl in *Otherwise than Being*, but this mode of calling freedom into question speaks to the specifically phenomenological concern of Levinas's early work on Husserl.

9. I have in mind here Heidegger's marginal notation to Husserl, in the context of the debate over the *Encyclopedia Britannica* article: "does not a world belong to the essence of the pure ego?" (Hua XI, 274).

10. This is what John Llewelyn proposes in his *Emmanuel Levinas: The Genealogy of Ethics* (New York: Routledge, 1995), 55ff: "But in the works available to him at that date Levinas judges Husserl's philosophy to be too intellectualist" (56). As we contest this characterization, we also note that the question is not particularly pressing for Llewelyn.

11. Though *Formal and Transcendental Logic* was available before the publication of *Theory of Intuition*, Levinas says that he was unable to consult

it for *Theory and Intuition* due to its late publication in the *Jahrbuch* (TIPH, 10/ translation unfortunately drops the remark).

12. Levinas makes little use of the texts available in 1940 that were not available in 1930. *Formal and Transcendental Logic* and *The Crisis of European Sciences and Transcendental Phenomenology* are cited, but the former only eight times and always alongside the *Logical Investigations,* and the latter only in the section on "Phenomenology and Knowledge" (ŒH, 42–44). Indeed, Levinas himself notes that there is virtually no departure from the central theses of *Logical Investigations* and *Formal and Transcendental Logic* (ŒH, 11n4). The *Crisis* text, Levinas notes, only underscores (though in a "particularly clear manner" [42]) the link between freedom and intentionality and does not first establish such a linkage. Thus, we can focus here on the specifically phenomenological (and thus not philological) motivations of the 1940 text and its rethinking of the conclusions of the *Theory of Intuition.*

13. We note here Levinas's interesting remark that this general problem of relating the theoretical to the concrete also takes the particular form of translating *(traduire)* idealized essences into the language of the concrete world (TIPH, 174n108/119n108). Levinas acknowledges that he owes insight into this problem to conversations with Husserl. This is of course the problem raised by Fink in 1933 and taken up in §10 "Phenomenologizing as Predication" of Husserl and Fink's *Sixth Cartesian Meditation* (trans. Ronald Bruzina [Bloomington: Indiana University Press, 1994], 84–100). Such facts suggest that Levinas was privy to (if not a part of) the discussion of the problems of transcendental language, problems that prefigure Derrida's work on Husserl.

14. E.g., EeI, 22–23/32.

15. In this context, it is of note that only one section earlier Husserl had announced that "[w]e now give preference everywhere . . . to positional forms" (Hua III, 239/277), which compromises the positive exposition of axiological intentionality. In *Ideas I,* Husserl only indicates the boundaries of axiological intentionality, without taking up the nonpositional aspect of the practical attitude. *Ideas II* begins to fill in that gap, though Levinas himself is here only noting the formal possibilities that Husserl indicates.

16. *Pace* the formulations of *Theory of Intuition,* where Levinas writes that ". . . even if the constitution of these [axiological] objects in life is heterogeneous to the constitution of theoretical objects, theoretical objects must still serve as their basis" (TIPH, 191/133). The turn to the concrete gives a first position to this heterogeneity. Also of note is Derrida's citation of this passage from Levinas when discussing the teleology of Reason in Husserl's phenomenology. See Jacques Derrida, *Introduction to Husserl's The Origin of Geometry,* trans. John Leavey (Lincoln: University of Nebraska Press, 1989), 136n162.

17. This is a problem that Levinas will address in "Intentionalité et Sensation" (see chapter 4, §1 below).

18. Leonard Lawlor claims that this is the sort of reading we find in Derrida's *Voice and Phenomenon;* see Lawlor's essay, "Phenomenology and Metaphysics: Deconstruction in *Le voix et le phénomène*," *Journal of the British Society for Phenomenology* 27, no. 2 (May 1996): 116–136. His formulations of the character of Derrida's strategy, though in a wholly different context, have influenced my present characterization of Levinas's work on Husserl.

19. Though my present concerns are with the work up to and including *Totality and Infinity,* this so-called "obsession" with representation recurs even as late as 1984. See "Ethics as First Philosophy," where Levinas writes that, in Husserl's construal of intentionality, ". . . representation or objectivization is the incontestable model" (EFP, 77).

20. It is to be noted in this context that the analyses up through *Totality and Infinity* lack the diachronic conception of time that, beginning with the 1965 essay "Intentionalité et Sensation," will lead to the characterization of sensibility as the nonintentional source of intentionality. In 1959, intentionality simply marks the insistence on relationality.

Chapter Three: The Subject in Question

1. Thematization will be employed as the modality of manifestation that bears within it the possibility of idealism. *Kath auto* and expression will be employed as styles of manifestation that break with the necessity and possibility of constitution (which, as we will see, bears on the problem of *Sinngebung*).

2. On this point, see Robert Bernasconi, "Re-Reading *Totality and Infinity,*" in *The Question of the Other,* eds. Charles Scott and Arleen Dallery (Albany: State University of New York Press, 1989), 23–34. On the transcendental character of Levinas's work, see Theodore de Boer, "An Ethical Transcendental Philosophy." In *Face-to-Face with Levinas,* ed. Richard Cohen. Albany: SUNY Press, 1986, 83–116. Our exposition will attempt to further de Boer's reading of the transcendental back into Levinas's work, but with a decisive modification of de Boer's strategy. De Boer's lack of attention to the language of empiricism limits his ability to see both the function of sense-bestowal from the outside, which sets out from the position of the exterior/sensible, and the instability the empirical language imports to the issue of foundation.

3. For a basic account of Levinas's critique of the Husserlian notion of *ego cogito,* see Maria Schafstedde, *Der Selbe und der Andere: Zur Erkenntnistheorie und Ethik be Husserl und Levinas.* Kassel: IAG, 1993, 39ff.

4. E.g., see his remark that in the relation established by the Same in representation "the distinction between me and the object, between the interior and exterior, is effaced" (TeI, 96/124). Reversing this effacement comprises the central theme of the text.

5. Cf., Ludwig Landgrebe, "The Problem of Passive Constitution," trans. Donn Welton, in his *The Phenomenology of Edmund Husserl*, ed. and trans. Donn Welton (Ithaca: Cornell University Press, 1980).

6. Cf., Eugen Fink, "L'analyse intentionnelle et le problème de la pensée spéculative," in his *Problèmes actuels de la Phénoménologie* (Paris: Desclée de Brower, 1952).

7. It is worth noting here Levinas's remarks in "Réflexions sur la 'technique' phénoménologique" that "all givens *(toute donnée)* . . . are moments of the work of *Sinngebung*," which refers to the constitution of empirical objects as unities (RTP, 123).

8. On this problem, also see Fink's remarks to Cairns regarding the necessary relation of *habitus* to *Urstiftung*, which reiterates the points made here. In Dorion Cairns, *Conversations with Husserl and Fink* (The Hague: Martinus Nijhoff, 1976), 13f.

9. This conception of idealism leads Husserl to structurally distinguish his idealism from the failed idealisms of the Moderns. Cf., Hua XVII, §100 for Husserl's "Historico-Critical Remarks" on the history of transcendental philosophy.

10. See James Hart's remarks on maternal language in the opening pages of his *Person and World* (The Hague: Martinus Nijhoff, 1990).

11. Paul Davies offers a sensitive account of patience in his "A Fine Risk: Reading Blanchot Reading Levinas," in Simon Critchley and Robert Bernasconi, eds., *Re-Reading Levinas* (Bloomington: Indiana University Press), 1990, 214ff., showing quite clearly how patience leads to passivity and exposure to the other person.

12. For an elaboration of this problem of the relation of totality to the concept of infinity, see Bernasconi, "Re-Reading *Totality and Infinity*," 23–27.

13. On the logic of "alteration," see Paul Davies, "The Face and the Caress," in *Modernity and the Hegemony of Vision*, ed. David Michael Levin (Berkeley: University of California Press, 1993), 252–272, *passim*, especially 256–266.

14. Jill Robbins, "Tracing Responsibility in Levinas's Ethical Thought," in *Ethics as First Philosophy*, ed. Adriaan Peperzak (New York and London: Routledge, 1995), 175–176.

15. Again, this is the question of transcendence thought radically. If *kath auto* is only a modification of adequation, adequate evidence of this nonadequation can be given; this is the force of Husserl's notion of an Idea in the Kantian sense. See Burt C. Hopkins's defense of Husserl on this issue in his "Husserl and Derrida on the Origin of Geometry," in J. Claude Evans and William McKenna, eds., *Derrida and Phenomenology* (Dordrecht: Kluwer Academic Publishers, 1995), 76ff.

16. Robbins, "Tracing Responsibility," 176.

17. Alphonso Lingis, "The Sensuality and the Sensitivity," in *Face-to-Face with Levinas*, ed. Richard Cohen (Albany: State University of New York Press, 1986), 227.

18. Edith Wyschogrod, "Doing before Hearing: On the Primacy of Touch," in *Textes pour Emmanuel Lévinas*, ed. François Laruelle (Paris: Éditions Jean-Michel Place, 1980), 182.

19. Cf., Alphonso Lingis, *Deathbound Subjectivity* (Bloomington: Indiana University Press, 1989), 142–145.

20. Cf., Adriaan Peperzak, "Transcendence," in *Ethics as First Philosophy*, 189. Also see, Adriaan Peperzak, *To the Other* (West Lafayette: Purdue University Press, 1993), 68.

21. *Republic*, 529b. Cornford translation.

22. Simon Critchley, *The Ethics of Deconstruction* (Oxford: Basil Blackwell Publishers, 1992), 3–13.

23. It may be objected here that the possibility of the withdrawal or absence of the Desired and the Enjoyed renders the relation, at some level, troubled. This is true, but the point here is that the Desired and the Enjoyed, unlike the face of the Other, do not call freedom into question. Rather, Desire and Enjoyment displace the transcendental, which is a necessary precondition of the ethical relation, though not a sufficient condition. Only the face poses the unanswerable question.

24. Let us forestall an objection. It is true that in *Totality and Infinity* Levinas will describe the welcome of the Other as an expression of the ". . . simultaneity of activity and passivity" (TeI, 62/89). But we are here seeking the *primordial* institution of sense in the face-to-face. The welcome is already a response to the questioning enacted by the facing face, hence the welcome already presupposes this first sense of ethics. We here maintain that it is passivity that designates the position of the subject in the constitution of the sense of the face-to-face, since the sense constituted is imposed on the subject from the outside. In this imposition, the very freedom that would underpin activity is "put in question."

25. Also, see his remarks regarding the relation of separation as a relation of unicity to unicity (PEA, 233).

26. On the alteration of sensibility as Enjoyment and Desire in the interruptive effect of the face, see Paul Davies, "The Face and Caress," 259.

27. Elisabeth Weber, "The Notion of Persecution in Levinas's *Otherwise than Being, or Beyond Essence*," in *Ethics as First Philosophy*, 74. Though Weber's paper is concerned with the terms persecution and trauma in the context of *Otherwise than Being* it is illuminating with regard to the issues raised here, insofar as in both texts the subject is insufficient to its origin—a logic that structures trauma as such.

28. E.g., ". . . the face of the Other is concrete and therefore deformalizes Descartes' notion of infinity" (TeI, 21/50). On this point, see Bernasconi's "Re-reading *Totality and Infinity*," 33.

29. Here we should remark on a tension, often noted by readers of *Totality and Infinity*, between the contestation of the position of the I and the apparent sense in which the Other appears to an already formed I (see, for example, Robert Bernasconi, "'Only the Persecuted . . .': Language of the Oppressor, Language of the Oppressed," in *Ethics as First Philosophy*, 77–86, esp. 79. Our analysis of the problem of sense aims at giving an account of how the I is already outside itself, constituted from the outside. The moral summons is a creative, originary, donative event where the I is already split in its identity. The bestowal of sense from the face in moral consciousness gives birth to the I, thus the Other does not in fact confront an already formed subject. This is not to say Levinas is unambiguous on this issue, but our recovery of the transcendental problem of sense has attempted to render an account of the subject outside itself within the logic of *Totality and Infinity*.

Chapter Four: Sensation, Trace, Enigma

1. Deciding the question of whether the discovery of sensibility—with all its radical implications—is an unwitting find or a conscious transgression is a quite significant decision. Indeed, it is the very question of whether Levinas is offering a "double reading" of Husserl or if Levinas may be indicating that Husserl himself conceives of phenomenology as an offense to metaphysics. On the first strategy, albeit in a different context, see Robert Bernasconi, "The Trace of Levinas in Derrida," in *Derrida and Differance*, eds. David Wood and Robert Bernasconi (Evanston: Northwestern University Press, 1988), 13–30 *passim.*, esp. 16–19. On the second strategy, also in a different context, see Leonard Lawlor, "Phenomenology and Metaphysics: Deconstruction in *La voix et le phénomène*," *Journal of the British Society for Phenomenology* 27, no. 2 (May 1996): 116–136. My own position vis-à-vis Levinas's reading of Husserl following *Totality and Infinity* will lean toward the double-reading strategy, though with the notion of "explicit transgression" still intact.

2. Lawlor, "Phenomenology and Metaphysics," 116–136.

3. It is important to note here that nonintentional will not mean that what is determined as nonintentional has no relation to the ego. Rather, it merely designates a modality of relation that does not articulate itself in terms of the intentionality proper to idealism.

4. Michel Henry has characterized the phenomenological investigation of materiality as one of the principle points for the renewal of phenomenology. Cf. his *Phénoménologie matérielle* (Paris: PUF, 1990). Henry's conclusions, however, will differ significantly from those of Levinas. While both will want

to complicate the coincidence of the *Ur-impression* with what is constituted by transcendental subjectivity, Henry, unlike Levinas, will continue to use the language of pure immanence. While this is, for Henry, an immanence different from that of idealism, it is not readily assimilable to Levinas's rendering of the same matter as transcendence. For a good account of the relation between Henry and Levinas, see François-David Sebbah, "Aux limites de l'intentionalité: M. Henry et E. Lévinas, lecteurs des *Leçons sur la conscience intime du temps,*" *Alter,* no. 2 (1994): 245–260.

5. In this task, we distinguish our project from that of James Dodd in his "Phenomenon and Sensation: A Reflection on Husserl's Concept of *Sinngebung,*" *Man and World* 29, no. 4 (October 1996): 419–439. There, Dodd emphasizes the fundamental continuity between the sensation itself and its appearance. Levinas will want to mark the point of alteration and discontinuity of the same relation. Dodd claims that the nonintentional aspect of sensation has been almost universally rejected (430n29), noting that Levinas is an exception to this "almost," but Dodd overstates the case. The nonintentional component of sensation has actually been the stepping off point for the radical phenomenologies of Levinas, Henry, and Derrida, which actually shows the vitality of this notion and points to horizons perhaps unsuspected and unseeable by Dodd and those defending the idealist prerogative in general.

6. On this point, see Burt C. Hopkins, *Intentionality in Husserl and Heidegger: The Problem of the Original Method and Phenomenon of Phenomenology* (Dordrecht: Kluwer Academic Publishers, 1992), 21–31. Hopkins's account makes quite clear the reflective context in which the immanent/transcendent distinction comes to the fore, a context that eliminates the interior/exterior presuppositions of the natural attitude. Of course, the task of Levinas's reflections on time is precisely the attempt to reinsert a renewed conception of the exterior that is neither reflective in Husserl's sense nor a return to the notion of an exterior that only makes sense within the natural attitude. It is therefore misleading to claim, as has de Boer, that the Levinasian notion of alterity is a "surmounting of the natural attitude" (Theodor de Boer, "An Ethical Transcendental Philosophy," in Richard Cohen, ed., *Face-to-Face with Levinas* (Albany: State University of New York Press, 1986), 83–116.

7. Cf., Jacques Derrida, "'Genèse et structure' et la phénoménologie," in *L'ecriture et la différence* (Paris: Éditions du Seuil, 1967), 229–252; "'Genesis and Structure' and Phenomenology," trans. Alan Bass, in *Writing and Difference* (Chicago: University of Chicago Press, 1978), 154–231. There, concerning the relation of the sensual material named *hyle* and the ideality of form, Derrida writes that ". . . if he [Husserl] keeps to the constituted *hyle-morphic* correlation, it is that his analyses are still developed . . . from within a constituted temporality" (243/163).

8. Recall here that Levinas will write in *Otherwise than Being* that he "will have to indicate the element in which this *concerning* occurs" (AE, 15/12–13). Our suggestion here is that the double character of sensuous is that medium.

9. As Levinas will put it elsewhere, the most primoridial stratum of time is the process of "dephasing," that is, the movement of constituted time outside itself to the "hither-side," at its origin. See AE, 11/9, 41ff/32ff, 86/68, 90/72, 207/162.

10. Levinas's evocation of a facticity that precedes the subject's self-presence should not fail to remind us of the function of a fundamental facticity in genetic phenomenology. See Hua XVII, 318/318.

11. Cf., Jacques Derrida, *Le voix et le phénomène* (Paris: PUF, 1967), 15–16, 67–77; *Speech and Phenomena*, trans. David Allison (Evanston: Northwestern University Press, 1973), 16, 60–69. Also, in "'Genesis and Structure' and Phenomenology," Derrida notes that ". . . the constitution of the other and of time refers phenomenology to a zone in which its 'principle of principles' . . . is radically put into question" (244/164).

12. Cf., Jacques Derrida, "Violence et métaphysique," in *L'écriture et la différence* (Paris: Éditions du Seuil, 1967), 224ff; "Violence and Metaphysics," trans. Alan Bass, in *Writing and Difference* (Chicago: University of Chicago Press, 1988), 151ff. Empiricism will be avoided in Levinas's temporal articulation of the beyond being. This forges precisely the third way sought by Levinas, a way of leaving the philosophy of identity without renouncing philosophy as such in favor of its opposite—empiricism. Rather, to evoke Derrida, this exiting of philosophy take place through the "infidelity" of an "abusive investigation" (see, "'Genesis and Structure' and Phenomenology," 154).

13. We might say that this attempts to free the analysis from the limitations of the phenomenology of our worldly being that are presented in the Second Book of the *Ideas* (cf., Hua IV, §§48–62), as well as from the existential categories that are elaborated in *Being and Time*.

14. Notable in the revision of "Trace of the Other" as "Meaning and Sense" is Levinas's linking of gratitude with Heidegger's attempt to "think/thank" Being, which indicates the significance of these considerations of alterity as ingratitude for Heidegger's later work—a certain critique of Thinking by way of the beyond being.

15. Precisely and quite literally, we might add, in the sense of upsetting or overturning one's plans.

16. Ultimately, the signifyingness of the trace will have to be grounded in impressional sense, for, as we noted in our "Introduction," signification always signifies a sense. This necessity of grounding the trace in the logic of impressional sense is explicated in chapter 5 in our reading of *Otherwise than Being*.

17. This already proposes a response to Derrida's questions regarding the specter of ontologism in "Violence and Metaphysics."

Chapter Five: Impressions of Sense

1. This reading will be supplemented with various essays by Levinas clustered around the publication of *Otherwise than Being*, as his work after 1974 continues the interest in time and passivity. Also, many of the essays on Husserl following 1974 fill out the phenomenological context of the logic of *Otherwise than Being*.

2. On this work of reduction, see Adriaan Peperzak's comments in *To the Other* (West Lafayette: Purdue University Press, 1993), 218ff, as well as those by Simon Critchley in *The Ethics of Deconstruction* (Oxford: Basil Blackwell Publishers, 1992), 8, 164. Both briefly indicate the essential function of the reduction, but continue to put it in brackets, which tends to obscure the positivity of the reduction Levinas now finds in Husserl's work.

3. On this point, see also William J. Richardson, "The Irresponsible Subject," in *Ethics as First Philosophy*, ed. Adriaan Peperzak (New York: Routledge, 1995), 128.

4. DCV, 57. In this passage from "De la conscience à la veille," Levinas refers us to the analyses in chapter 4 of *Otherwise than Being*. This reference, in addition to other philosophical concerns, should allow us to link unreservedly the problem of awakening with the genetic problem of sense.

5. See also Husserl's comments on the possibility of awakening as reactivation and recollection (Hua IX, 210n1/161n1). These remarks push us into the consideration of time as the element of sleep/awakening/wakefulness taken up below.

6. On this point in Husserl, see Kathleen Haney's interpretation in *Intersubjectivity Revisited* (Athens: Ohio University Press, 1994), esp. 25–78, and my remarks on her project in "Review Essay: *Intersubjectivity Revisited*," *Husserl Studies* 12 (1995): 82–86, 88–90.

7. John Brough, "The Emergence of an Absolute Consciousness in Husserl's Early Writings on Time-Consciousness," in *Husserl: Expositions and Appraisals*, eds. Frederick Elliston and Peter McCormick (Notre Dame: University of Notre Dame Press, 1977), 83.

8. Cf., AE, 135/106 for the list of structural terms that Levinas says "describe responsibility for others."

9. Cf., Hua III, 163n1/194n26, where Husserl defers to the time-consciousness lectures as the grounds of the analyses being carried out.

10. For a full treatment of this issue, see Brough, *passim*.

11. Hans-Georg Gadamer, "The Phenomenological Movement," in *Philosophical Hermeneutics*, trans. and ed. David Linge (Berkeley: University of

California Press, 1976), 166. Nathalie Depraz reads the C manuscripts with a view to Levinas's work in her *Transcendance et incarnation* (Paris: Vrin, 1995), especially 249–260.

12. Gadamer, "The Phenomenological Movement," 166. On this, see also Ludwig Landgrebe's account of the primal flow of time and consciousness in "The Problem of Teleology and Corporeality in Phenomenology and Marxism," in *Phenomenology and Marxism*, eds. B. Waldenfels, J. Broekman, and E. Pazanin (London: Routledge & Kegan Paul, 1984), 74ff.

13. Hua XV, 670, my emphasis. This is a passage from Ms. C I, September 21–22, 1934. See James Mensch's comments on this passage, as well as on the general tension between Absolute Consciousness and Absolute Flow in his *Intersubjectivity and Transcendental Idealism* (Albany: State University of New York Press, 1988), 207–212.

14. Cf., M. A. Bera, ed., *Husserl, Cahiers de Royaumont* (Paris: Éditions de Minuit, 1959), 323. Gadamer agrees with van Breda's reply to Hyppolite that such a notion is unthinkable for Husserl (Van Breda: "Pour Husserl, cette solution est impensable," Ibid.; Gadamer, 168). Levinas will claim that this pre-egoic life, which is the locus of the pre-history of the I, is unthinkable but necessary for Husserl, and therein lies the essence of Levinas's reading of Husserlian phenomenology in this context.

15. On this aspect of Husserl's reflections, see J. Claude Evans's "The Myth of Absolute Consciousness," in *Crises in Continental Philosophy*, eds. Charles Scott and Arleen Dallery (Albany: State University of New York Press, 1990), 35–43, esp. 36–38. Evans ultimately argues for the abandonment of this element of Husserl's phenomenology for reasons not unlike those offered by Levinas, viz., in the name of purging Husserl's phenomenology of unwarranted metaphysical speculations. We might add that this is the very imperative of a presuppositionless science of subjectivity, which makes Levinas's criticisms of Husserl intimately phenomenological.

16. Cf., Landgrebe, "The Problem of Teleology," 56ff.

17. On this point, see Leonard Lawlor's account of phenomenology as a transgression of metaphysics in "Phenomenology and Metaphysics: Deconstruction in *La voix et le phénomène*," *Journal of the British Society for Phenomenology* 27, no. 2 (May 1996): 116–127.

18. Cf., Landgrebe, "The Problem of Teleology," 57–59, 74–77.

19. Ibid., 57.

20. On this problem of translation and the general connection between will and meaning, see John Llewelyn, "Meanings Reserved, Re-served, and Reduced," *Southern Journal of Philosophy* XXXII, Supplemental Volume (1993): 38–42.

21. See Hua IV, 145ff/152ff for the original statement of the touching-touched issue. Merleau-Ponty more famously accounts for this "reversability" in both *Phénoménologie de la perception* (Paris: Gallimard, 1945), 190; *Phenomenology of Perception,* trans. Colin Smith London: (City: Routledge & Kegan Paul, 1962), 93 and *Le visible et l'invisible* (Paris: Gallimard, 1964), 191ff; *The Visible and the Invisible* trans. Alphonso Lingis. (Evanston: Northwestern University Press, 1968), 146ff. See Levinas's remarks on the issue, HS, 148–150/99–101.

22. See, AE, 41–42/33; Hua X, 99–101/105–107. Specifically, Husserl will write of the primal impression that "it does not arise as something produced but through *genesis spontanea;* it is primal generation" (Hua X, 100/106). Levinas will quote these very words, with explicit approval, in *Otherwise than Being* (AE, 41–42/33).

23. On this point, see Philip Maloney's "Substitution and Transcendental Subjectivity," *Man and World* (1996): 122–130.

24. Paul Celan, "Der Meridian," in *Der Meridian und andere Proza* (Frankfurt am Main: Suhrkamp, 1994), 61; "The Meridian," trans. Rosemarie Waldrop, in *Collected Prose* (New York: Sheep Meadow Press, 1986), 54.

Selected Bibliography

Aubay, Francois. "Conscience, immanence, et non-présence: Emmanuel Levinas, lecteur de Husserl." *Alter* 1 (1993): 293–318.

Bernasconi, Robert. "The Trace of Levinas in Derrida." In *Derrida and Differance*, eds. David Wood and Robert Bernasconi. Evanston: Northwestern University Press, 1988, 13–30.

―――. "Levinas: Philosophy and Beyond." In *Philosophy and Non-Philosophy since Merleau-Ponty*, ed. Hugh Silverman. New York: Routledge, 1988, 232–258.

―――. "Re-Reading *Totality and Infinity*." In *The Question of the Other*, eds. Charles Scott and Arleen Dallery. Albany: State University of New York Press, 1989, 22–34.

―――. "Seeing Double: *Destruktion* and Deconstruction." In *Dialogue and Deconstruction: The Gadamer-Derrida Encounter*, eds. Diane P. Michelfelder and Richard E. Palmer. Albany: State University of New York Press, 1989, 233–250.

―――. "One-Way Traffic: The Ontology of Decolonization and Its Ethics." In *Ontology and Alterity in Merleau-Ponty*, eds. Galen Johnson and Michael Smith. Evanston: Northwestern University Press, 1990, 67–80.

―――. "'Only the Persecuted . . .' Language of the Oppressor, Language of the Oppressed." In *Ethics as First Philosophy*, ed. Adriaan Peperzak. New York: Routledge, 1995, 77–86.

————. *Between Levinas and Derrida.* Unpublished manuscript, forthcoming.

Bernasconi, Robert and Simon Critchley, eds. *Re-Reading Levinas.* Bloomington: Indiana University Press, 1990.

Bernasconi, Robert and David Wood, eds. *The Provocation of Levinas.* New York: Routledge, 1995.

Bernet, Rudolf. *La vie du sujet.* Paris: PUF, 1994.

————. "Preface." In Nathalie Depraz, *Transcendance et incarnation.* Paris: Vrin, 1995.

Caputo, John. *Against Ethics.* Bloomington: Indiana University Press, 1993.

Casey, Edward. "Levinas on Memory and the Trace." In *The Collegium Phaenomenologicum: The First Ten Years*, eds. Moneta, Sallis, and Taminiaux. Dordrecht: Kluwer Academic Publishers, 1988, 240–255.

Chanter, Tina. *The Ethics of Eros.* New York: Routledge, 1994.

————. "Feminism and the Other." In *The Provocation of Levinas,* eds. Robert Bernasconi and David Wood. New York: Routledge, 1995.

Cohen, Richard, "Emmanuel Levinas: Happiness Is a Sensational Time." *Philosophy Today* 25, no. 3 (1981): 196–203.

————, ed. *Face-to-Face with Levinas.* Albany: State University of New York Press, 1986.

————. "Absolute Positivity and Ultrapositivity: Husserl and Levinas." In *The Question of the Other*, eds. Charles Scott and Arleen Dallery. Albany: State University of New York Press, 1989, 35–43.

————. "Levinas, Rosenzweig, and the Phenomenologies of Husserl and Heidegger." *Philosophy Today* 32, no. 2 (Summer 1988): 165–178.

————. *Elevations.* Chicago: University of Chicago Press, 1995.

Colette, Jacques. "Lévinas et la phénoménologie husserlienne." In *Emmanuel Levinas, Les Cahiers de La Nuit Surveilée No. 3,* ed. J. Rolland. Lagrasse: Verdier, 1984, 19–36.

Critchley, Simon. *The Ethics of Deconstruction*. Oxford: Basil Blackwell Publishers, 1992.

Davies, Paul. "The Face and the Caress." In *Modernity and the Hegemony of Vision*, ed. David Michael Levin. Berkeley: University of California Press, 1993, 252–272.

De Boer, Theodor. "An Ethical Transcendental Philosophy." In *Face-to-Face with Levinas*, ed. Richard Cohen. Albany: State University of New York Press, 1986, 83–116.

De Greef, Jan. "Levinas et la phénoménologie." *Revue de Métaphysique et de Morale* 76, no. 4 (Octobre–Décembre 1971): 448–465.

Depraz, Nathalie. *Transcendance et incarnation*. Paris: Vrin, 1995.

Derrida, Jacques. "Violence et métaphysique: Essai sur la pensée d'Emmanuel Levinas." In *L'écriture et la différence*. Paris: Éditions du Seuil, 1967, 117–228; "Violence and Metaphysics: An Essay on the Thought of Emmanuel Levinas." In *Writing and Difference*, trans. Alan Bass. Chicago: University of Chicago Press, 1988, 79–153.

———. *La voix et le phénomène*. Paris: PUF, 1967; *Speech and Phenomena*, trans. David Allison. Evanston: Northwestern University Press, 1973.

Descombes, Vincent. *Modern French Philosophy*, trans. L. Scott-Fox and J. M. Harding. Cambridge: Cambridge University Press, 1980.

Evans, J. Claude. "The Myth of Absolute Consciousness." In *Crises in Continental Philosophy*, eds. Charles Scott and Arleen Dallery. Albany: State University of New York Press, 1990, 35–43.

Fink, Eugen. "L'analyse intentionelle et le problème de la pensée spéculative." In his *Problèmes actuels de la Phénoménologie*. Paris: Desclée de Brower, 1952.

———. "Die phänomenologische Philosophie Edmund Husserls in der Gegenwärtigen Kritik," in *Studien zur Phänomenologie: 1930–1939*. The Hague: Martinus Nijhoff, 1966; "The Phenomenological Philosophy of Edmund Husserl and Contemporary Criticism," trans. R. O. Elveton. In *The Phenomenology of Husserl*, ed. R. O. Elveton. Chicago: Quadrangle, 1970.

————. *The Sixth Cartesian Meditation,* trans. Ronald Bruzina. Bloomington: Indiana University Press, 1994.

Gadamer, Hans-Georg. *Philosophical Hermeneutics*, trans. David Linge. Berkeley: University of California Press, 1976.

Guillamaud, Patrice. "L'autre et l'immanence." *Revue de Métaphysique et de Morale* 94 (1989): 251–272.

Haney, Kathleen. *Intersubjectivity Revisited: Phenomenology and the Other.* Athens: Ohio University Press, 1994.

Heidegger, Martin. *Being and Time,* trans. Edward Robinson and John Macquarrie. New York: Harper and Row, 1980.

————. *History of the Concept of Time,* trans. Ted Kisiel. Bloomington: Indiana University Press, 1984.

Henry, Michel, "Quatre principes de la phénomenologie." *Revue de Metaphysique et de Morale* 96, no. 1 (1991): 12–18.

————. *Phénoménologie matérielle.* Paris: PUF, 1990.

Hering, Jean. "Review of *La théorie de l'intuition dans la phénoménologie de Husserl.*" *Revue Philosophique de la France et de l'Etranger* CXIII (1932), 5–6: 474–481.

Hopkins, Burt. "On the Paradoxical Inception and Motivation of Transcendental Philosophy in Plato and Husserl." *Man and World* 24 (1991): 27–47.

————. *Intentionality in Husserl and Heidegger.* Dordrecht: Kluwer Academic Publishers, 1991.

Ingarden, Roman. *On the Motives Which Led Husserl to Transcendental Idealism,* trans. Arnór Hannibalsson. The Hague: Martinus Nijhoff, 1975.

Krewani, Wolfgang. "Le temps comme transcendance vers l'autre: La notion du temps dans la philosophie d'E. Levinas." *Archives de Philosophie* 44 (1981): 529–560.

Landgrebe, Ludwig. *The Phenomenology of Edmund Husserl*, ed. and trans. Donn Welton. Ithaca: Cornell University Press, 1980.

————. "The Problem of Teleology and Corporeality in Phenomenology and Marxism," trans. J. Claude Evans. In *Phenomenology and*

Marxism, eds. B. Waldenfels, J. Broekman, and E. Pazanin. London: Routledge & Kegan Paul, 1984, 53–81.

Lawlor, Leonard. *Imagination and Chance: The Difference between the Thought of Ricœur and Derrida*. Albany: State University of New York Press, 1992.

———. "Phenomenology and Metaphysics: Deconstruction in *La voix et le phénomène*." *Journal of the British Society for Phenomenology* 27, no. 2 (May 1996): 116–136.

Libertson, Joseph. "Intentionality and Sensation." *Tijdschrift voor Filosofie* 41, no. 3 (1979): 485–502.

———. *Proximity*. The Hague: Martinus Nijhoff, 1988.

Lingis, Alphonso. *Libido*. Bloomington: Indiana University Press, 1985.

———. "The Sensuality and the Sensitivity." In *Face-to-Face with Levinas*, ed. Richard Cohen. Albany: State University of New York Press, 1986, 219–230.

———. *Phenomenological Explanations*. Dordrecht: Martinus Nijhoff, 1986.

———. *Deathbound Subjectivity*. Bloomington: Indiana University Press, 1989.

Llewelyn, John. "Levinas, Derrida, and Others, vis-à-vis." In *Beyond Metaphysics?* Atlantic Highlands: Humanities Press, 1985, 185–206.

———. "Meanings Reserved, Re-served, and Reduced." *Southern Journal of Philosophy* XXXII, Supplemental Volume (1993): 27–54.

———. *Emmanuel Levinas: The Genealogy of Ethics*. New York: Routledge, 1995.

Lyotard, Jean-François. *The Differend*, trans. Georges Van Den Abbeele. Minneapolis: University of Minnesota Press, 1988.

MacDonald, Michael. "'Jewgreek and Greekjew': The Concept of the Trace in Derrida and Levinas." *Philosophy Today* 35, no. 3 (Fall 1991): 215–227.

Maloney, Philip. "Substitution and Transcendental Subjectivity." *Man and World* (1996): 122–130.

Manning, Robert. *Interpreting Otherwise than Heidegger.* Pittsburgh: Duquesne University Press, 1993.

Marbach, Eduard. *Das Problem des Ich in der Phänomenologie Husserls.* The Hague: Martinus Nijhoff, 1974.

Marion, Jean-Luc. *Réduction et donation.* Paris: PUF, 1990.

———. "L'autre philosophie première et la question de la donation." *Philosophie* 49, no. 1 (Mars 1996): 68–83.

McKenna, William. *Husserl's "Introductions to Phenomenology."* The Hague: Martinus Nijhoff, 1982.

Mensch, James. *Intersubjectivity and Transcendental Idealism.* Albany: State University of New York Press, 1988.

Meyer-Drawe, Käte. "Totalität und Unendlichkeit. Das Levinas-Kolloquium im Husserl-Archiv in Leuven vom 10. bis zum 12. März 1983." In *Studien zum Problem der Technik*, ed. E. W. Orth, *Phänomenologische Forschungen.* Freiburg/München: Verlag Karl Alber, 1983, 148–157.

Mohanty, J. N. *Husserl and Frege.* Bloomington: Indiana University Press, 1982.

———. *The Possibility of Transcendental Philosophy.* The Hague: Martinus Nijhoff, 1988.

———. *Transcendental Phenomenology.* Philadelphia: Temple University Press, 1989.

Mortley, Raoul. *French Philosophers in Conversation.* London: Routledge, 1991.

Peperzak, Adriaan. "Beyond Being." *Research in Phenomenology* 8 (1978): 239–261.

———. "Phenomenology-Ontology-Metaphysics: Levinas's Perspective on Husserl and Heidegger." *Man and World* 16, no. 2 (1983): 113–127.

———. "From Intentionality to Responsibility: Levinas's Philosophy of Language." In *The Question of the Other*, eds. Charles Scott and Arleen Dallery. Albany: State University of New York Press, 1989, 3–21.

———. "The One for the Other: The Philosophy of Emmanuel Levinas." *Man and World* 24, no. 4 (1992): 427–459.

———. *To the Other: An Introduction to the Philosophy of Emmanuel Levinas.* West Lafayette: Purdue University Press, 1993.

———. *Ethics as First Philosophy.* New York: Routledge, 1995.

Reed, Charles William. "Levinas's Question." In *Face-to-Face with Levinas*, ed. Richard Cohen. Albany: State University of New York Press, 1986, 73–82.

Richardson, William J. "The Irresponsible Subject." In *Ethics as First Philosophy*, ed. Adriaan Peperzak. New York: Routledge, 1995, 123–135.

Ricœur, Paul. "L'originaire de la question-en-retour dans le Krisis de Husserl." In *Textes pour Emmanuel Levinas*, ed. François Laruelle. Paris: Éditions Jean-Michel Place, 1980, 167–178.

Robbins, Jill. "Tracing Responsibility in Levinas's Ethical Thought." In *Ethics as First Philosophy*, ed. Adriaan Peperzak. New York: Routledge, 1995, 173–184.

Schafstedde, Maria. *Der Selbe und der Andere.* Kaesseler Philosophische Schriften. Kaessler: IAG, 1993.

Schroeder, Brian. *Altared Ground.* New York: Routledge, 1996.

Sebbah, Francois-David. "Éviel et naissance." *Alter* 1 (1993): 213–240.

———. "Aux limites de l'intentionalité: M. Henry et E. Levinas, lecteurs des *Lecons sur la conscience intime du temps*." *Alter* 2 (1994): 245–260.

Strasser, Stephan. "Emmanuel Levinas (b. 1906): Phenomenological Philosophy." In Herbert Spiegelberg, *The Phenomenological Movement.* The Hague: Martinus Nijhoff, 1982, 612–649.

———. "Antiphénoménologie et phénoménologie dans la philosophie d'Emmanuel Levinas." *Revue Philosophique de Louvain* 75 (Février, 1977): 101–125.

Tallon, Andrew. "Nonintentional Affectivity, Affective Intentionality, and the Ethical in Levinas's Philosophy." In *Ethics as First Philosophy*, ed. Adriaan Peperzak. New York: Routledge, 1995, 107–122.

Vasey, Craig R. "Emmanuel Levinas: From Intentionality to Proximity." *Philosophy Today* 25, no. 3 (1981): 178–195.

Weber, Elizabeth. "The Notion of Persecution in Levinas's *Otherwise than Being, or Beyond Essence*." In *Ethics as First Philosophy*, ed. Adriaan Peperzak. New York: Routledge, 1995, 69–76.

Wyschgrod, Edith. *Emmanuel Levinas: The Problem of Ethical Metaphysics*. The Hague: Martinus Nijhoff, 1974.

———. "Doing before Hearing: On the Primacy of Touch." In *Textes pour Emmanuel Levinas*, ed. François Laruelle. Paris: Éditions Jean-Michel Place, 1980, 179–203.

———. "Exemplary Individuals." *Philosophy and Theology* 1 (1986): 9–31.

Index